DUBLIN STREETFINDER
COLOUR ATLAS & GUIDE

CONTENTS

TOURIST AND TRAVEL INFORMATION

Air

Dublin Airport

Tel: 01 814 1111.

Web: www.dublin-airport.com

Frequent direct flights operate between Dublin and many airports in Britain, Europe and North America. Internal flights are available to Cork, Galway, Kerry, Shannon, and Sligo (Aer Lingus Tel: 01 844 4777) and Donegal and the Aran Islands (Aer Arann Tel: 01 814 5240). Other operators include British Airways (Tel: 1800 626 747), British Midland (Tel: 01 283 8833) and Ryanair (Tel: 01 677 4422). The airport is 12km (8 miles) north of the city centre with a frequent 'Airlink' express coach service operating between the airport, the central bus station in Store Street (Bus Áras) and the two mainline rail stations, Connolly and Heuston. It runs every 15 or 20 minutes from 07.00–23.00. There are also local bus services from the airport to various destinations in and around Dublin and a luxury private 'Aircoach' service (Tel: 01 844 7118) into the city centre, stopping en-route near some of the main hotels and operating every 15 mins from 05.30–23.30.

Web: www.dublinbus.ie or www.aircoach.ie

Services at Dublin airport include Travel Information, Tourist Information and Bureau de Change.

Passenger and Vehicle Ferries

Numerous modern ferries and high-speed services with drive-on drive-off facilities cross the Irish Sea from Britain (Liverpool, Holyhead and Isle of Man) to Dublin.

Irish Ferries (Dublin–Holyhead). Tel: 01 638 3333 or Lo Call 1890 31 31 31 or from UK: 08705 17 17 17.

Web: www.irishferries.com

Email: info@irishferries.ie

Merchant Ferries (Dublin–Liverpool). Tel: 01 819 2999 or from UK: 0870 600 4321.

Web: www. merchant–ferries.com

P & O European Ferries (Dublin–Liverpool).
Tel: 1800 409 049 or from UK: 0870 24 24 777.

Web: www.poirishsea.com

Steam Packet/Seacat (Dublin–Liverpool).
Tel: 1800 55 17 43 or from UK: 08705 523 523.

Web: www.steam–packet.com

Stena Line
(Dún Laoghaire–Holyhead & Dublin–Holyhead).
Tel: 01 204 7700/7777
or from UK: 08705 70 70 70.

Web: www.stenaline.com

Email: info@stenaline.com

Dublin Port and Dún Laoghaire have bus and taxi services to the city centre although on busy sailings it may be prudent to pre-book a taxi. The ferry terminal at Dún Laoghaire is also linked to the city by the DART rail service with a 15 minute journey time.

Tourist Information

Dublin Tourism Centre, Suffolk Street. Tel: 01 605 7700. Open: (July and August) Mon–Sat 09.00–18.30, Sun 10.30–14.30; (Sept–June) Mon–Sat 09.00–17.30. Open bank holidays 10.30–14.30; closed 25 & 26 Dec & 1 Jan.

Formerly St. Andrew's Church, the centre provides details of visitor attractions and events in the city as well as acting as a ticket and accommodation bureau. Transport and tour information, exchange facilities and a café are also on hand.

Other tourist information and reservation centres in Dublin (walk-in only) are located at:

Dublin Airport. Open: Mon–Sun 08.00–22.00 (closes 22.30 July & Aug). Open bank holidays except 25 & 26 Dec & 1 Jan.

Dún Laoghaire Ferry Terminal. Open: Mon–Sat 10.00–18.00. Open bank holidays except 25 & 26 Dec & 1 Jan.

Baggott Street Bridge. Open: Mon–Fri 09.30–17.00. Closed bank holidays.

The Square Shopping Centre, Tallaght. Open: Mon–Sat 09.30–17.00. Closed bank holidays.

For accommodation reservations in Dublin and Ireland contact Ireland Reservations. Tel from within Ireland: 1800 668 668; universal freephone: 00800 668 668 66; freephone from USA: 011 800 668 668 66.

Official tourism website for Dublin:

Web: www.visitdublin.com

Email: information@dublintourism.ie
or reservations@dublintourism.ie

Irish Tourist Board Website:

Web: www.ireland.travel.ie

Information regarding heritage sites and events in Dublin and elsewhere in Ireland can be obtained from Dúchas, The Heritage Service.
Tel: LoCall: 1890 47 48 47

Web: www.heritageireland.ie

Email: info@heritageireland.ie

KEY TO MAP SYMBOLS

M2	Motorway/ under construction	P	Car park
N6	National primary road	i	Tourist information centre
		+	Church
N55	National secondary road	PO Lib	Public service building (appropriate name shown)
R95	Regional road		Leisure / Tourism
	Other road		Administration / Law
	Track		Health / Hospital
	Ferry		Education
	City boundary		Other / Notable building
24	Postcode number		Built up area
	Postal boundary		Park / Garden / Sports ground / Public open space
	Railway station		Cemetery
	Bus / Coach station		Lake / River

Scale of main mapping: 1:15,000 (4 inches to 1 mile) approx.

0 0.25 0.5 0.75 1 km

0 1/4 1/2 mile

Published by Collins
An imprint of HarperCollins*Publishers*
77-85 Fulham Palace Road, Hammersmith, London W6 8JB

The HarperCollins website address is: www.**fire**and**water**.com

Bartholomew website address is: www.bartholomewmaps.com

Based on Ordnance Survey Ireland Mapping with the permission of the Government © Government of Ireland

Printed in Hong Kong

ISBN 0 00 449085 1 NI 10663 NDD

e-mail: roadcheck@harpercollins.co.uk

KEY TO MAP PAGES

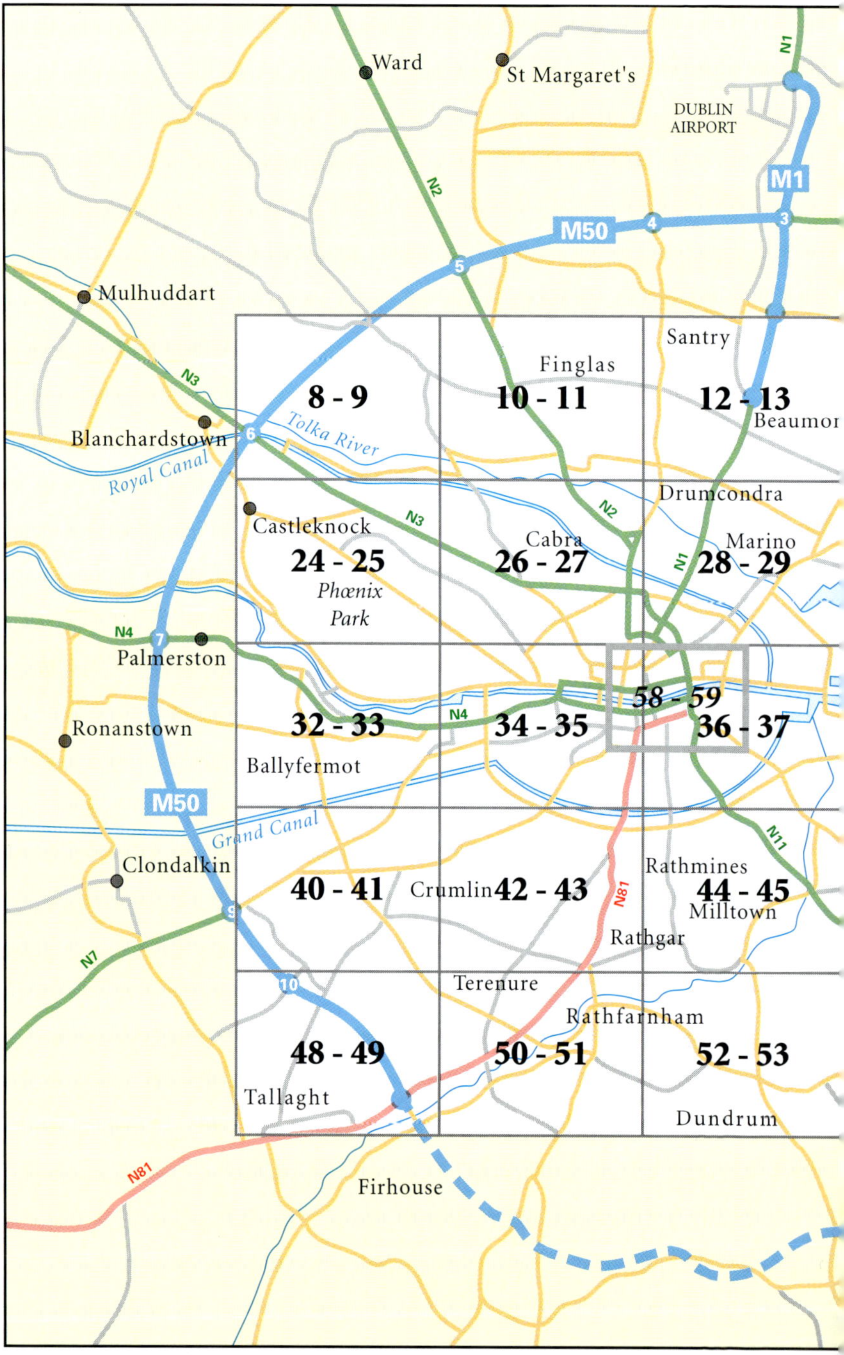

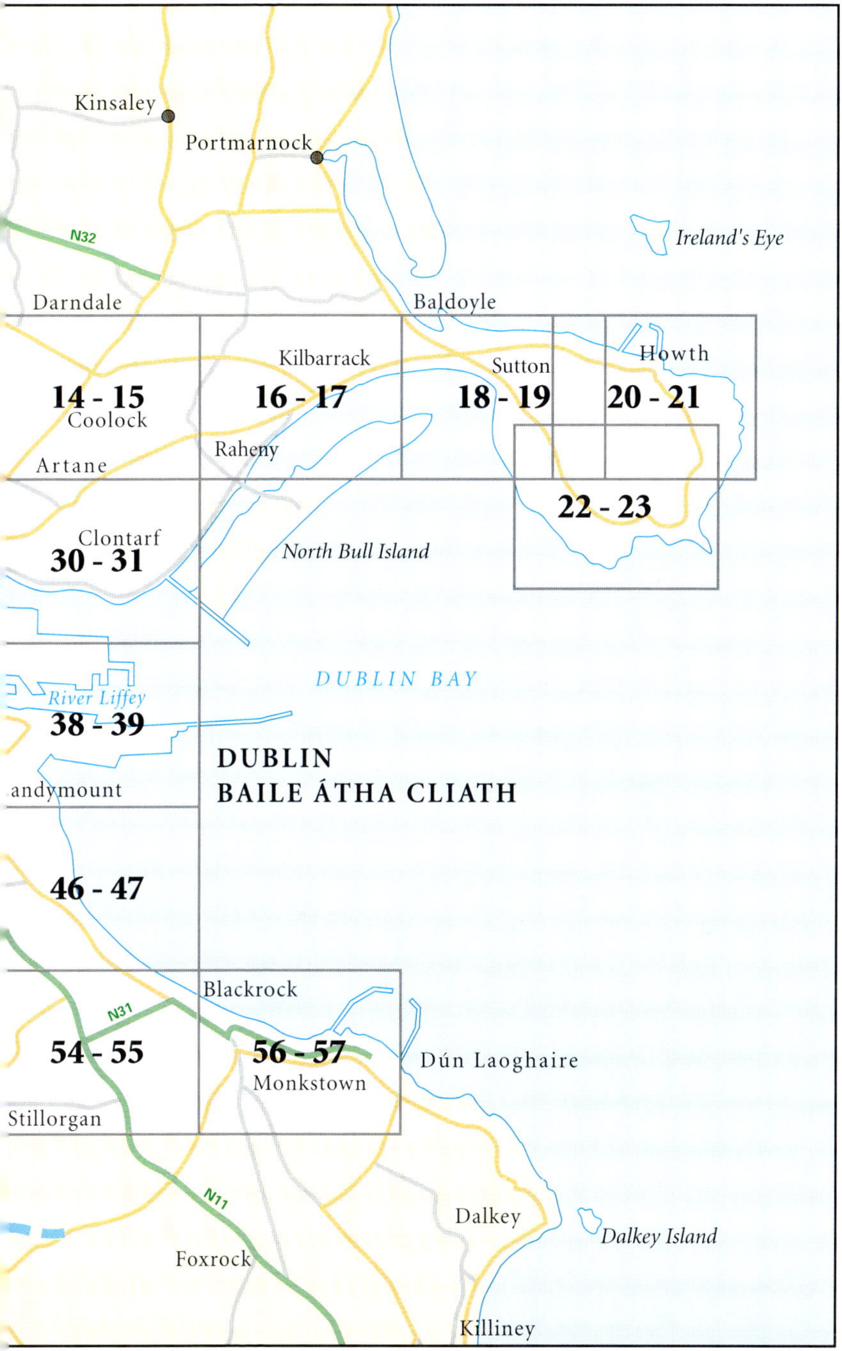
Kinsaley
Portmarnock
N32
Ireland's Eye
Darndale
Baldoyle
Kilbarrack
Sutton
Howth
14 - 15
Coolock
16 - 17
18 - 19
20 - 21
Artane
Raheny
22 - 23
Clontarf
30 - 31
North Bull Island
DUBLIN BAY
River Liffey
38 - 39
DUBLIN
BAILE ÁTHA CLIATH
andymount
46 - 47
Blackrock
N31
54 - 55
56 - 57
Dún Laoghaire
Monkstown
Stillorgan
N11
Dalkey
Dalkey Island
Foxrock
Killiney

CAVAN
LONGFORD
WESTMEATH
OFFALY
LAOIS
Ballinagh
Carrickaboy
Moylett
Baillieborough
Kingscourt
Moyer
341
Arvagh
Moyne
Gorteen
Erne
Lough Rynn Estate & Gardens
Rinn Lough
R201
R202
R198
R165
R154
R196
R191
R178
R164
N3
N55
New Inn
Killinkere
Teevurcher
Lough Gowna
Kilnaleck
Crosserlough
Ballyjamesduff
Dromod
Ballinamuck
Aghnacliff
Clooneagh
Cloonagh
Aghadowry
Roosky
Drumlish
R194
Mount Nugent
Virginia
Mullagh
Lough Sheelin
Lough Ramor
Lisduff
Moynalty
Pipers Town
Bunlahy
R394
R195
Ryefield
Ross
Newtown Forbes
Ballinalee
Granard
Finnea
Oldcastle
Carlanstown
Whitehall
St. Mel's Cathedral
Carriglass Manor
Castletown
Millbrook
Megalithic Cemetery
276
Slieve na Calliagh
Kells (Ceanannus)
High Crosses
Longford
N4
Lisryan
R395
Coole
Drumone
Crossakeel
Edgeworthstown
Tullynally Castle
Fore Priory
Cross Keys
Kilskeer
R393
Danesfort
Castlepollard
Fordstown
Moydow
Lough Derravaragh
Lough Lene
N52
Clonmellon
Boherard
R398
Royal Canal
Rathowen
Lackan
Drumcree
Keenagh
Carrickboy
Ballinalack
Multyfarnham
Athboy
R397
Barry
Inny
Lough Iron
Ballynafid
Crookedwood
Delvin
N51
Foygh
Ballynacarrigy
Abbeyshrule
Lough Owel
Monilea
Terrin
Kildalkey
Ballymahon
Cloghbrack
Deel
Tang
Moyvore
Rathconrath
Cathedral
Cloghan
R156
Ballivor
Cloncullen
R392
Mullingar (An Muileann gCearr)
Killucan
Uisneach
184
R391
Gainestown
Rathmolyon
Glassan
R390
Ballymore
Lough Ennell
Coralstown
R160
Drumraney
R161
Longwood
Gaybrook
Kinnegad
Clonard
Streamstown
R400
Moyvoughly
Castletown Geoghegan
Killaskillen
Moyvalley
N6
Rochfortbridge
R401
Johnstown Bridge
Fardrum
Moate
Horseleap
Ballinagore
Garr
Castlejordan
Tober
Tyrrellspass
Kilbeggan
Newtownlow
Carbury
Kilshanroe
Ballynahowen
Clara
R436
Rhode
Edenderry
Windmill
Grand Canal
Durrow
Croghan
Ballyfore
Togher
Ballycumber
N80
Bog of Allen
R403
Tullamore (Tulach Mhór)
Daingean
Allenwood
Brosna
Rahan
R402
Ballykilleen
Lullymore
Robertstown
Ferbane
Charleville Castle
Clonbullogue
Killinthomas
Scraggan
R420
Ballinagar
R414
Kilmeague
N62
R357
Geashill
Brackagh
Rathangan
Blue Ball
Killeigh
Bracknagh
R419
Milltown
Cloghan
Kilcavan
KILDARE
Broughal
R421
Mountbolus
Clonygowan
Cushina
St Brigid's Cathedral
Round Tower
Barrow
Kilcormac
Portarlington
Kildare
Galros
R422
Two Mile Bridge
R423
Japanese Gardens
Rapemills
Clonaslee
Rosenallis
Jamestown
Monasterevan
The Curragh
Rath
Cadamstown
Ballybrittas
Crosskeys
Castle Demesne
Mountmellick
N7
R440
Kinnitty
New Inn
Nurney
Calverstown
Slieve Bloom Mts
Crinkill
Clareen
Vicarstown
R415
Ballyfin
R447
Kilberry
Arderin
529
Ballydavis
M7
R427
Fontstown
Sharavogue
Drimmo
Portlaoise
Rock of Dunamase
N78
R417
Ardscull
Boherphuca
Mountrath
Stradbally
R428
White Castle
Nealstown
Athy
High Cross
Brosna
N8
Cashel
R418
Priory (remains)
Coolrain
Castletown
Damer House
R425
Timahoe
Ballylynan
Kilkea
Roscrea
Kilmorony

ROUTE PLANNING MAP

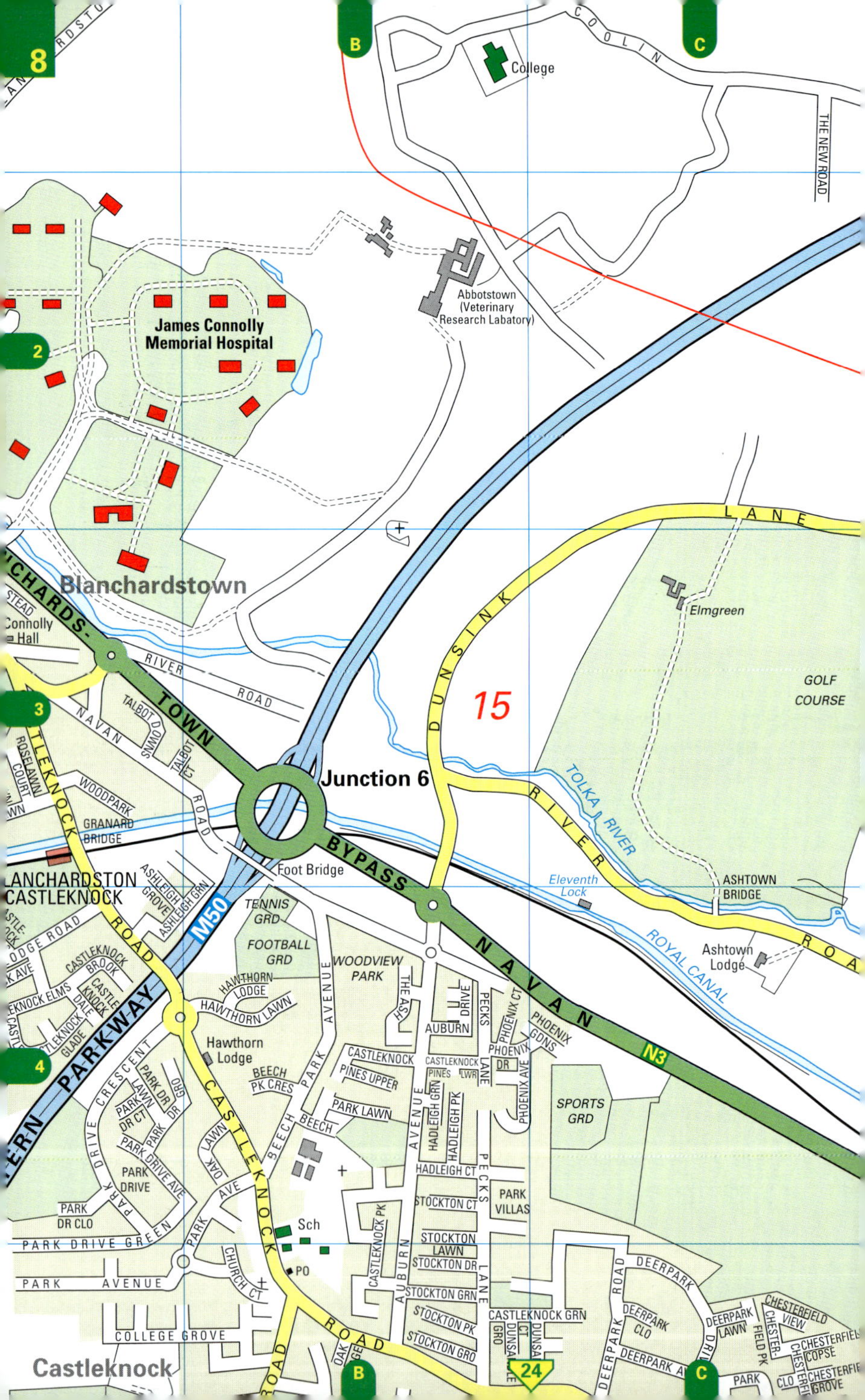

B
C
2
3
4
College
COOLIN
THE NEW ROAD
James Connolly Memorial Hospital
Abbotstown (Veterinary Research Labatory)
Blanchardstown
Connolly Hall
RIVER ROAD
TOWN
NAVAN
TALBOT DOWNS
TALBOT CT
ROAD
ROSELAWN COURT
WOODPARK
GRANARD BRIDGE
BLANCHARDSTOWN CASTLEKNOCK
ASHLEIGH GROVE
ASHLEIGH GRN
Junction 6
BYPASS
Foot Bridge
M50
LANE
DUNSINK
15
Elmgreen
GOLF COURSE
TOLKA RIVER
RIVER
ROAD
Eleventh Lock
ASHTOWN BRIDGE
ROYAL CANAL
Ashtown Lodge
NAVAN
N3
TENNIS GRD
FOOTBALL GRD
WOODVIEW PARK
AVENUE
THE ASH
AUBURN
DRIVE
PECKS
PHOENIX CT
PHOENIX GDNS
PHOENIX DR
PHOENIX AVE
HAWTHORN LODGE
HAWTHORN LAWN
Hawthorn Lodge
PARKWAY
CASTLEKNOCK BROOK
CASTLEKNOCK DALE
CASTLEKNOCK GLADE
CASTLEKNOCK ELMS
CRESCENT
PARK DR
PARK LAWN
PARK DR CT
PARK DRIVE AVE
PARK DRIVE
PARK DR CLO
PARK DRIVE GREEN
PARK AVENUE
BEECH PK CRES
BEECH PARK
CASTLEKNOCK PINES UPPER
CASTLEKNOCK PINES LWR
PARK LAWN
HADLEIGH GRN
HADLEIGH PK
HADLEIGH CT
SPORTS GRD
STOCKTON CT
STOCKTON LAWN
STOCKTON DR
STOCKTON GRN
STOCKTON PK
STOCKTON GRO
PARK VILLAS
CASTLEKNOCK PK
OAK LAWN
Sch
PO
CHURCH CT
COLLEGE GROVE
Castleknock
CASTLEKNOCK ROAD
CASTLEKNOCK GRN
DUNSANDLE GRO
DUNSANDLE CT
24
DEERPARK ROAD
DEERPARK
DEERPARK CLO
DEERPARK AVE
DEERPARK LAWN
DEERPARK DRIVE
CHESTERFIELD VIEW
CHESTERFIELD PK
CHESTERFIELD COPSE
CHESTERFIELD GROVE
PARK

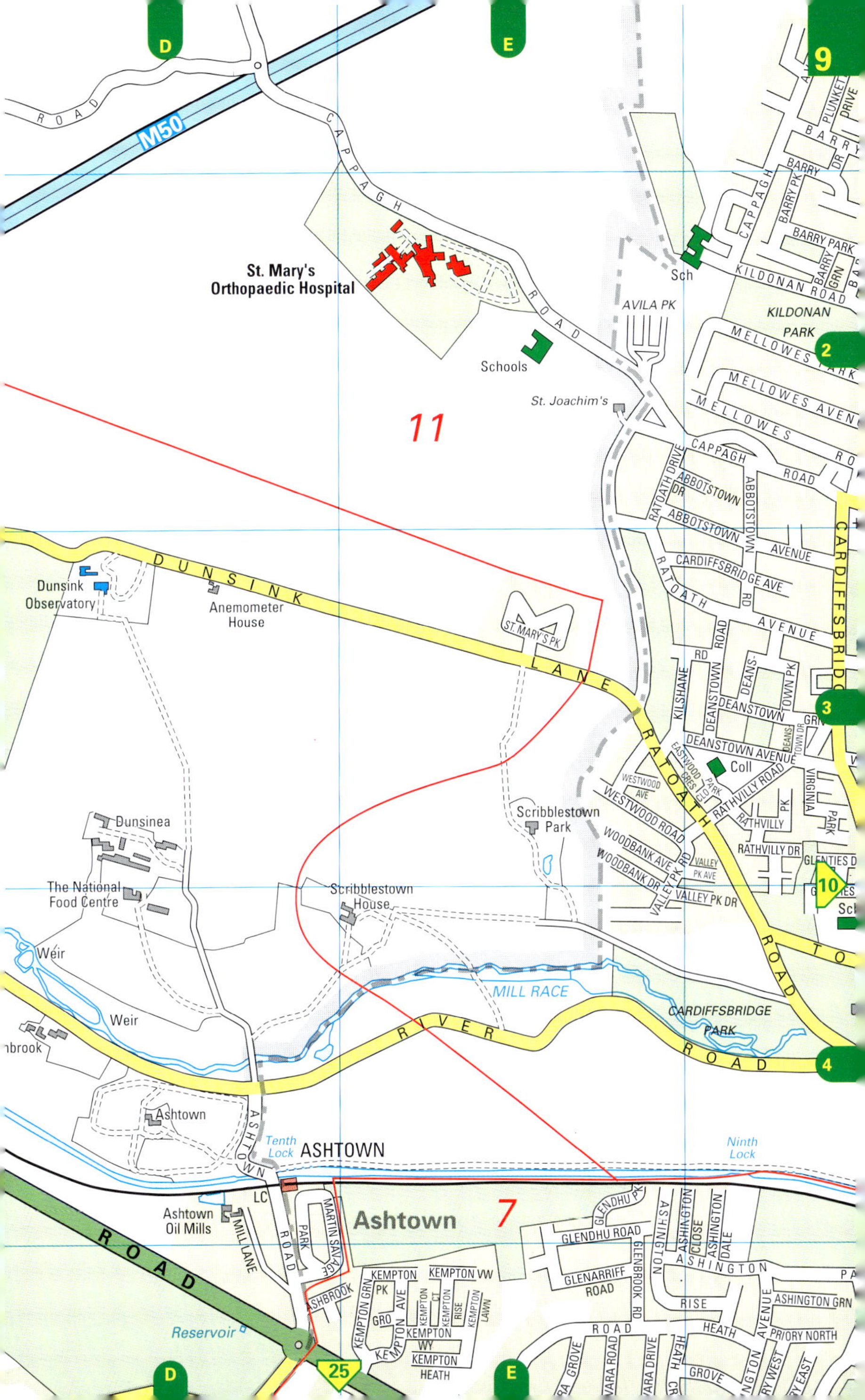
D
E
9
M50
ROAD
CAPPAGH ROAD
St. Mary's
Orthopaedic Hospital
Schools
St. Joachim's
11
AVILA PK
Sch
PLUNKETT DRIVE
BARRY DR
BARRY
BARRY PK
BARRY PARK
BARRY GRN
CAPPAGH
KILDONAN ROAD
KILDONAN PARK
2
MELLOWES PARK
MELLOWES AVENUE
MELLOWES
CAPPAGH ROAD
RATOATH DRIVE
ABBOTSTOWN DR
ABBOTSTOWN
ABBOTSTOWN AVENUE
CARDIFFSBRIDGE AVE
RATOATH RD
AVENUE
CARDIFFSBRID
DUNSINK LANE
Dunsink
Observatory
Anemometer
House
ST. MARY'S PK
KILSHANE RD
DEANSTOWN ROAD
DEANSTOWN PK
DEANSTOWN GRN
DEANSTOWN AVENUE
DEANSTOWN DR
3
EASTWOOD CRES
CLO
PARK
Coll
RATHVILLY ROAD
RATHVILLY PK
RATHVILLY DR
VIRGINIA
PARK
GLENTIES D
10
Sch
WESTWOOD AVE
WESTWOOD ROAD
WOODBANK AVE
WOODBANK DR
VALLEY PK RD
VALLEY PK AVE
VALLEY PK DR
Scribblestown
Park
Dunsinea
The National
Food Centre
Scribblestown
House
Weir
Weir
MILL RACE
RATOATH ROAD
CARDIFFSBRIDGE
PARK
RIVER ROAD
4
nbrook
Ashtown
ASHTOWN
Tenth
Lock
ASHTOWN
Ninth
Lock
LC
Ashtown
Oil Mills
MILL LANE
ROAD
MARTIN SAVAGE PARK
Ashtown
7
GLENDHU PK
GLENDHU ROAD
GLENARRIFF
ROAD
GLENBROOK RD
ASHINGTON
ASHINGTON CLOSE
ASHINGTON DALE
ASHINGTON
RISE
ASHINGTON GRN
AVENUE
HEATH
PRIORY NORTH
ROAD
ASHBROOK
KEMPTON
KEMPTON VW
KEMPTON GRN
PK
GRO
AVE
KEMPTON CT
KEMPTON RISE
KEMPTON LAWN
KEMPTON WY
KEMPTON HEATH
ROAD
Reservoir
25
E
D

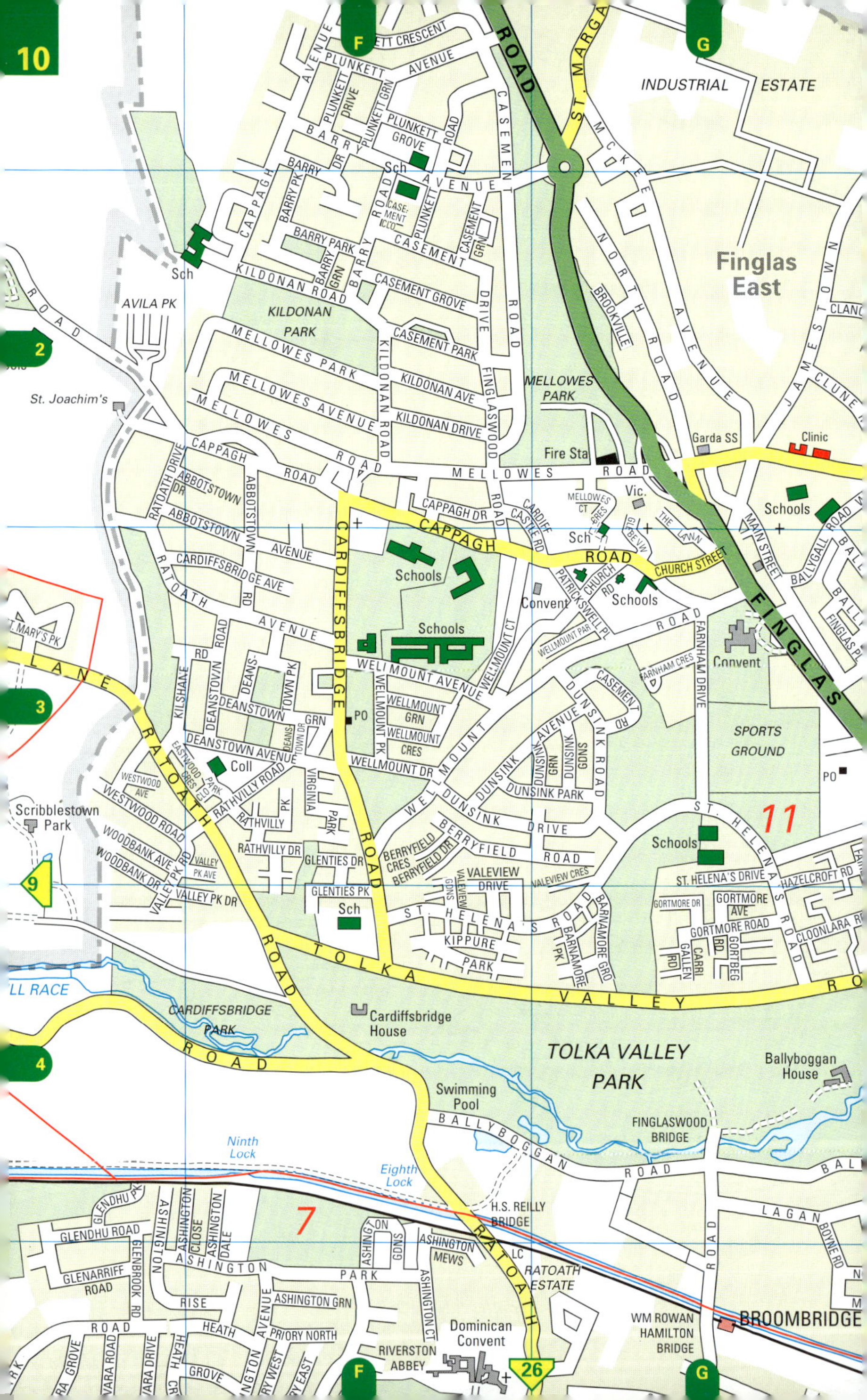
F
G
INDUSTRIAL ESTATE
Finglas East
PLUNKETT CRESCENT
PLUNKETT AVENUE
PLUNKETT DRIVE
PLUNKETT GRN
PLUNKETT GROVE
PLUNKETT ROAD
BARRY DR
BARRY AVENUE
BARRY PK
BARRY PARK
BARRY GRN
BARRY ROAD
CASEMENT ROAD
CASEMENT AVENUE
CASEMENT GRN
CASEMENT CLO
CASEMENT GROVE
CASEMENT PARK
CASEMENT DRIVE
CAPPAGH AVENUE
KILDONAN ROAD
KILDONAN PARK
KILDONAN AVE
KILDONAN DRIVE
Sch
AVILA PK
ROAD
2
St. Joachim's
MELLOWES PARK
MELLOWES AVENUE
MELLOWES ROAD
FINGLASWOOD ROAD
ROAD
ST. MARGARET'S
McKEE
NORTH ROAD
NORTH AVENUE
BROOKVILLE
JAMESTOWN
CLUNE
CLANC
Garda SS
Clinic
Fire Sta
Vic.
MELLOWES CT
MELLOWES CRES
GLEBE VIEW
THE LAWN
Schools
MAIN STREET
BALLYGALL ROAD
CHURCH STREET
FINGLAS
CAPPAGH ROAD
CAPPAGH DR
CARDIFF CASTLE RD
ABBOTSTOWN DR
ABBOTSTOWN AVENUE
ABBOTSTOWN
ABBOTSTOWN RD
RATOATH DRIVE
CARDIFFSBRIDGE AVE
RATOATH AVENUE
CARDIFFSBRIDGE ROAD
Convent
PATRICKSWELL PL
CHURCH RD
WELLMOUNT PAR
WELLMOUNT CT
WELLMOUNT AVENUE
WELLMOUNT GRN
WELLMOUNT CRES
WELLMOUNT PK
WELLMOUNT DR
WELLMOUNT ROAD
FARNHAM CRES
FARNHAM DRIVE
DUNSINK ROAD
DUNSINK AVENUE
DUNSINK GRN
DUNSINK GDNS
DUNSINK PARK
DUNSINK DRIVE
CASEMENT RD
SPORTS GROUND
PO
11
ST. MARY'S PK
LANE
3
KILSHANE RD
DEANSTOWN ROAD
DEANSTOWN AVENUE
DEANSTOWN PK
DEANSTOWN DR
DEANSTOWN GRN
Coll
EASTWOOD CRES
EASTWOOD CLO
EASTWOOD PARK
RATHVILLY ROAD
RATHVILLY PK
RATHVILLY DR
VIRGINIA PARK
WESTWOOD AVE
WESTWOOD ROAD
Scribblestown Park
WOODBANK AVE
WOODBANK DR
VALLEY PK RD
VALLEY PK AVE
VALLEY PK DR
9
GLENTIES DR
GLENTIES PK
BERRYFIELD CRES
BERRYFIELD DR
BERRYFIELD ROAD
VALEVIEW DRIVE
VALEVIEW GDNS
VALEVIEW CRES
ST. HELENA'S ROAD
ST. HELENA'S DRIVE
KIPPURE PARK
KIPPURE PK
BARNAMORE PK
BARNAMORE GRO
HAZELCROFT RD
GORTMORE DR
GORTMORE AVE
GORTMORE ROAD
CARRIGALLEN RD
GORTBEG RD
CLOONLARA RD
RATOATH ROAD
TOLKA VALLEY ROAD
RACE
CARDIFFSBRIDGE PARK
ROAD
4
Cardiffsbridge House
TOLKA VALLEY PARK
Ballyboggan House
Swimming Pool
BALLYBOGGAN ROAD
FINGLASWOOD BRIDGE
Ninth Lock
Eighth Lock
H.S. REILLY BRIDGE
LC
7
GLENDHU PK
GLENDHU ROAD
GLENARRIFF ROAD
GLENBROOK RD
ASHINGTON CLOSE
ASHINGTON DALE
ASHINGTON PARK
ASHINGTON GDNS
ASHINGTON MEWS
ASHINGTON CT
ASHINGTON GRN
ASHINGTON AVENUE
ASHINGTON RISE
ASHINGTON HEATH
RATOATH ESTATE
LAGAN ROAD
BOYNE RD
BROOMBRIDGE
WM ROWAN HAMILTON BRIDGE
PRIORY NORTH
Dominican Convent
RIVERSTON ABBEY
26
GROVE

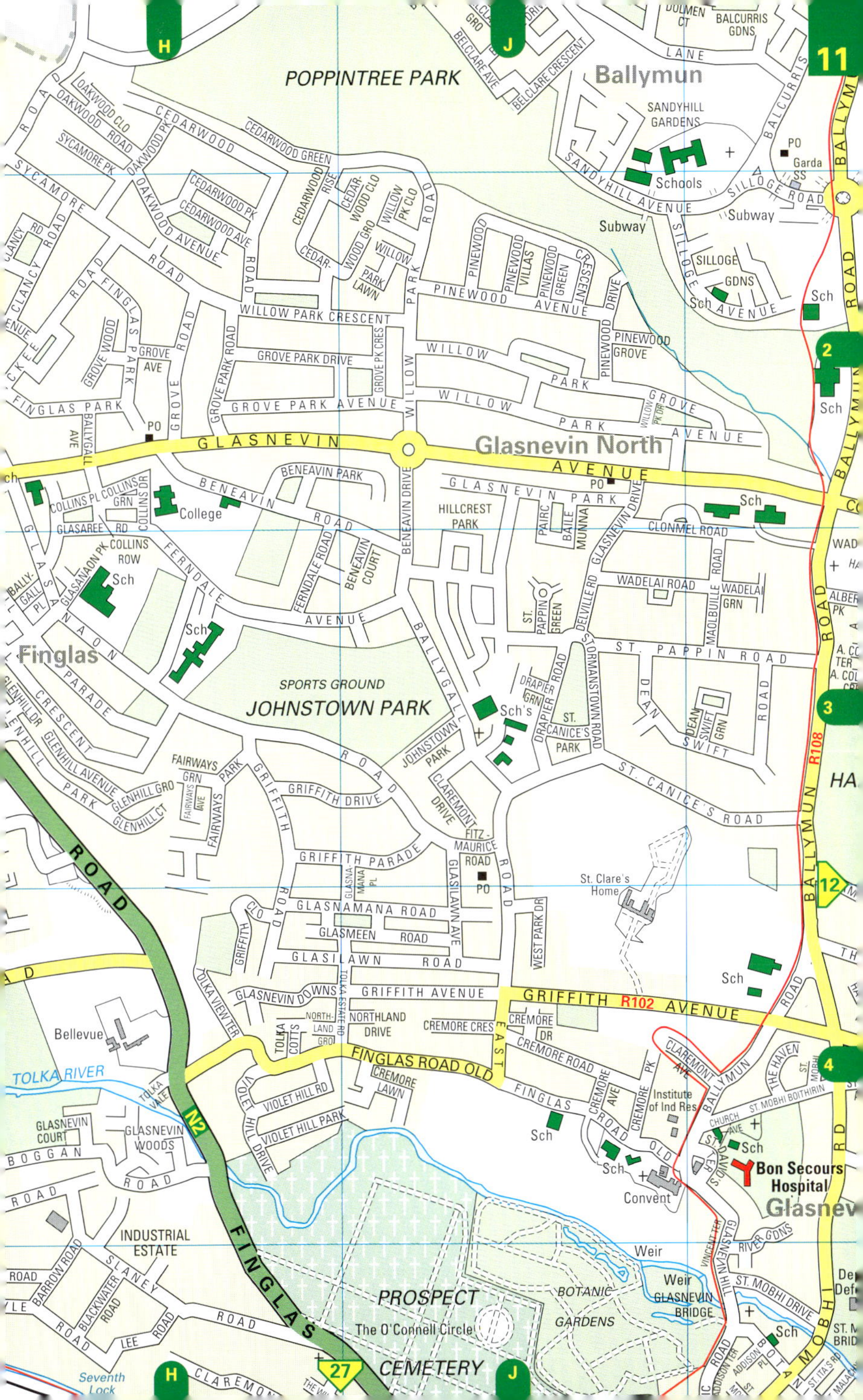
H
J
POPPINTREE PARK
Ballymun
DOLMEN CT
BALCURRIS GDNS
LANE
BELCLARE CRESCENT
BELCLARE AVE
SANDYHILL GARDENS
Schools
SANDYHILL AVENUE
SILLOGE ROAD
PO
Garda
SS
BALCURRIS
Subway
Subway
SILLOGE
SILLOGE GDNS
SILLOGE AVENUE
Sch
Sch
OAKWOOD CLO
OAKWOOD ROAD
SYCAMORE PK
OAKWOOD PK
CEDARWOOD
CEDARWOOD GREEN
CEDARWOOD RISE
CEDARWOOD CLO
WILLOW PK CLO
ROAD
CEDARWOOD PK
CEDARWOOD AVE
OAKWOOD AVENUE
ROAD
SYCAMORE ROAD
CLANCY RD
CLANCY ROAD
FINGLAS PARK
CEDAR-WOOD GRO
WILLOW PARK LAWN
PINEWOOD
PINEWOOD VILLAS
PINEWOOD GREEN
CRESCENT
PINEWOOD AVENUE
PINEWOOD DRIVE
WILLOW PARK CRESCENT
GROVE ROAD
GROVE WOOD
GROVE AVE
GROVE PARK ROAD
GROVE PARK DRIVE
GROVE PK CRES
WILLOW PARK
PINEWOOD GROVE
GROVE PARK AVENUE
WILLOW PARK GROVE
WILLOW PK DR
PARK AVENUE
FINGLAS PARK
BALLYGALL AVE
PO
GLASNEVIN
Glasnevin North
AVENUE
2
Sch
BENEAVIN PARK
BENEAVIN ROAD
BENEAVIN DRIVE
GLASNEVIN PARK
PO
Sch
CLONMEL ROAD
HILLCREST PARK
PAIRC BAILE MUNNA
GLASNEVIN DRIVE
COLLINS PL
COLLINS GRN
COLLINS DR
College
GLASAREE RD
GLASANAON PK
COLLINS ROW
BALLYGALL PL
Sch
FERNDALE ROAD
BENEAVIN COURT
FERNDALE AVENUE
ST. PAPPIN GREEN
DELVILLE RD
WADELAI ROAD
WADELAI GRN
MAOLBUILLE ROAD
WAD
ALBERT PK
Finglas
GLASANAON ROAD
Sch
PARADE
CRESCENT
ST. PAPPIN ROAD
STORMANSTOWN ROAD
SPORTS GROUND
JOHNSTOWN PARK
BALLYGALL ROAD
Sch's
DRAPIER GRN
DRAPIER ROAD
ST. CANICE'S PARK
DEAN SWIFT GRN
DEAN SWIFT
A. CO TER
A. COL
3
R108
HA
GLENHILL DR
GLENHILL ROAD
GLENHILL AVENUE
GLENHILL PARK
GLENHILL GRO
GLENHILL CT
FAIRWAYS GRN
FAIRWAYS AVE
FAIRWAYS PARK
GRIFFITH ROAD
JOHNSTOWN PARK
ST. CANICE'S ROAD
GRIFFITH DRIVE
CLAREMONT DRIVE
FITZ-MAURICE ROAD
ROAD
BALLYMUN ROAD
ROAD
GRIFFITH PARADE
GLASNAMANA PL
GLASILAWN AVE
PO
St. Clare's Home
12
GRIFFITH CLO
GLASNAMANA ROAD
GLASMEEN ROAD
GLASILAWN ROAD
WEST PARK DR
TOLKA VIEW TER
GLASNEVIN DOWNS
TOLKA ESTATE RD
GRIFFITH AVENUE
GRIFFITH R102 AVENUE
Sch
TH
NORTHLAND GRO
NORTHLAND DRIVE
CREMORE CRES
CREMORE DR
EAST
Bellevue
TOLKA COTTS
FINGLAS ROAD OLD
CREMORE ROAD
CLAREMONT AVE
THE HAVEN
ST. MOBHI
4
TOLKA RIVER
TOLKA VALE
VIOLET HILL RD
VIOLET HILL DRIVE
VIOLET HILL PARK
CREMORE LAWN
FINGLAS ROAD OLD
CREMORE AVE
CREMORE PK
Institute of Ind Res
BALLYMUN
ST. MOBHI BOITHIRIN
CHURCH AVE
Sch
GLASNEVIN COURT
GLASNEVIN WOODS
N2
BOGGAN ROAD
Sch
Sch
Convent
ST. DAVID'S TER
Bon Secours Hospital
Glasnev
ROAD
INDUSTRIAL ESTATE
FINGLAS ROAD
RIVER GDNS
Weir
Weir
GLASNEVIN BRIDGE
VINCENT TER
GLASNEVIN HILL
ST. MOBHI DRIVE
Def
ROAD
BARROW ROAD
SLANEY ROAD
BLACKWATER ROAD
LEE ROAD
PROSPECT
BOTANIC
GARDENS
The O'Connell Circle
Sch
ST. M BRID
MOBHI
RD
Seventh Lock
H
CLAREMONT
27
CEMETERY
J
ADDISON TER
ADDISON PL
BOTANIC
ST. ITA'S RD

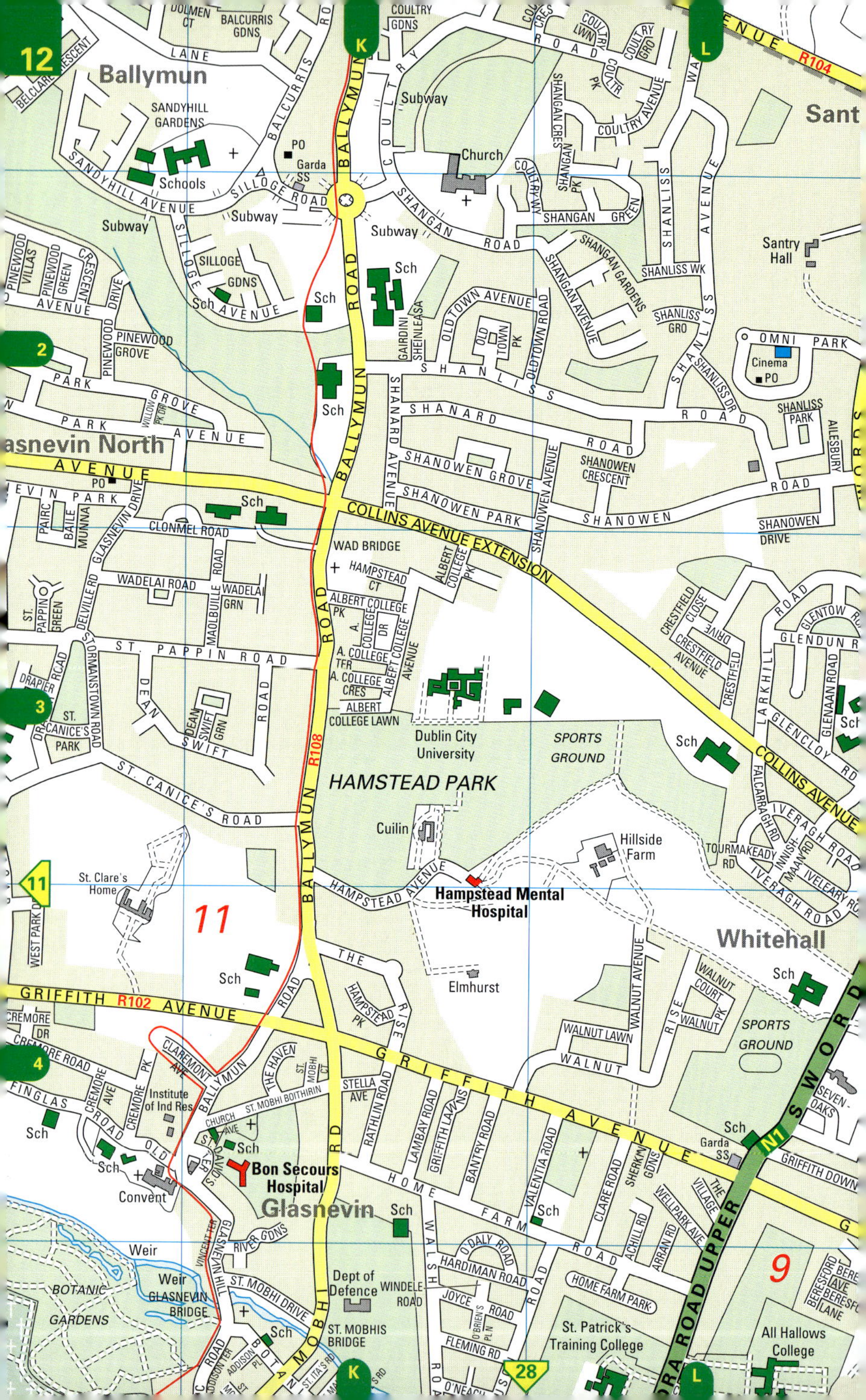
Ballymun
Sandyhill Gardens
Schools
Sandyhill Avenue
Sillogue Road
Subway
PO
Garda SS
Ballymun Road
Coultry Gdns
Coultry Road
Coultry Avenue
Church
Shangan Road
Shangan Green
Shangan Gardens
Shangan Avenue
Shanliss Avenue
Shanliss Wk
Shanliss Gro
Shanliss Road
Shanliss Dr
Shanliss Park
Santry Hall
Omni Park
Cinema
Sillogue Gdns
Sillogue Avenue
Sch
Pinewood Villas
Pinewood Green
Pinewood Crescent
Pinewood Avenue
Pinewood Drive
Pinewood Grove
Oldtown Avenue
Oldtown Road
Old Town Pk
Gairdini Sheinleasa
Shanard Road
Shanard Avenue
Shanowen Grove
Shanowen Park
Shanowen Avenue
Shanowen Crescent
Shanowen Road
Shanowen Drive
Glasnevin North
Park Avenue
Grove
Collins Avenue
Collins Avenue Extension
Glasnevin Park
Pairc Baile Munna
Glasnevin Drive
Clonmel Road
Wad Bridge
Hampstead Ct
Albert College Pk
Albert College Dr
Albert College Avenue
A. College Tfr
A. College Cres
Albert College Lawn
Wadelai Road
Wadelai Grn
Maolbuille Road
Delville Rd
St. Pappin Green
St. Pappin Road
Stormanstown Road
Drapier Road
St. Canice's Park
St. Canice's Road
Dean Swift Road
Dean Swift Grn
Dublin City University
Sports Ground
Hamstead Park
Cuilin
Hillside Farm
Crestfield Close
Crestfield Drive
Crestfield Avenue
Larkhill Road
Glentow Rd
Glendun Rd
Glenaan Road
Glencloy Rd
Falcarragh Rd
Iveragh Road
Innishmaan Rd
Iveleary Rd
Tourmakeady Rd
St. Clare's Home
11
Hampstead Avenue
Hampstead Mental Hospital
Elmhurst
Whitehall
West Park Dr
R108
Ballymun Road
The Rise
Hampstead Pk
Walnut Avenue
Walnut Lawn
Walnut Rise
Walnut Court
Walnut Pk
Sports Ground
Griffith Avenue
R102
Cremore Dr
Cremore Road
Cremore Ave
Cremore Pk
Claremont Ave
Finglas Road
Old
Institute of Ind Res
The Haven
St. Mobhi Ct
St. Mobhi Boithirin
Church Ave
Stella Ave
Rathlin Road
Lambay Road
Griffith Lawns
Bantry Road
Valentia Road
Clare Road
Sherkin Gdns
Achill Rd
Arran Rd
Wellpark Ave
The Village
Griffith Downs
Seven Oaks
Garda SS
N1
Swords Road
Drumcondra Road Upper
Convent
St. David's
Bon Secours Hospital
Glasnevin
Home Farm Road
Home Farm Park
Hardiman Road
O'Daly Road
Joyce Road
O'Brien's Pl N
Fleming Rd
Walsh Road
Windele Road
Dept of Defence
River Gdns
Vincent Ter
Glasnevin Hill
St. Mobhi Drive
St. Mobhis Bridge
Mobhi Rd
Weir
Glasnevin Bridge
Botanic Gardens
Addison Pl
Botanic Road
St. Ita's Rd
St. Patrick's Training College
All Hallows College
Beresford Lane
Beresford Ave
9
28
Santry
R104
K
L
2
3
4

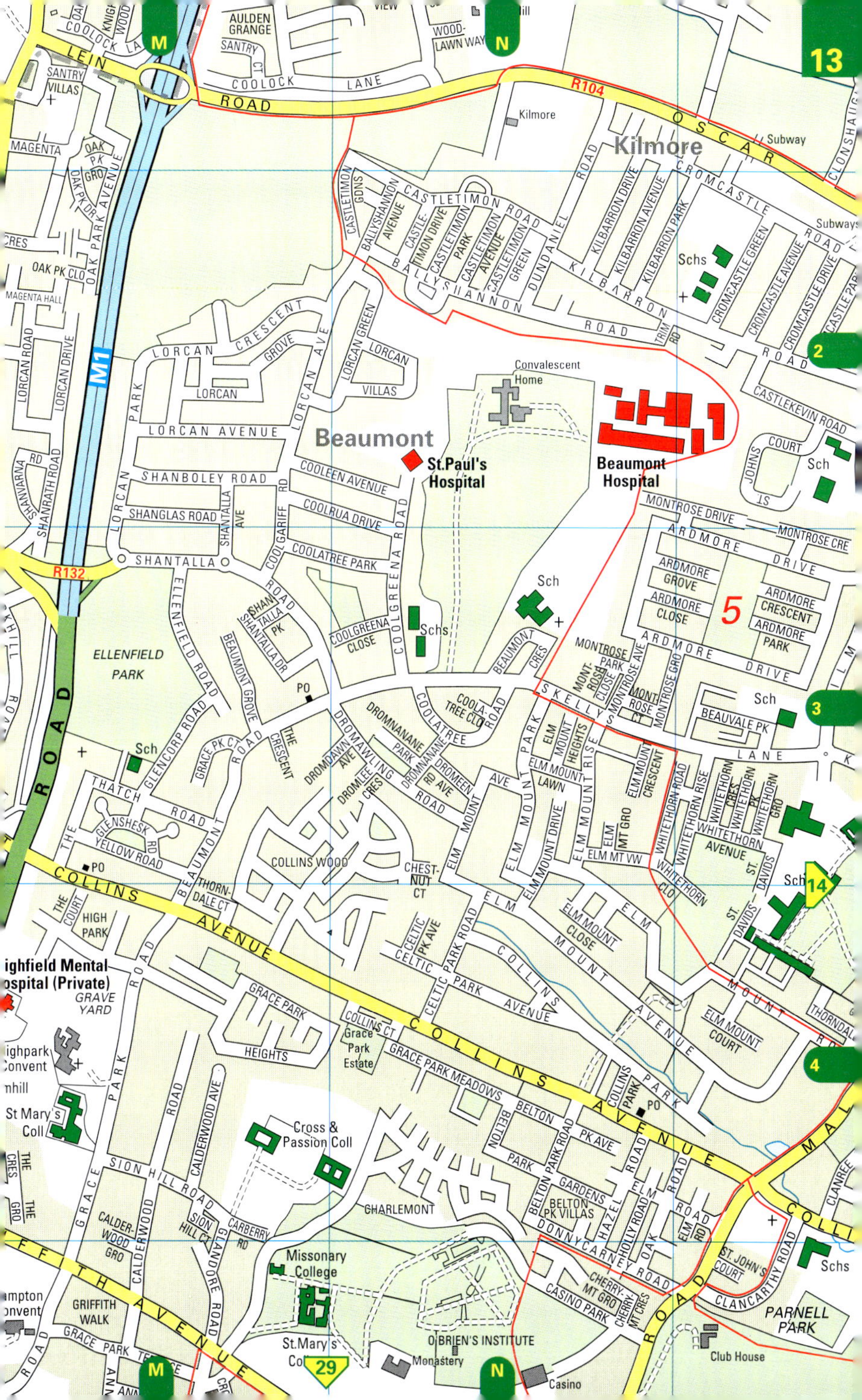
M
N
Kilmore
Beaumont
St.Paul's Hospital
Beaumont Hospital
Convalescent Home
5
2
3
4
14
29
ELLENFIELD PARK
PARNELL PARK
Cross & Passion Coll
Missonary College
O'BRIEN'S INSTITUTE
Highfield Mental Hospital (Private)
COLLINS AVENUE
OSCAR ROAD
COOLOCK LANE
SANTRY RD
R104
R132
M1
GRIFFITH AVENUE
CHARLEMONT
Club House
Casino
Monastery

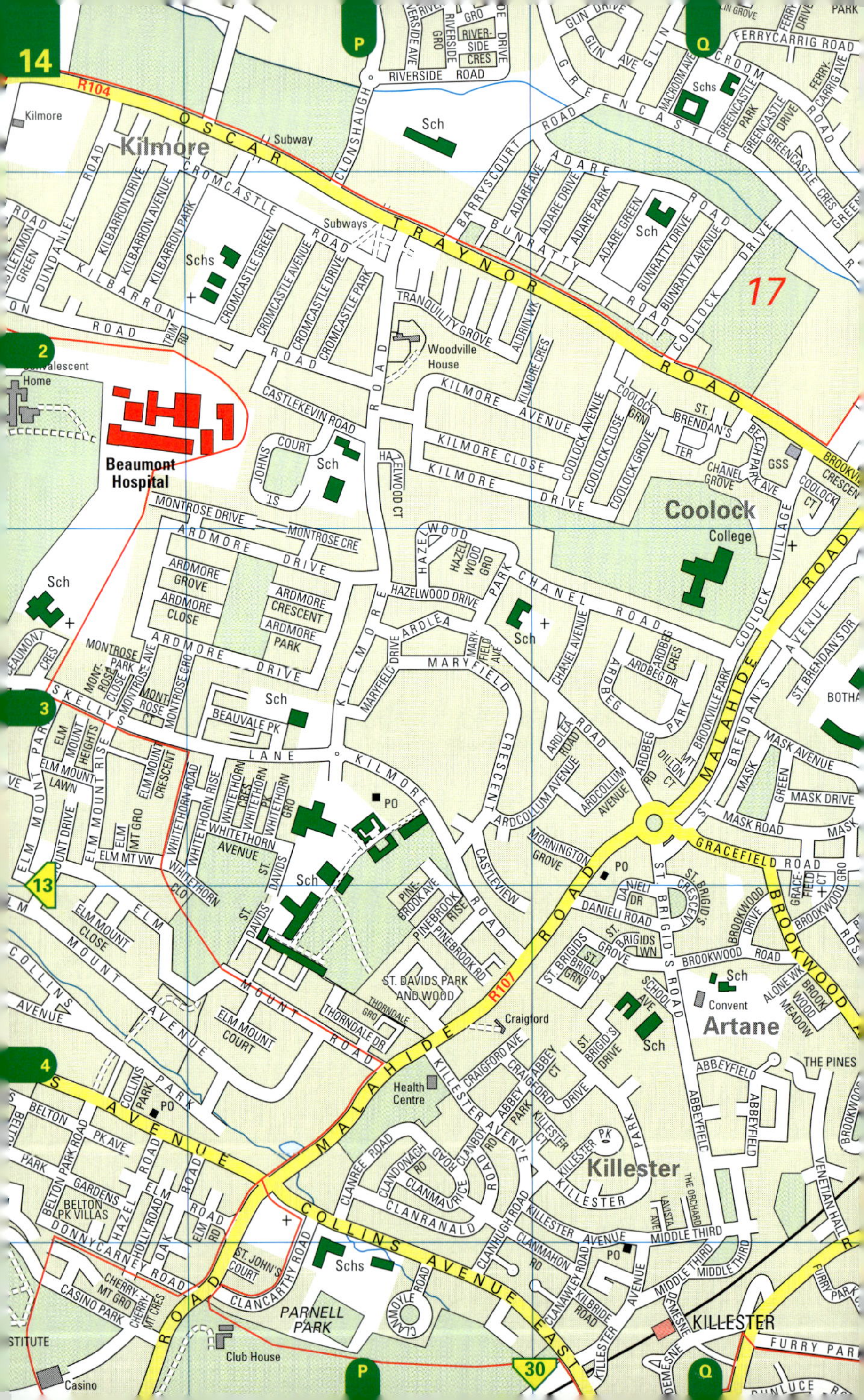
P
Q
17
2
3
4
13
30
R104
R107
Kilmore
Coolock
Artane
Killester
KILLESTER
OSCAR TRAYNOR ROAD
CROMCASTLE ROAD
KILBARRON ROAD
KILBARRON DRIVE
KILBARRON AVENUE
KILBARRON PARK
DUNDANIEL ROAD
CROMCASTLE GREEN
CROMCASTLE AVENUE
CROMCASTLE DRIVE
CROMCASTLE PARK
TRIM RD
CLONSHAUGH ROAD
RIVERSIDE ROAD
RIVERSIDE AVE
RIVERSIDE GRO
RIVERSIDE CRES
GLIN DRIVE
GLIN AVE
GREENCASTLE ROAD
GREENCASTLE PARK
GREENCASTLE DRIVE
GREENCASTLE CRES
MACROOM AVE
CROOM
FERRYCARRIG ROAD
FERRYCARRIG AVE
BARRYSCOURT ROAD
ADARE ROAD
ADARE AVE
ADARE DRIVE
ADARE PARK
ADARE GREEN
BUNRATTY ROAD
BUNRATTY DRIVE
BUNRATTY AVENUE
COOLOCK DRIVE
TRANQUILITY GROVE
ALDRIN WK
Woodville House
KILMORE ROAD
KILMORE AVENUE
KILMORE CRES
KILMORE CLOSE
KILMORE DRIVE
COOLOCK AVENUE
COOLOCK CLOSE
COOLOCK GROVE
COOLOCK GRN
ST. BRENDAN'S TER
CHANEL GROVE
BEECH PARK AVE
GSS
BROOKVILLE CRESCENT
COOLOCK CT
COOLOCK VILLAGE
College
Convalescent Home
Beaumont Hospital
CASTLEKEVIN ROAD
ST. JOHNS COURT
HAZELWOOD CT
MONTROSE DRIVE
MONTROSE CRE
ARDMORE DRIVE
ARDMORE GROVE
ARDMORE CLOSE
ARDMORE CRESCENT
ARDMORE PARK
HAZELWOOD
HAZELWOOD GRO
HAZELWOOD DRIVE
CHANEL ROAD
ARDLEA
MARYFIELD DRIVE
MARYFIELD AVE
MARYFIELD CRESCENT
CHANEL AVENUE
ARDBEG ROAD
ARDBEG DR
ARDBEG CRES
ARDBEG PARK
ARDBEG RD
MALAHIDE ROAD
ST. BRENDAN'S AVENUE
ST. BRENDAN'S DR
BOTHAR
BEAUMONT CRES
MONTROSE PARK
MONTROSE CLOSE
MONTROSE AVE
MONTROSE GRO
MONTROSE CT
SKELLYS LANE
BEAUVALE PK
ELM MOUNT PARK
ELM MOUNT HEIGHTS
ELM MOUNT RISE
ELM MOUNT CRESCENT
ELM MOUNT LAWN
ELM MOUNT DRIVE
ELM MT GRO
ELM MT VW
ELM MOUNT CLOSE
ELM MOUNT AVENUE
ELM MOUNT COURT
ELM MOUNT ROAD
WHITETHORN ROAD
WHITETHORN RISE
WHITETHORN CRES
WHITETHORN PK
WHITETHORN GRO
WHITETHORN AVENUE
WHITETHORN CLO
ST. DAVIDS
PO
PINEBROOK AVE
PINEBROOK RISE
PINEBROOK RD
ST. DAVIDS PARK AND WOOD
THORNDALE GRO
THORNDALE DR
CASTLEVIEW
ARDCOLLUM AVENUE
ARDLEA ROAD
MORNINGTON GROVE
DILLON CT
BROOKVILLE PARK
MASK AVENUE
MASK GREEN
MASK DRIVE
MASK ROAD
GRACEFIELD ROAD
GRACEFIELD CT
BROOKWOOD CT
BROOKWOOD DRIVE
BROOKWOOD ROAD
BROOKWOOD
ST. BRIGID'S CRESCENT
ST. BRIGID'S ROAD
DANIELI DR
DANIELI ROAD
ST. BRIGIDS GROVE
BRIGIDS LWN
ST. BRIGIDS GRN
ST. BRIGIDS CT
ST. BRIGID'S DRIVE
SCHOOL AVE
Convent
ALONE WK
BROOKWOOD MEADOW
Craigford
CRAIGFORD AVE
CRAIGFORD DRIVE
ABBEY CT
ABBEY PARK
ABBEYFIELD
THE PINES
KILLESTER AVENUE
KILLESTER CT
KILLESTER PK
KILLESTER PARK
Health Centre
COLLINS AVENUE
COLLINS PARK
COLLINS AVENUE EAST
BELTON PARK ROAD
BELTON PK AVE
BELTON PARK GARDENS
BELTON PK VILLAS
DONNYCARNEY ROAD
HAZEL ROAD
HOLLY ROAD
ELM ROAD
OAK ROAD
ELM RD
CLANREE ROAD
CLANDONAGH RD
CLANMAURICE ROAD
CLANBOY ROAD
CLANRANALD ROAD
CLANHUGH ROAD
CLANMAHON RD
CLANAWLEY ROAD
KILBRIDE ROAD
CLANMOYLE ROAD
CLANCARTHY ROAD
ST. JOHN'S COURT
PARNELL PARK
Club House
CHERRY MT GRO
CHERRY MT CRES
CASINO PARK
Casino
STITUTE
THE ORCHARD
LAVISTA AVE
MIDDLE THIRD
DEMESNE
FURRY PARK
VENETIAN HALL
DUNLUCE
Schs
Sch
Subway
Subways

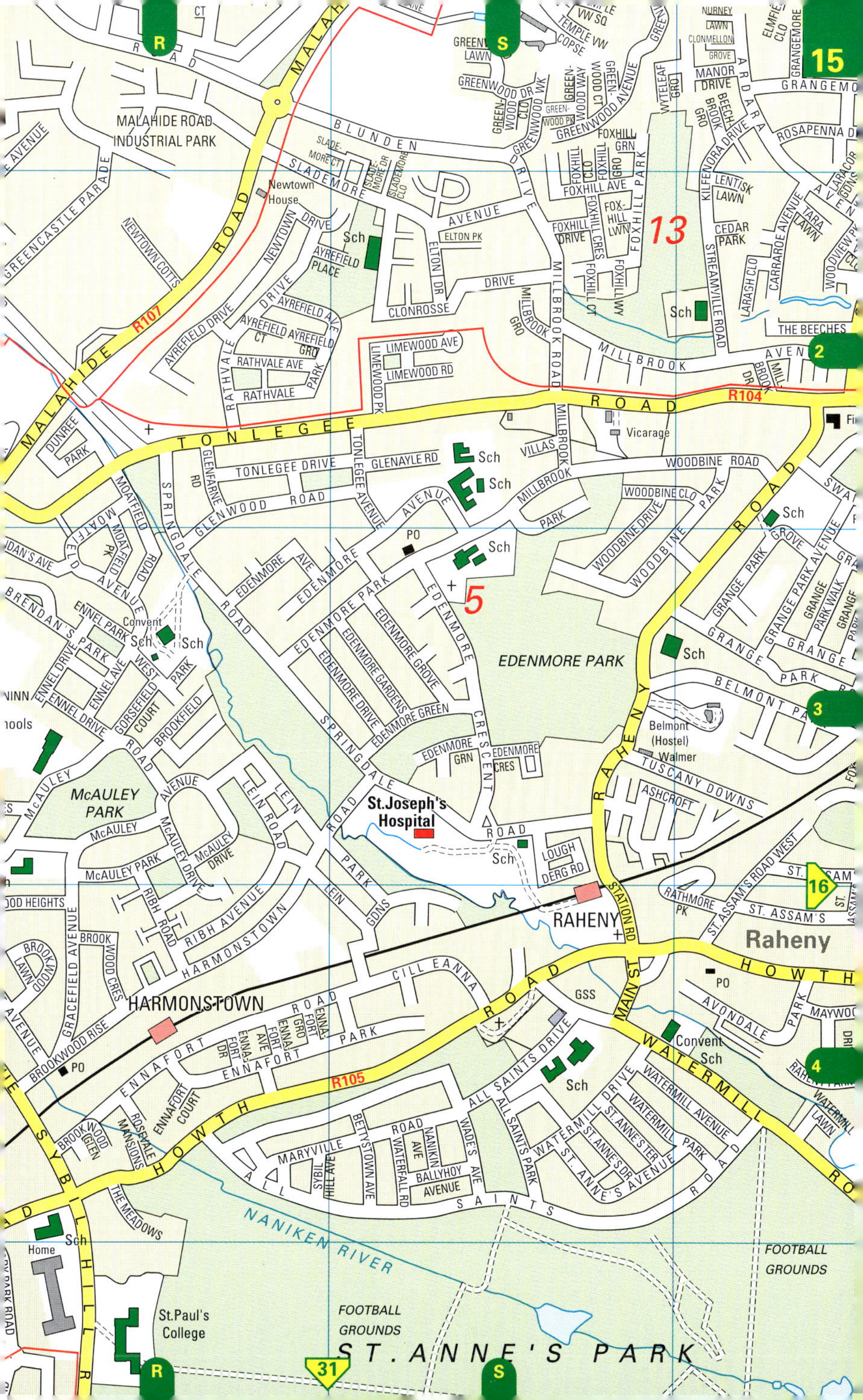
R
S
MALAHIDE ROAD INDUSTRIAL PARK
MALAHIDE ROAD
R107
BLUNDEN DRIVE
SLADEMORE
Newtown House
GREENCASTLE PARADE
NEWTOWN COTTS
NEWTOWN DRIVE
AYREFIELD PLACE
AYREFIELD DRIVE
AYREFIELD AVE
AYREFIELD CT
AYREFIELD GRO
RATHVALE
RATHVALE AVE
RATHVALE PARK
Sch
ELTON PK
ELTON DR
AVENUE
CLONROSSE DRIVE
GREENWOOD DR
GREENWOOD AVENUE
TEMPLE VW
FOXHILL AVE
FOXHILL DRIVE
FOXHILL CRES
FOXHILL PARK
FOXHILL GRN
FOXHILL CT
FOXHILL LWN
FOXHILL WY
13
MILLBROOK ROAD
MILLBROOK GRO
MILLBROOK AVENUE
KILFENORA DRIVE
STREAMVILLE ROAD
ARDARA
GRANGEMORE
ROSAPENNA DR
LENTISK LAWN
CEDAR PARK
CARRAROE AVENUE
TARA LAWN
LARASH CLO
WOODVIEW PK
THE BEECHES
LIMEWOOD AVE
LIMEWOOD RD
LIMEWOOD PK
TONLEGEE ROAD
R104
2
Vicarage
DUNREE PARK
TONLEGEE DRIVE
TONLEGEE AVENUE
GLENAYLE RD
GLENFARNE RD
GLENWOOD ROAD
MILLBROOK VILLAS
WOODBINE ROAD
WOODBINE CLO
WOODBINE DRIVE
WOODBINE PARK
RAHENY ROAD
MOATFIELD AVENUE
MOATFIELD ROAD
MOATFIELD PK
SPRINGDALE ROAD
EDENMORE AVE
EDENMORE PARK
EDENMORE AVENUE
EDENMORE GARDENS
EDENMORE DRIVE
EDENMORE GROVE
EDENMORE GREEN
EDENMORE CRESCENT
EDENMORE GRN
EDENMORE CRES
PO
5
EDENMORE PARK
GRANGE PARK
GRANGE PARK AVENUE
GRANGE PARK WALK
GRANGE PARK GROVE
BELMONT PARK
3
Belmont (Hostel)
Walmer
TUSCANY DOWNS
ASHCROFT
BRENDAN'S AVE
ENNEL PARK
ENNEL DRIVE
ENNEL AVE
Convent
GORSEFIELD COURT
BROOKFIELD
WEST PARK
McAULEY PARK
McAULEY ROAD
McAULEY AVENUE
McAULEY DRIVE
LEIN ROAD
LEIN PARK
LEIN GDNS
St.Joseph's Hospital
ROAD
LOUGH DERG RD
RIBH AVENUE
RIBH ROAD
HARMONSTOWN ROAD
GRACEFIELD AVENUE
BROOKWOOD CRES
BROOKWOOD LAWN
BROOKWOOD RISE
HARMONSTOWN
RAHENY
STATION RD
ST. ASSAM'S ROAD WEST
ST. ASSAM'S
RATHMORE PK
16
Raheny
HOWTH ROAD
MAIN ST
PO
GSS
AVONDALE PARK
CILL EANNA
ENNAFORT ROAD
ENNAFORT PARK
ENNAFORT DR
ENNAFORT AVE
ENNAFORT GRO
ENNAFORT COURT
R105
ALL SAINTS DRIVE
ALL SAINTS PARK
Convent Sch
WATERMILL ROAD
WATERMILL DRIVE
WATERMILL AVENUE
WATERMILL PARK
WATERMILL LAWN
ST. ANNE'S TER
ST. ANNE'S DR
ST. ANNE'S AVENUE
4
MARYVILLE ROAD
SYBIL HILL AVE
BETTYSTOWN AVE
WATERFALL RD
NANIKIN AVE
BALLYHOY AVENUE
WADE'S AVE
ALL SAINTS ROAD
BROOKWOOD GLEN
ROSEVALE MANSIONS
THE MEADOWS
SYBIL HILL ROAD
NANIKEN RIVER
Home
Sch
St.Paul's College
FOOTBALL GROUNDS
FOOTBALL GROUNDS
ST. ANNE'S PARK
31

T
U
13
2
15
3
4
5
GRANGE ABBEY DRIVE
GRANGE ABBEY CRESCENT
GRANGE ABBEY GROVE
ELMFIELD LWN
ELMFIELD CRES
ELMFIELD CLO
GRANGEMORE CRES
GRANGEMORE DR
GRANGEMORE ROAD
GRANGEMORE GROVE
GRANGEMORE LAWN
GRANGEMORE AVE
NURNEY LAWN
CLONMELLON GROVE
MANOR DRIVE
ARDARA AVENUE
TEMPLE VW SQ
TEMPLE VW COPSE
GREENWOOD AVENUE
GREENWOOD CT
GREENWOOD WAY
GREENWOOD PK
GREENWOOD WK
GREENWOOD CLO
GREENWOOD DR
WYTELEAF GRO
BEECHBROOK GRO
ROSAPENNA DRIVE
FOXHILL GRN
FOXHILL CLO
FOXHILL AVE
FOXHILL LWN
FOXHILL DRIVE
FOXHILL CRES
FOXHILL CT
FOXHILL WY
FOXHILL PARK
KILFENORA DRIVE
LENTISK LAWN
CEDAR PARK
STREAMVILLE ROAD
CARRAROE AVENUE
TARA LAWN
LARACOR GDNS
KILMORONY CLO
LARAGH CLO
WOODVIEW PK
WOODVIEW CLO
HOWTH VW PK
THE BEECHES
GRANGE ROAD
Sch
PO
THE DONAHIES
NEWBROOK ROAD
NEWBROOK AVE
DONAGHMEDE PARK
CARNDONAGH PARK
CARNDONAGH DRIVE
CARNDONAGH ROAD
CARNDONAGH LWN
DONAGHMEDE ROAD
HOLYWELL CRESCENT
HOLYWELL ROAD
DONAGHMEDE AVE
DONAGHMEDE PARK
DONAGHMEDE DRIVE
MILLBROOK ROAD
MILLBROOK AVENUE
MILLBROOK DR
ST. DONAGH'S ROAD
ST. DONAGH'S CRES
ST. DONAGH'S PK
R104
KILBARRACK ROAD
HOWTH JUNCTION
KILBARRACK PARADE
KILBARRACK WAY
INDUSTRIAL ESTATE
Fire Sta
Subway
Vicarage
MILLBROOK VILLAS
WOODBINE ROAD
WOODBINE CLO
WOODBINE PARK
WOODBINE DRIVE
MOUNT OLIVE ROAD
MOUNT OLIVE PARK
MOUNT OLIVE GROVE
SWANS NEST ROAD
SWANS NEST CT
SWANS NEST AVE
Schs
KILBARRACK
GRANGE PARK GROVE
GRANGE PARK AVENUE
GRANGE PARK PARADE
GRANGE PARK WALK
GRANGE PARK DRIVE
GRANGE PARK RISE
GRANGE PK GRN
GRANGE PK CLO
GRANGE PARK CRESCENT
GRANGE PARK ROAD
EDENMORE PARK
BRIARFIELD ROAD
BRIARFIELD GROVE
BRIARFIELD VILLAS
THORNVILLE ROAD
THORNVILLE PARK
THORNVILLE DRIVE
THORNVILLE AVE
GREENDALE ROAD
GREENDALE AVENUE
Health Centre
RAHENY ROAD
BELMONT PARK
Belmont (Hostel)
Walmer
TUSCANY DOWNS
ASHCROFT
ROSE GLEN ROAD
ROSE GLEN AVENUE
FOXFIELD GREEN
FOXFIELD CRES
FOXFIELD ST. JOHN
FOXFIELD GROVE
FOXFIELD HEIGHTS
CEDAR WALK
FOXFIELD AVENUE
FOXFIELD DRIVE
FOXFIELD ROAD
FOXFIELD LAWN
FOXFIELD PARK
LOUGHDERG RD
RAHENY
STATION RD
RATHMORE PK
ST. ASSAM'S ROAD WEST
ST. ASSAM'S PARK
ST. ASSAM'S AVENUE
ST. ASSAM'S DR
ST. ASSAM'S RD EAST
Raheny
HOWTH ROAD
R105
FOXS LANE
MAIN ST
GSS
ORCHARD ROAD
AVONDALE PARK
MAYWOOD AVENUE
MAYWOOD GROVE
MAYWOOD PARK
MAYWOOD DRIVE
MAYWOOD RD
MAYWOOD CLO
MAYWOOD CRESCENT
MAYWOOD LANE
BETTYGLEN
Convent Sch
RAHENY PARK
WATERMILL ROAD
WATERMILL DRIVE
WATERMILL AVENUE
WATERMILL PARK
WATERMILL LAWN
ALL SAINTS PARK
ST. ANNE'S TER
ST. ANNE'S DR
ST. ANNE'S AVENUE
THE VILLAGE
THE COURT
THE GROVE
JAMES LARKIN ROAD
FOOTBALL GROUNDS
E'S PARK

Talavera
STAPOLIN ESTATE
V
W
Sch
LARK HILL BRIDGE
ADMIRAL
WILLIE
NOLAN RD
St. Mary's Orth. Hospital
REILLYS LA
PAROCHIAL AVE
COLLEGE ST
BACK LA
Sch
STRAND ROAD
ST
WARRENHOUSE ROAD
PO
Coll
DUBLIN STREET
BROOKSTONE RD
GEORGIAN HAMLET
Sch
Schs
GRANGE PARK
GRANGE RISE
GRANGE AVENUE
ROAD
SEAGRANGE AVE
SEAGRANGE DR
SEAGRANGE ROAD
ABBEY PARK
MARIAN PARK
SEAGRANGE PARK
TUSCANY PARK
MEADOWBROOK AVENUE
MEADOWBROOK LAWN
MEADOWBROOK PARK
TURNBERRY
WARREN GREEN
BALDOYLE INDUSTRIAL ESTATE
GRANGE CLOSE
GRANGE DRIVE
GRANGE WAY
SEAGRANGE
SEACLIFF DR
SEACLIFF AVENUE
SEACLIFF RD
PARKVALE
MOYCLARE PARK
MOYCLARE AVE
MOYCLARE ROAD
MOYCLARE CLO
BURROWFIELD ROAD
JAMES MCCORMACK GARDENS
2
BAYSIDE
BAYSIDE BOULEVARD
BAYSIDE WALK
VERBENA PK
VERBENA GRO
Sch
VERBENA AVENUE
SARTO LAWN
NORTH
BAYSIDE PARK
SUTTON
SUTTON PARK
RAILWAY AVENUE
THE CRES
BINN EADAIR VIEW
SUTTON PARK
SUTTON COURT
SEAFIELD CT
LAWNS
BALDOYLE ROAD
BAYSIDE SQ NORTH
BAYSIDE SQ EAST
BAYSIDE SQ S
BAYSIDE SQ WEST
BAYSIDE SQ S
PO
SARTO PARK
SUTTON GROVE
SUTTON DOWNS
KILBARRACK CEMETERY
ROAD
R105
Yacht Club
Kilbarrack
PACELLI AVENUE
SARTO ROAD
SARTO PARK
SARTO RISE
RONCALLI ROAD
JAMES JOYCE CT
BAYSIDE BOULEVARD S
R104
ROAD
DEL VAL CT
DEL VAL AVE
BEACH VIEW
ROSBEG CT
HILLSIDE VW
DUBLIN
SUTTON S
3
MARGARET'S AVENUE
ROAD
18
4
Nature Reserve and Bird Sanctuary
North Bull Island
ST. ANNE'S GOLF COURSE
Club House
V
W

X
Y
2
3
4
17
Baldoyle
Orth. Hospital
NOLAN RD
Sch
REILLYS LA
COLLEGE ST
CHIAL AVE
PARO-
BACK LA
GEORGIAN HAMLET
Coll
DUBLIN STREET
PO
Schs
AVENUE
TURNBERRY
MEADOWBROOK
MEADOWBROOK LAWN
MEADOWBROOK PARK
WARREN GREEN
WARRENHOUSE ROAD
STRAND ROAD
STATION ROAD
MOYCLARE PARK
MOYCLARE AVE
MOYCLARE ROAD
MOYCLARE CLO
BURROWFIELD ROAD
JAMES MCCORMACK GARDENS
LC
SUTTON
SUTTON PARK
SUTTON PARK LAWNS
SEAFIELD CT
BALDOYLE ROAD
RAILWAY AVENUE
THE CRES
BINN EADAIR VIEW
THE COURT
Sch
Sutton
ROAD
R105
Yacht Club
RRACK ETERY
Gush Point
Club House
GOLF COURSE
GOLF LINKS
Suncroft
BURROW ROAD
LAUDERS LA
GOLF LINKS
PO
DUBLIN
GREENFIELD ROAD
SPORTS GROUND
CHURCH ROAD
Marine Hotel
Sch
SUTTON STRAND
SUTTON CREEK
North Bull Island

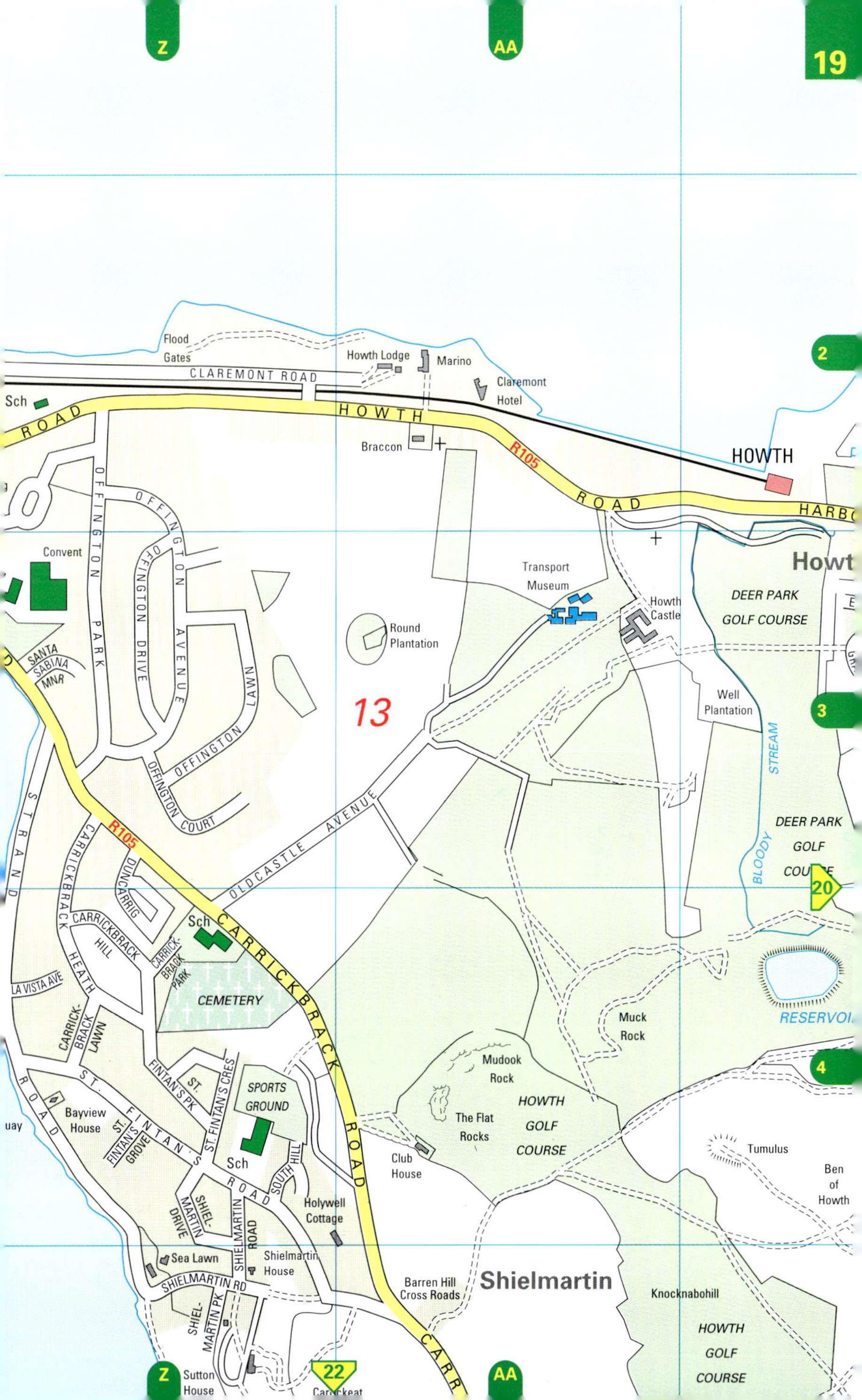

Z
AA
2
3
4
20
22
Flood Gates
CLAREMONT ROAD
Howth Lodge
Marino
Claremont Hotel
Sch
HOWTH ROAD
R105
Braccon
HOWTH
ROAD
HARBO
Howt
DEER PARK GOLF COURSE
Transport Museum
Howth Castle
Round Plantation
Well Plantation
13
OFFINGTON PARK
OFFINGTON AVENUE
OFFINGTON DRIVE
OFFINGTON LAWN
OFFINGTON
OFFINGTON COURT
Convent
SANTA SABINA MNR
STRAND ROAD
OLDCASTLE AVENUE
STREAM
BLOODY
DEER PARK GOLF COURSE
CARRICKBRACK HEATH
CARRICKBRACK HILL
DUNCARRIG
CARRICKBRACK PARK
CARRICKBRACK ROAD
Sch
CEMETERY
LA VISTA AVE
CARRICKBRACK LAWN
RESERVOI
Muck Rock
Mudook Rock
The Flat Rocks
HOWTH GOLF COURSE
FINTAN'S PK
ST. FINTAN'S CRES
SPORTS GROUND
Sch
ST. FINTAN'S ROAD
ST. FINTAN'S GROVE
Bayview House
uay
SOUTH HILL
Club House
Tumulus
Ben of Howth
Holywell Cottage
SHIELMARTIN DRIVE
SHIELMARTIN ROAD
Sea Lawn
Shielmartin House
SHIELMARTIN RD
SHIELMARTIN PK
Barren Hill Cross Roads
Shielmartin
Knocknabohill
HOWTH GOLF COURSE
Sutton House
Carrickeat
CARR

AA
BB
2
3
4
CLAREMONT ROAD
Howth Lodge
Marino
Claremont Hotel
HOWTH ROAD
R105
Braccon
HOWTH
West Pier
HOWTH HARBOUR
HARBOUR ROAD
Promenade
Howth
Transport Museum
Round Plantation
Howth Castle
DEER PARK GOLF COURSE
Garda S.S.
CHURCH
EVORA PARK
ST. LAWRENCE RD
GRACE O'MALLEY ROAD
TER
Sch
TUCKETT'S LA
ST. PETER'S TER
GRACE O'MALLEY DRIVE
BALGLASS ESTATE
BALKILL PK
Well Plantation
BLOODY STREAM
DEER PARK GOLF COURSE
OFFINGTON LAWN
OFFINGTON COURT
AVENUE
OLDCASTLE AVENUE
19
Sch
CARRICKBRACK ROAD
CARRICKBRACK PARK
CEMETERY
Muck Rock
RESERVOIR
Howth Tennis Ground
Old Plantation
Pav
Mudook Rock
The Flat Rocks
HOWTH GOLF COURSE
Club House
SPORTS GROUND
Sch
ST. FINTAN'S CRES
ST. FINTAN'S PK
SOUTH HILL
ROAD
SHIELMARTIN DRIVE
SHIELMARTIN ROAD
Holywell Cottage
Sea Lawn
Shielmartin House
SHIELMARTIN RD
SHIELMARTIN PK
Tumulus
Ben of Howth
Loughoreen
Black Linn
Barren Hill Cross Roads
Shielmartin
Knocknabohill
HOWTH GOLF COURSE
22
Sutton House
Carrickeat
Black Heath

CC
DD
2
3
4
23
13
BALSCADDEN BAY
East Pier
Martello Tower
Puck's Rocks
Nose of Howth
Kilrock
Elsinore
BALSCADDEN ROAD
KILROCK LANE
ASGARD PK
NASHVILLE PARK
NASHVILLE RD
ABBEY STREET
MAIN STREET
THORMANBY ROAD
GRAYSBROOK
ASGARD ROAD
COWBOOTER LANE
CLIFF WALK
Cannon Rock Cottage
CANNON ROCK VIEW
UPPER CLIFF RD
THORMANBY LAWNS
DUNGRIFFAN ROAD
MARINERS COVE
WOODCLIFF HEIGHTS
CASANA VIEW
GREYS LANE
Rookstown
THORMANBY LODGE
THORMANBY WOODS
Ashville
Highfield
Bearna
Oakley Park
Green Ivy
Piper's Gut
WINDGATE ROAD
KITESTOWN ROAD
R105
St.Patrick's
NEW ROAD
RISE
WINDGATE
Fox Hole
The Haven
PO
BAILEY GRN RD
BRACK ROAD
Bay View
Old Baily
Highro

Z
20
AA
4
5
6
OFFINGTON
OFFINGTON COURT
R105
OLDCASTLE AVENUE
STRAND ROAD
CARRICKBRACK HEATH
DUNCARRIG
CARRICKBRACK HILL
CARRICK-BRACK PARK
Sch
CARRICKBRACK ROAD
CEMETERY
LA VISTA AVE
13
CARRICK-BRACK LAWN
FINTAN'S PK
ST.
ST. FINTAN'S CRES
SPORTS GROUND
ST. FINTAN'S ROAD
Old Quay
Bayview House
ST. FINTAN'S GROVE
Sch
SOUTH HILL
SHIEL-MARTIN DRIVE
SHIELMARTIN ROAD
Holywell Cottage
Sea Lawn
Shielmartin House
SHIELMARTIN RD
SHIEL-MARTIN PK
Sutton House
Carrickeat
Martello Tower
Barren Hill Cross Roads
Shielmartin
Club House
Mudook Rock
The Flat Rocks
HOWTH GOLF COURSE
Muck Rock
Somali
BALSAGGART STREAM
Pumping House
Shearwater
CLIFF WALK
The Cliffs
Sheep Hole
Worn Hole

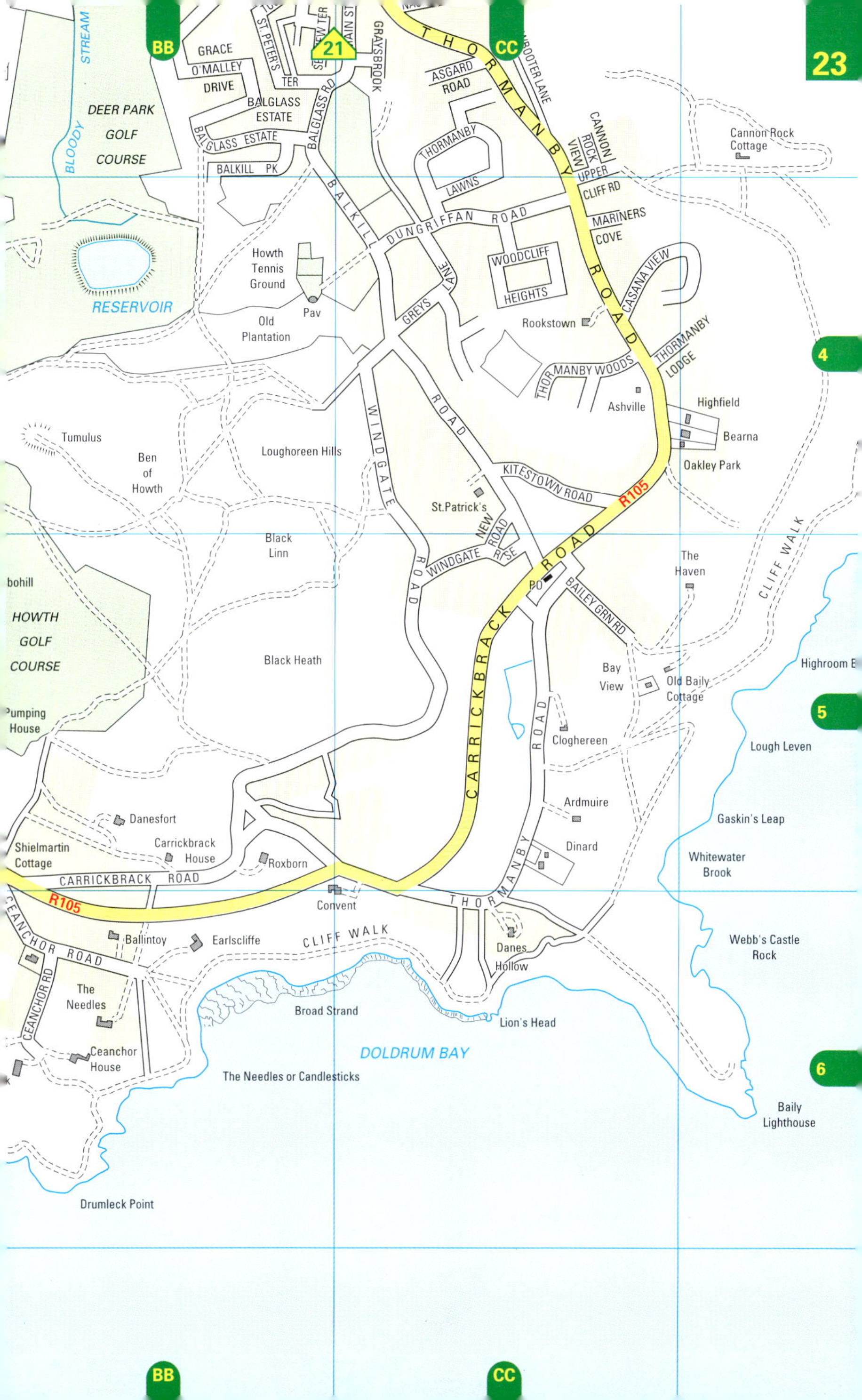
BB
CC
21
GRACE O'MALLEY DRIVE
ST. PETER'S TER
GRAYSBROOK
THORMANBY ROAD
ASGARD ROAD
BOOTER LANE
DEER PARK GOLF COURSE
BLOODY STREAM
BALGLASS ESTATE
BALGLASS RD
BALKILL PK
BALKILL
THORMANBY LAWNS
CANNON ROCK VIEW
UPPER CLIFF RD
MARINERS COVE
Cannon Rock Cottage
DUNGRIFFAN ROAD
WOODCLIFF HEIGHTS
CASANA VIEW
Howth Tennis Ground
Pav
RESERVOIR
Old Plantation
GREYS LANE
Rookstown
THORMANBY WOODS
THORMANBY LODGE
4
Ashville
Highfield
Bearna
Oakley Park
Tumulus
Ben of Howth
Loughoreen Hills
WINDGATE ROAD
KITESTOWN ROAD
R105
St.Patrick's
NEW ROAD RISE
Black Linn
CARRICKBRACK ROAD
The Haven
CLIFF WALK
PO
BAILEY GRN RD
bohill
HOWTH GOLF COURSE
Black Heath
Bay View
Old Baily Cottage
Highroom B
Pumping House
5
Cloghereen
Lough Leven
Ardmuire
Gaskin's Leap
Danesfort
Shielmartin Cottage
Carrickbrack House
Roxborn
Dinard
Whitewater Brook
THORMANBY ROAD
Convent
Ballintoy
Earlscliffe
CEANCHOR ROAD
CEANCHOR RD
Webb's Castle Rock
Danes Hollow
The Needles
Broad Strand
Lion's Head
Ceanchor House
DOLDRUM BAY
6
The Needles or Candlesticks
Baily Lighthouse
Drumleck Point

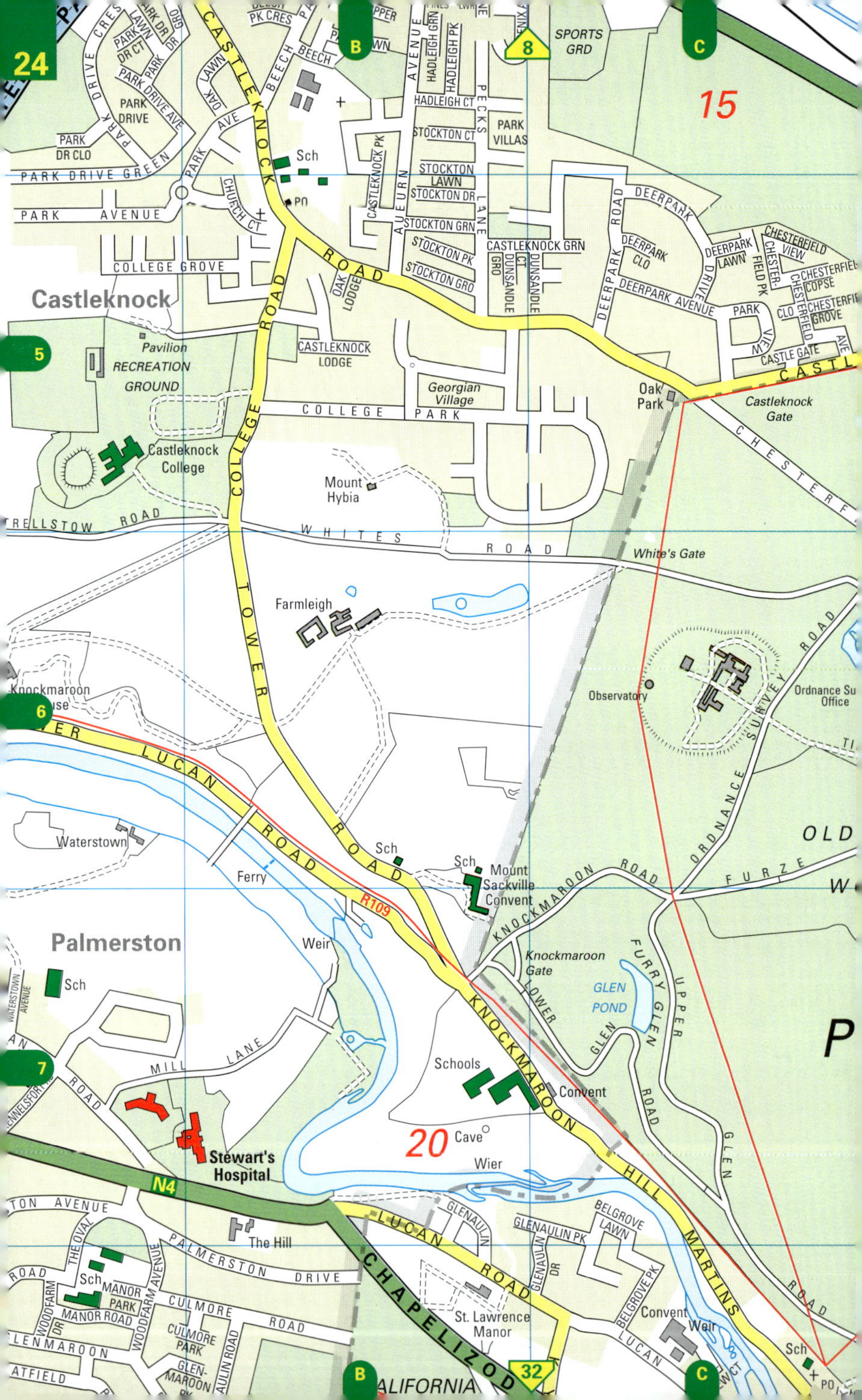
B
C
8
15
SPORTS GRD
PK CRES
BEECH
PARK DRIVE CRES
PARK LAWN
PARK DR CT
PARK DRIVE AVE
PARK DRIVE
PARK DR CLO
PARK DRIVE GREEN
PARK AVENUE
PARK AVE
OAK LAWN
CHURCH CT
CASTLEKNOCK ROAD
Sch
PO
AVENUE
HADLEIGH GRN
HADLEIGH PK
HADLEIGH CT
PECKS LANE
PARK VILLAS
STOCKTON CT
CASTLEKNOCK PK
AUBURN
STOCKTON LAWN
STOCKTON DR
STOCKTON GRN
STOCKTON PK
STOCKTON GRO
CASTLEKNOCK GRN
DUNSANDLE GRO
DUNSANDLE CT
DEERPARK
DEERPARK ROAD
DEERPARK CLO
DEERPARK AVENUE
DEERPARK LAWN
DEERPARK DRIVE
CHESTERFIELD VIEW
CHESTERFIELD PK
CHESTERFIELD COPSE
CHESTERFIELD CLO
CHESTERFIELD GROVE
CHESTERFIELD AVE
PARK VIEW
CASTLE GATE
COLLEGE GROVE
OAK LODGE
Castleknock
5
Pavilion
RECREATION GROUND
CASTLEKNOCK LODGE
COLLEGE ROAD
Georgian Village
COLLEGE PARK
Oak Park
Castleknock Gate
CHESTERFIELD
Castleknock College
Mount Hybia
TRELLSTOW ROAD
WHITES ROAD
White's Gate
TOWER ROAD
Farmleigh
Observatory
Ordnance Survey Office
SURVEY ROAD
Knockmaroon House
6
LUCAN ROAD
Waterstown
Ferry
Sch
Mount Sackville Convent
KNOCKMAROON ROAD
FURZE ROAD
ORDNANCE
OLD
R109
Palmerston
Weir
Knockmaroon Gate
LOWER GLEN
GLEN POND
FURRY GLEN
UPPER GLEN ROAD
P
WATERSTOWN AVENUE
7
MILL LANE
ROAD
Schools
Convent
KNOCKMAROON HILL
20
Cave
Wier
Stewart's Hospital
N4
MARTINS
GLEN ROAD
ROAD
AVENUE
THE OVAL
The Hill
PALMERSTON DRIVE
GLENAULIN
GLENAULIN PK
GLENAULIN DR
BELGROVE LAWN
BELGROVE PK
MANOR PARK
MANOR ROAD
WOODFARM DR
WOODFARM AVENUE
CULMORE ROAD
CULMORE PARK
GLENAULIN ROAD
GLENMAROON
CHAPELIZOD
St. Lawrence Manor
Convent
Weir
LUCAN
ATFIELD
CALIFORNIA
32
PO

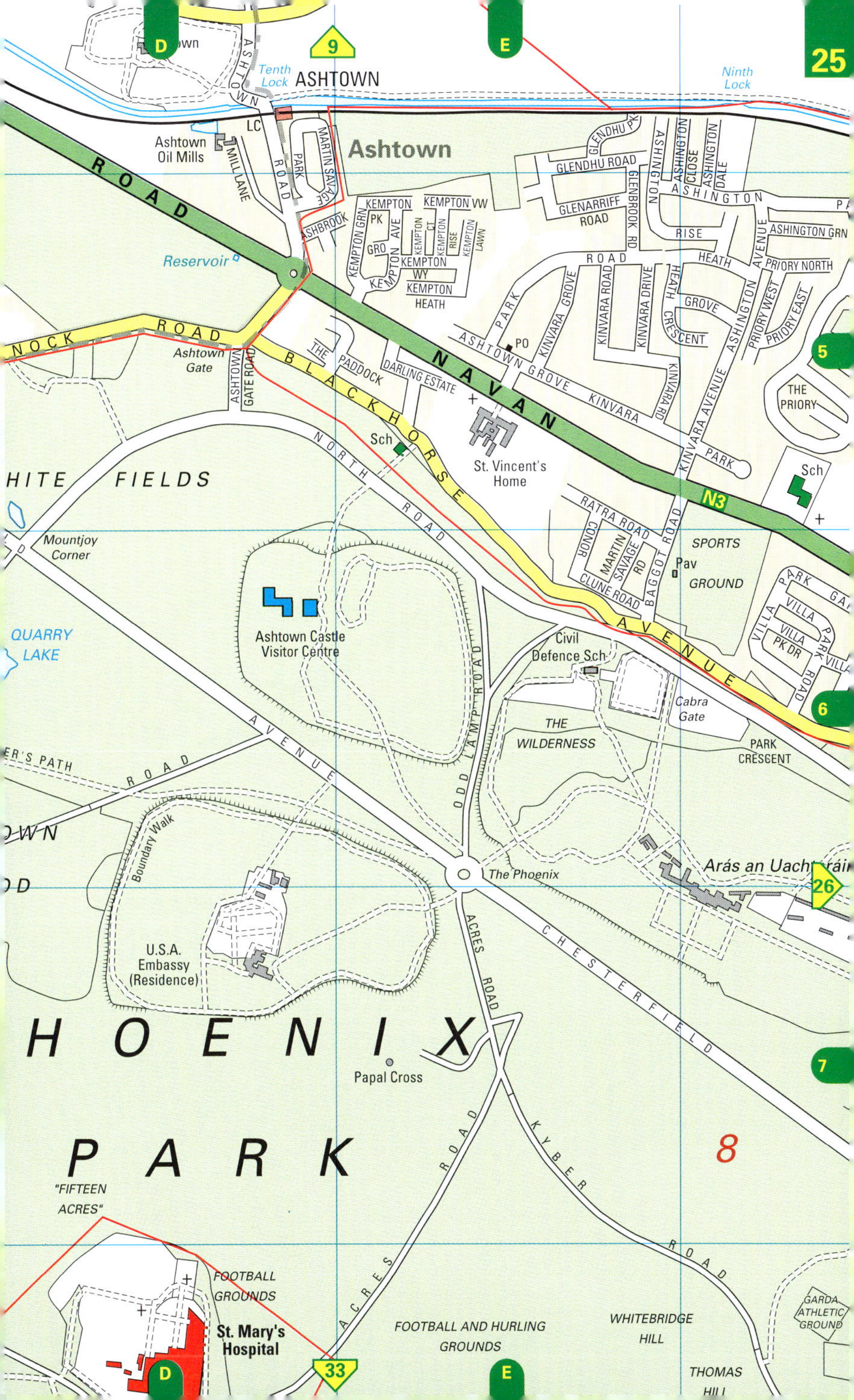

ASHTOWN
Tenth Lock
Ninth Lock
Ashtown
Ashtown Oil Mills
MILL LANE
ASHTOWN ROAD
PARK
MARTIN SAVAGE
LC
NAVAN ROAD
Reservoir
GLENDHU PK
GLENDHU ROAD
GLENARRIFF ROAD
GLENBROOK RD
ASHINGTON
ASHINGTON CLOSE
ASHINGTON DALE
ASHINGTON RISE
ASHINGTON HEATH
ASHINGTON GRN
ASHINGTON AVENUE
PRIORY NORTH
PRIORY WEST
PRIORY EAST
THE PRIORY
KEMPTON GRN
KEMPTON PK
KEMPTON VW
KEMPTON GRO
KEMPTON AVE
KEMPTON CT
KEMPTON RISE
KEMPTON LAWN
KEMPTON WY
KEMPTON HEATH
ASHBROOK
ASHTOWN GROVE
PARK ROAD
PO
KINVARA GROVE
KINVARA ROAD
KINVARA DRIVE
HEATH CRESCENT
HEATH GROVE
KINVARA RD
KINVARA AVENUE
KINVARA PARK
NOCK ROAD
Ashtown Gate
ASHTOWN GATE ROAD
THE PADDOCK
DARLING ESTATE
BLACKHORSE AVENUE
St. Vincent's Home
Sch
N3
HITE FIELDS
NORTH ROAD
Mountjoy Corner
QUARRY LAKE
Ashtown Castle Visitor Centre
RATRA ROAD
CONOR
MARTIN SAVAGE RD
CLUNE ROAD
BAGGOT ROAD
Pav
SPORTS GROUND
VILLA PARK GA
VILLA PARK ROAD
VILLA PK DR
VILLA
Civil Defence Sch
Cabra Gate
THE WILDERNESS
PARK CRESCENT
ODD LAMP ROAD
AVENUE
ER'S PATH
ROAD
OWN
D
Boundary Walk
The Phoenix
Arás an Uachtaráin
U.S.A. Embassy (Residence)
ACRES ROAD
CHESTERFIELD
PHOENIX PARK
Papal Cross
"FIFTEEN ACRES"
KYBER ROAD
8
FOOTBALL GROUNDS
St. Mary's Hospital
FOOTBALL AND HURLING GROUNDS
WHITEBRIDGE HILL
THOMAS HILL
GARDA ATHLETIC GROUND
D
E
9
26
33
5
6
7

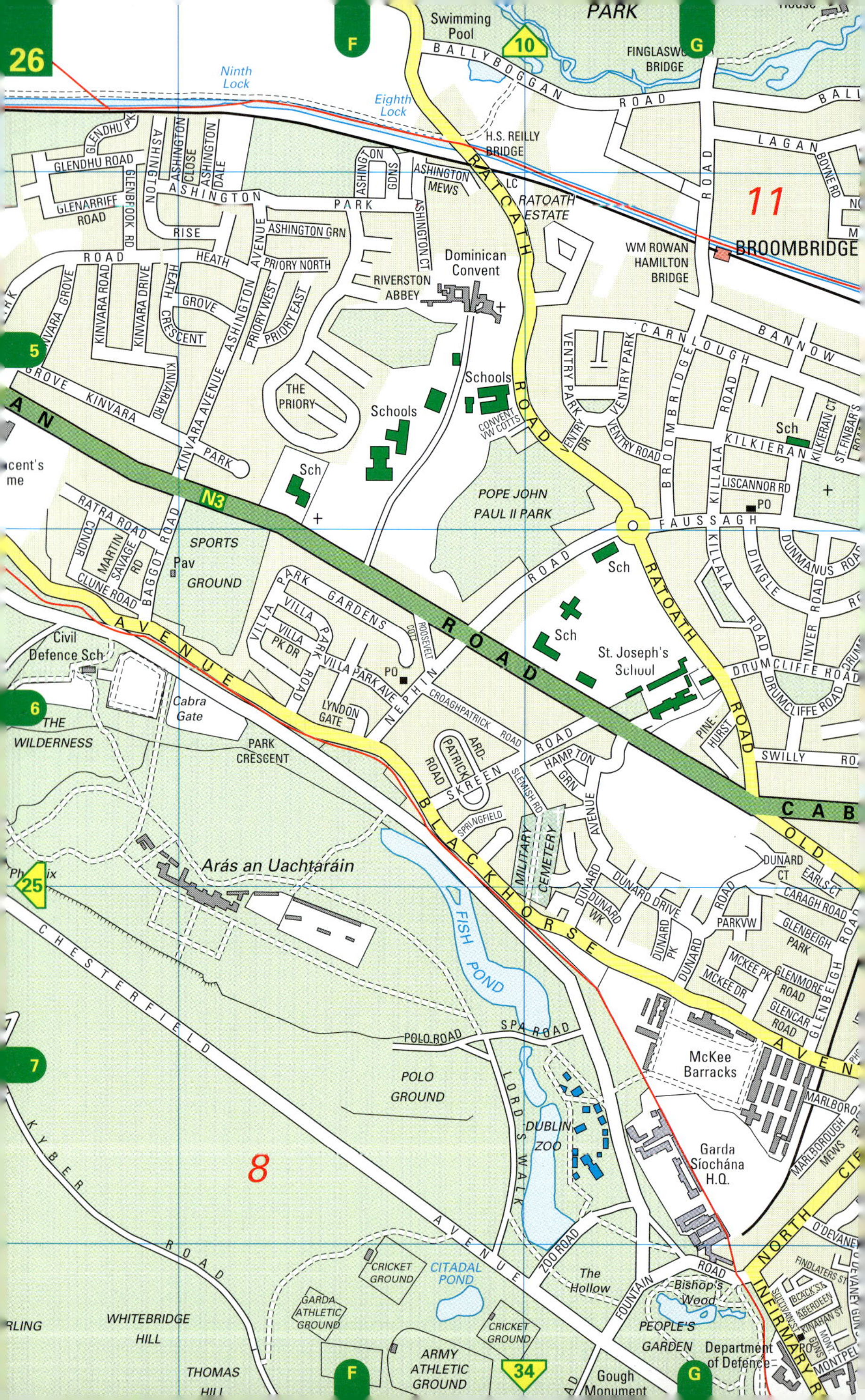
F
G
Swimming Pool
10
PARK
FINGLASWOOD BRIDGE
Ninth Lock
Eighth Lock
BALLYBOGGAN ROAD
H.S. REILLY BRIDGE
LAGAN ROAD
11
BROOMBRIDGE
WM ROWAN HAMILTON BRIDGE
GLENDHU PK
GLENDHU ROAD
ASHINGTON
ASHINGTON CLOSE
ASHINGTON DALE
GLENARRIFF ROAD
GLENBROOK RD
ASHINGTON PARK
ASHINGTON GDNS
ASHINGTON MEWS
ASHINGTON CT
ASHINGTON GRN
RATOATH ESTATE
RATOATH ROAD
LC
RISE
HEATH
ROAD
PRIORY NORTH
PRIORY WEST
PRIORY EAST
Dominican Convent
RIVERSTON ABBEY
KINVARA GROVE
KINVARA ROAD
KINVARA DRIVE
HEATH CRESCENT
GROVE
ASHINGTON AVENUE
CARNLOUGH
BANNOW
VENTRY PARK
VENTRY DR
VENTRY ROAD
BROOMBRIDGE ROAD
5
GROVE
KINVARA
KINVARA RD
KINVARA AVENUE
THE PRIORY
Schools
Schools
CONVENT VW COTTS
Sch
KILKIERAN
KILKIERAN CT
ST FINBAR'S
KILLALA ROAD
LISCANNOR RD
PO
cent's me
PARK
Sch
N3
POPE JOHN PAUL II PARK
FAUSSAGH
RATRA ROAD
CONOR
MARTIN SAVAGE RD
BAGGOT ROAD
Pav
SPORTS GROUND
ROAD
Sch
DUNMANUS ROAD
DINGLE ROAD
CLUNE ROAD
VILLA PARK GARDENS
VILLA PARK ROAD
VILLA PK DR
VILLA PARK AVE
ROOSEVELT COTT
ROAD
Sch
St. Joseph's School
INVER ROAD
DRUMCLIFFE ROAD
Civil Defence Sch
AVENUE
PO
NEPHIN
Cabra Gate
LYNDON GATE
CROAGHPATRICK ROAD
ROAD
PINEHURST
6
THE WILDERNESS
PARK CRESCENT
ARDPATRICK ROAD
SKREEN
SLEMISH RD
HAMPTON GRN
SWILLY RO
CAB
OLD
Phoenix
25
Arás an Uachtaráin
SPRINGFIELD
MILITARY CEMETERY
AVENUE
DUNARD CT
EARLS CT
CARAGH ROAD
DUNARD WK
DUNARD DRIVE
DUNARD ROAD
PARKVW
GLENBEIGH PARK
GLENBEIGH ROAD
BLACKHORSE
CHESTERFIELD
FISH POND
DUNARD PK
DUNARD
MCKEE PK
MCKEE DR
GLENMORE ROAD
GLENCAR ROAD
AVEN
POLO ROAD
SPA ROAD
McKee Barracks
7
POLO GROUND
LORD'S WALK
MARLBOROUGH
DUBLIN ZOO
Garda Síochána H.Q.
MARLBOROUGH MEWS
KYBER
8
NORTH CI
O'DEVANEY
AVENUE
ZOO ROAD
ROAD
ROAD
CRICKET GROUND
CITADAL POND
The Hollow
FOUNTAIN
Bishop's Wood
FINDLATERS ST
BLACK ST
ABERDEEN
NORTH INFIRMARY ROAD
GARDA ATHLETIC GROUND
WHITEBRIDGE HILL
CRICKET GROUND
PEOPLE'S GARDEN
SULLIVAN ST
KINAHAN ST
PO
MONT
MONTPEL
RLING
THOMAS HILL
ARMY ATHLETIC GROUND
34
Department of Defence
Gough Monument

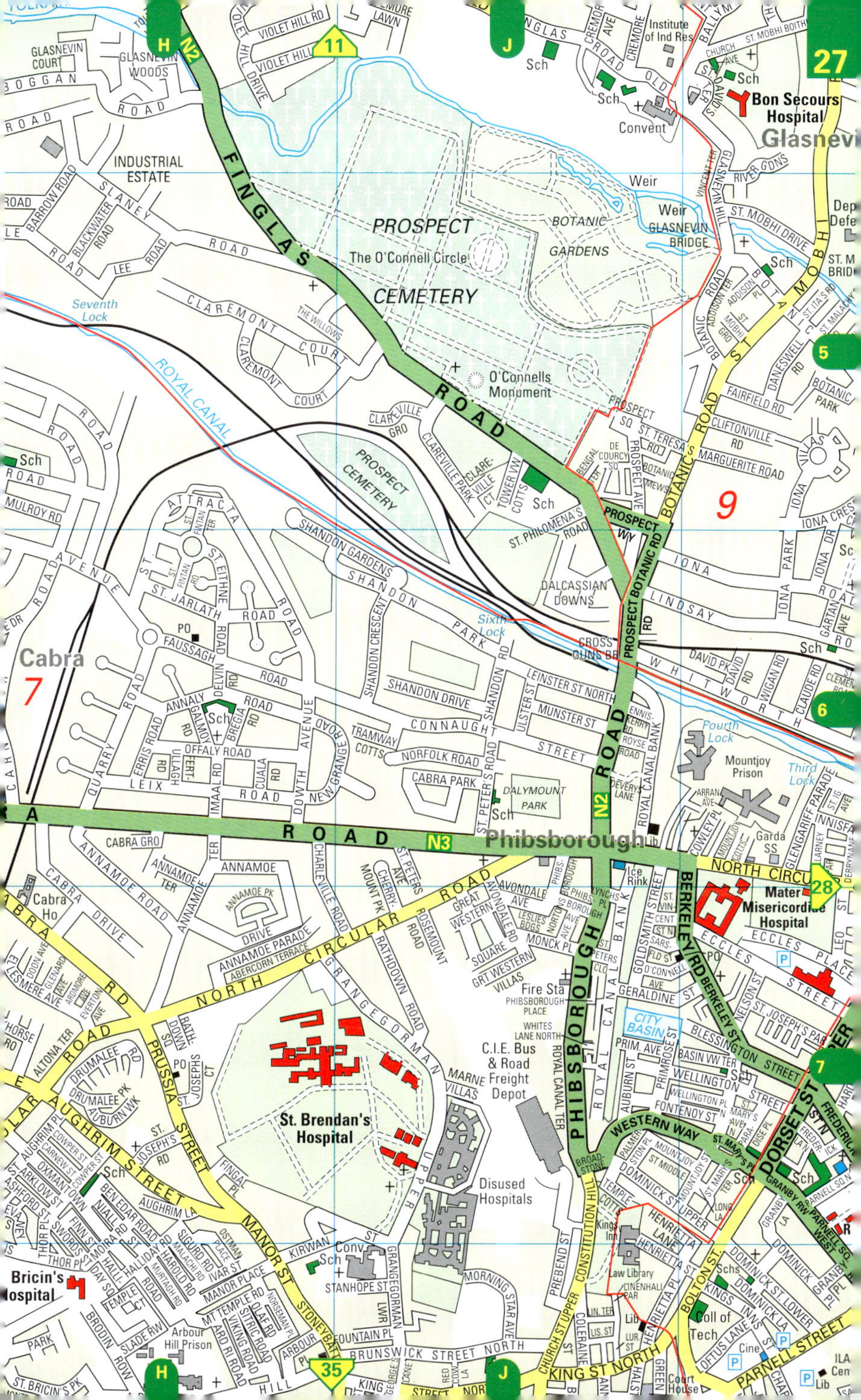

H
J
11
27
5
6
7
28
35
9
7
N2
N3
Glasnevin Court
Glasnevin Woods
Boggan Road
Industrial Estate
Barrow Road
Slaney Road
Blackwater Road
Lee Road
Seventh Lock
Royal Canal
Claremont Court
The Willows
Finglas Road
Prospect Cemetery
The O'Connell Circle
Botanic Gardens
O'Connells Monument
Weir
Glasnevin Bridge
Institute of Ind Res
Sch
Convent
Bon Secours Hospital
Glasnevin
St. Mobhi Drive
St. Mobhi Road
Botanic Road
Fairfield Rd
Cliftonville Rd
Marguerite Road
Iona Villas
Iona Road
Iona Cres
Iona Park
Iona Dr
Lindsay Road
Prospect Way
Prospect Botanic Rd
Prospect Sq
St. Teresa's Rd
De Courcy Sq
Prospect Ave
Botanic Mews
Bengal Ter
Clareville Gro
Clareville Park
Clareville Ct
Tower Vw Cotts
St. Philomena's Road
Dalcassian Downs
Sixth Lock
Cross Guns Br
Whitworth Road
David Pk
David Rd
Wigan Rd
Claude Rd
Fourth Lock
Third Lock
Mountjoy Prison
Cabra
Attracta
St. Fintan Ter
St. Eithne Rd
St. Jarlath Road
Faussagh Road
Shandon Gardens
Shandon Park
Shandon Crescent
Shandon Drive
Shandon Road
Leinster St North
Munster St
Connaught Street
Ulster St
Tramway Cotts
Norfolk Road
Cabra Park
Dalymount Park
St. Peter's Road
Delvin Rd
Annaly Rd
Galmoy Rd
Bregia Rd
Offaly Road
Ferris Road
Ullagh Rd
Fertiagh
Imaal Rd
Cuala Rd
Leix Road
Dowth Avenue
New Grange Road
Quarry Road
Cabra Road
Phibsborough
Royal Canal Bank
North Circular Road
Mater Misericordiae Hospital
Eccles Place
Eccles Street
Berkeley Rd
Berkeley St
Garda SS
Ice Rink
Cabra Gro
Annamoe Ter
Annamoe Road
Annamoe Pk
Annamoe Drive
Annamoe Parade
Abercorn Terrace
Charleville Road
Cherry Ave
Mount Pk
Rathdown Road
Rosemount Road
Great Western Square
Grt Western Villas
Avondale Ave
Monck Pl
Goldsmith Street
Geraldine St
City Basin
Blessington Street
St. Joseph's Par
Fire Sta
Phibsborough Place
Whites Lane North
C.I.E. Bus & Road Freight Depot
Grangegorman
Marne Villas
St. Brendan's Hospital
Disused Hospitals
Cabra Drive
Cabra Ho
Prussia Street
Drumalee Rd
Drumalee Pk
Auburn Wk
Aughrim Street
Aughrim La
Manor St
Manor Place
Kirwan St
Stanhope St
Stoneybatter
Arbour Hill Prison
Bricin's Hospital
St. Bricin's Pk
Brunswick Street North
Morning Star Ave
Constitution Hill
Church St Upper
King St North
Prebend St
Western Way
Dorset St
Dominick St Upper
Dominick St Lower
Henrietta Lane
Henrietta St
Kings Inns
Law Library
Bolton St
Coll of Tech
Parnell Street
Granby Row
Court House
Lib
Cine
Wellington Street
Fontenoy St
Primrose St
Auburn St
Broadstone
Royal Canal Ter

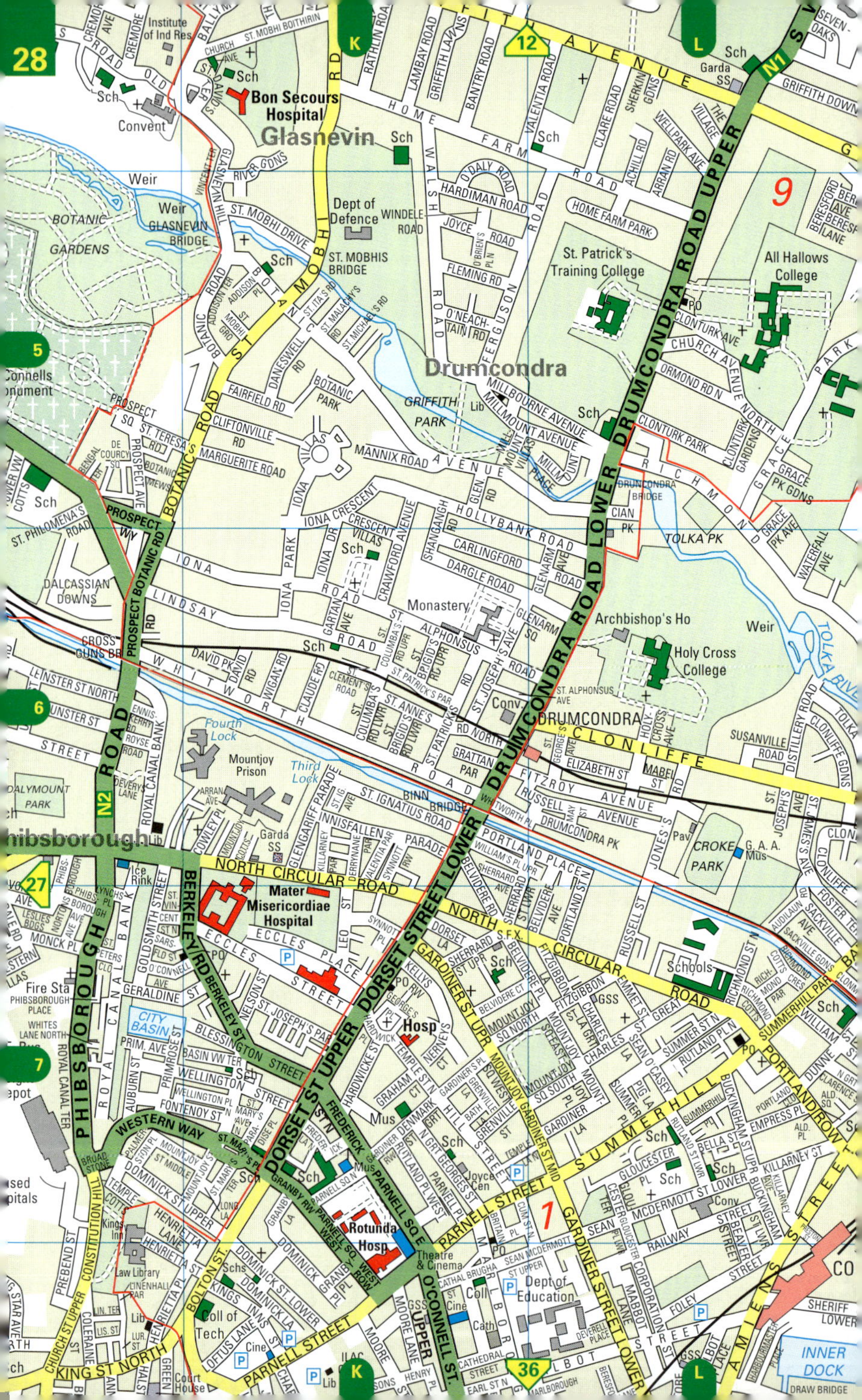

Glasnevin
Drumcondra
Phibsborough
Bon Secours Hospital
Mater Misericordiae Hospital
Rotunda Hosp
Mountjoy Prison
Botanic Gardens
Croke Park
Holy Cross College
Archbishop's Ho
All Hallows College
St. Patrick's Training College
Dept of Defence
Dept of Education
Tolka Pk
Griffith Park
City Basin
Monastery
Law Library
Kings Inns
Coll of Tech
Fire Sta
Convent
Institute of Ind Res
Dalcassian Downs
Dalymount Park
Fourth Lock
Third Lock
Binn Bridge
Cross Guns Br
St. Mobhis Bridge
Glasnevin Bridge
Drumcondra Bridge
Theatre & Cinema
Joyce Cen
Inner Dock
St. Mobhi Road
Botanic Road
Prospect Road
Phibsborough Road
Drumcondra Road Upper
Drumcondra Road Lower
Dorset Street Upper
Dorset Street Lower
North Circular Road
Whitworth Road
Clonliffe Road
Home Farm Road
Griffith Avenue
Richmond Road
Berkeley Road
Eccles Street
Western Way
Constitution Hill
King St North
Bolton St
Parnell Street
Parnell Sq
O'Connell St Upper
Gardiner St Upper
Gardiner Street Lower
Summerhill
Portland Row
Mountjoy Sq
Amiens Street
Sean McDermott St
Great Charles St
Iona Road
Lindsay Road
Hollybank Road
Mannix Road
Millmount Avenue
Clonturk Park
Grace Park Gdns
Jones's Rd
Russell St
Fitzroy Avenue
Clonliffe Gdns
N1
N2
12
27
36
5
6
7
9
1
K
L

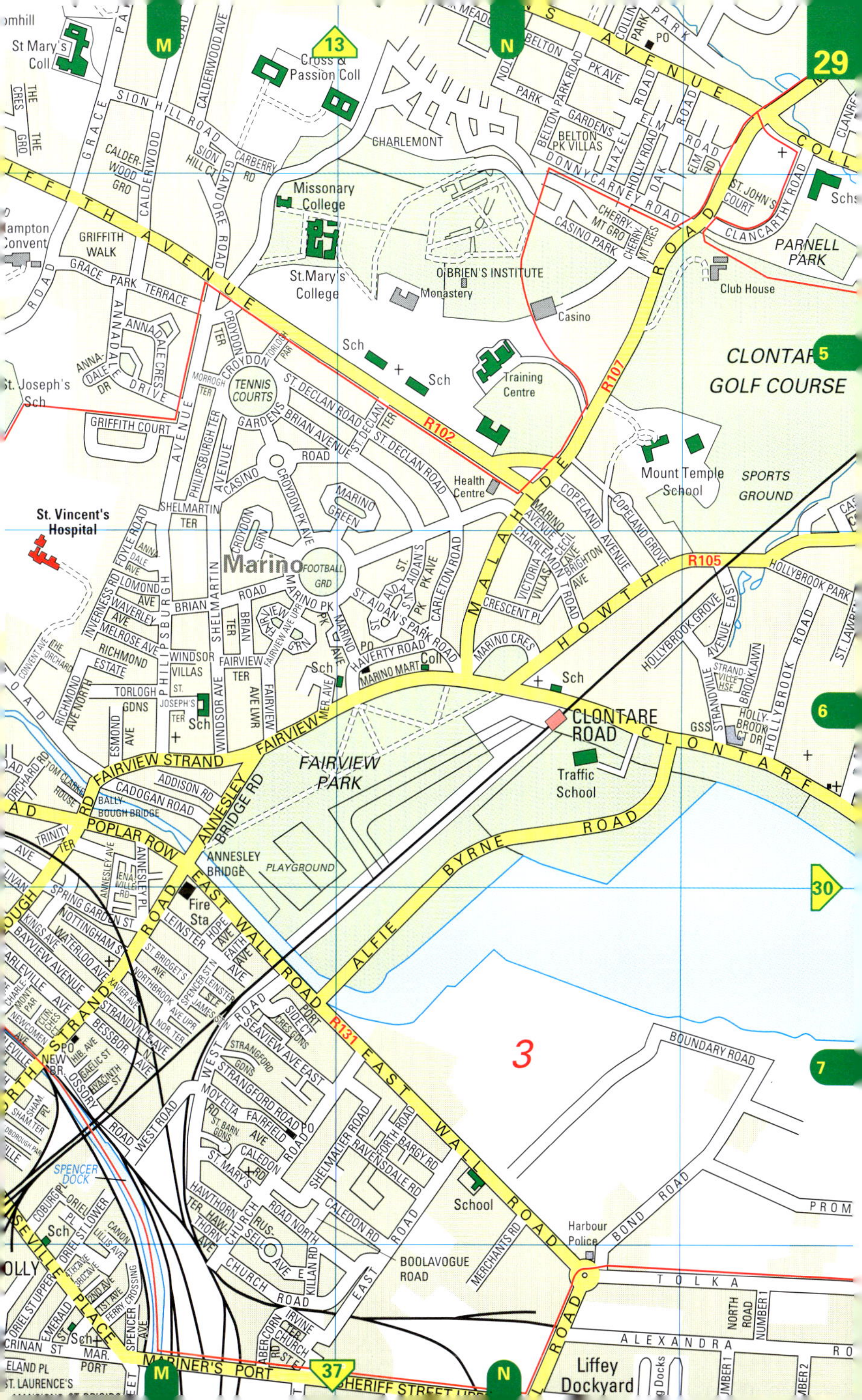

M
N
13
5
6
30
7
37
3
St Mary's Coll
Cross & Passion Coll
CHARLEMONT
BELTON PARK ROAD
BELTON PK AVE
BELTON PK VILLAS
GARDENS
DONNYCARNEY ROAD
HAZEL
HOLLY ROAD
ELM ROAD
OAK
COLLINS AVENUE
COLLINS PARK
PO
ST. JOHN'S COURT
CLANCARTHY ROAD
Schs
PARNELL PARK
Club House
SION HILL ROAD
SION HILL CT
CARBERRY RD
GLANDORE ROAD
CALDERWOOD AVE
CALDERWOOD
CALDERWOOD GRO
GRACE PARK
GRACE PARK TERRACE
GRIFFITH AVENUE
GRIFFITH WALK
Missonary College
St.Mary's College
O'BRIEN'S INSTITUTE
Monastery
Casino
CASINO PARK
CHERRYMT GRO
CHERRYMT CRES
Hampton Convent
ANNADALE
ANNADALE CRES
ANNADALE DRIVE
ANNADALE DR
St. Joseph's Sch
GRIFFITH COURT
CROYDON PARK
TENNIS COURTS
CROYDON GARDENS
TORLOGH PAR
MORROGH TER
PHILIPSBURGH TER
PHILIPSBURGH AVENUE
Sch
Training Centre
CLONTARF GOLF COURSE
R107
R102
ST. DECLAN ROAD
ST. DECLAN TER
BRIAN AVENUE
CASINO ROAD
Health Centre
MALAHIDE ROAD
Mount Temple School
SPORTS GROUND
COPELAND AVENUE
COPELAND GROVE
MARINO AVENUE
CHARLEMONT
CECIL AVE
BRIGHTON AVE
VICTORIA VILLAS
CRESCENT PL
MARINO CRES
SHELMARTIN TER
SHELMARTIN AVE
CROYDON GRN
CROYDON PK AVE
MARINO GREEN
Marino
FOOTBALL GRD
St. Vincent's Hospital
FOYLE ROAD
ANNADALE AVE
LOMOND AVE
WAVERLEY AVE
INVERNESS RD
MELROSE AVE
RICHMOND ESTATE
BRIAN ROAD
BRIAN TER
MARINO PK
FAIRVIEW AVE UPR
FAIRVIEW GRN
ST. AIDAN'S PK AVE
ST. AIDAN'S PARK ROAD
CARLETON ROAD
HAVERTY ROAD
MARINO MART
Coll
PO
HOWTH ROAD
R105
HOLLYBROOK PARK
HOLLYBROOK GROVE
HOLLYBROOK ROAD
AVENUE EAST
STRANDVILLE AVE
STRANDVILLE HSE
BROOKLAWN
HOLLYBROOK CT DR
GSS
CONVENT AVE
THE ORCHARD
RICHMOND AVE NORTH
TORLOGH GDNS
WINDSOR VILLAS
ST. JOSEPH'S TER
WINDSOR AVE
FAIRVIEW TER
FAIRVIEW AVE LWR
ESMOND AVE
CLONTARF ROAD
CLONTARF
Traffic School
FAIRVIEW STRAND
FAIRVIEW
FAIRVIEW PARK
ADDISON RD
CADOGAN ROAD
BALLY BOUGH BRIDGE
TOM CLARKE HOUSE
ANNESLEY BRIDGE RD
ANNESLEY BRIDGE
PLAYGROUND
ROAD
BYRNE
ALFIE
POPLAR ROW
TRINITY TER
ANNESLEY AVE
ANNESLEY PL
LEINSTER AVE
HOPE AVE
FAITH AVE
Fire Sta
EAST WALL ROAD
R131
SPRING GARDEN ST
NOTTINGHAM ST
WATERLOO AVE
KINGS AVE
BAYVIEW AVENUE
ST. BRIDGET'S AVE
NORTHBROOK AVE
XAVIER AVE
STRANDVILLE AVE
BESSBOR AVE
NORTH STRAND
NEW BR.
GAELIC ST
OSSORY ROAD
HYACINTH ST
SPENCER ST N
JAMES'S ST
NOR. TER
WEST ROAD
SEAVIEW AVE EAST
STRANGFORD GDNS
STRANGFORD ROAD
CHURCH ROAD
MOY ELTA RD
FAIRFIELD AVE
ST. BARN. GDNS.
CALEDON RD
ST. MARY'S RD
HAWTHORN TER
CHURCH RD
RUSSELL AVE E
KILLAN RD
SHELMALIER ROAD
RAVENSDALE RD
BARGY RD
FORTH ROAD
School
BOOLAVOGUE ROAD
MERCHANTS RD
Harbour Police
BOND ROAD
BOUNDARY ROAD
PROM
TOLKA
ALEXANDRA RO
NORTH ROAD NUMBER 1
Liffey Dockyard
SPENCER DOCK
COBURG PL
ORIEL PL
ORIEL ST LOWER
ORIEL ST UPPER
CANON LILLIS AVE
SEVILLE PLACE
EMERALD SQ
Sch
MAR. PORT
MARINER'S PORT
SHERIFF STREET
FERRY CROSSING
CRINAN ST
ST. LAURENCE'S

Killester
KILLESTER
CLONTARF GOLF COURSE
PARNELL PARK
Club House
Casino
Mount Temple School
SPORTS GROUND
Orthopaedic Hospital
Hospital
Clinic
CLONTARF ROAD
Traffic School
Clontarf Baths
Harbour Police
Liffey Dockyard
COLLINS AVENUE EAST
HOWTH ROAD
CLONTARF ROAD
CLONTARF PROMENADE
VERNON AVENUE
CASTLE AVENUE
KINCORA ROAD
ST. LAWRENCE ROAD
THE STILES
VICTORIA ROAD
MALAHIDE ROAD
BOUNDARY ROAD
PROMENADE ROAD
BOND ROAD
TOLKA QUAY
TOLKA QUAY ROAD
ALEXANDRA ROAD
EAST WALL ROAD
R107
R105
3
14
29
38
P
Q
5
6
7

31
R105
15
39
R
S
5
6
7
5
ST. ANNE'S PARK
FOOTBALL GROUNDS
FOOTBALL GROUNDS
FOOTBALL GROUNDS
NANIKEN RIVER
St.Paul's College
Pavilion
St.Anne's (Ruins)
Home
Sch
HOWTH
SYBIL HILL ROAD
BROOKWOOD GLEN
ROSEVALE MANSIONS
THE MEADOWS
MARYVILLE ROAD
SYBIL HILL AVE
BETTYSTOWN AVE
WATERFALL RD
NANIKIN AVE
BALLYHOY AVENUE
WADE'S AVE
ALL SAINTS ROAD
ALL SAINTS PARK
WATERMILL DRIVE
WATERMILL AVENUE
WATERMILL ROAD
ST. ANNE'S TER
ST. ANNE'S DR
ST. ANNE'S AVENUE
VERNON RISE
VERNON DR
VERNON AVENUE
VERNON HEATH
ESTATE
OAKLEY PK
SUNNYSIDE MWS
CASTILLA PARK
VERNON PARK
WOODSIDE
MOUNT PROSPECT DRIVE
MOUNT PROSPECT LAWNS
MOUNT PROSPECT PARK
MOUNT PROSPECT GROVE
MOUNT PROSPECT AVENUE
PARK LAWN
BAYMOUNT PARK
SEAPARK
THE OAKS
Convent
Manresa Retreat House
DOLLYMOUNT AVENUE
SEAFIELD GRO
Dollymount
THE MEWS
DOLLYMOUNT GROVE
ST. GABRIELS CT
ST. GABRIEL'S ROAD
PO
SEACOURT
DOLLYMOUNT PARK
DOLLYMOUNT RISE
SEAFIELD AVENUE
SEAPARK ROAD
SEAFIELD ROAD EAST
MERCHAMP
Schs
CHELSEA GARDENS
KINCORA ROAD
SEAPARK DRIVE
Seafield
SEAFIELD DOWN
DANES COURT
JAMES LARKIN ROAD
VERNON GDNS
VERNON GRO
CONQUER HILL TER
CONQUER HILL ROAD
KINCORA COURT
KINCORA RD
Clontarf
CLONTARF PARK
BRIAN BORU ST
TRAM TERRACE
VERNON COURT
FORTVIEW AVENUE
BRIAN BORU AVE
CONQUER
CLONTARF ROAD
Yacht Club Slipway
BULL BRIDGE
Coastguard Station
BULL WALL
ROYAL DUBLIN GOLF COURSE
Club House
TERMINAL ROAD NORTH
ALEXANDRA ROAD

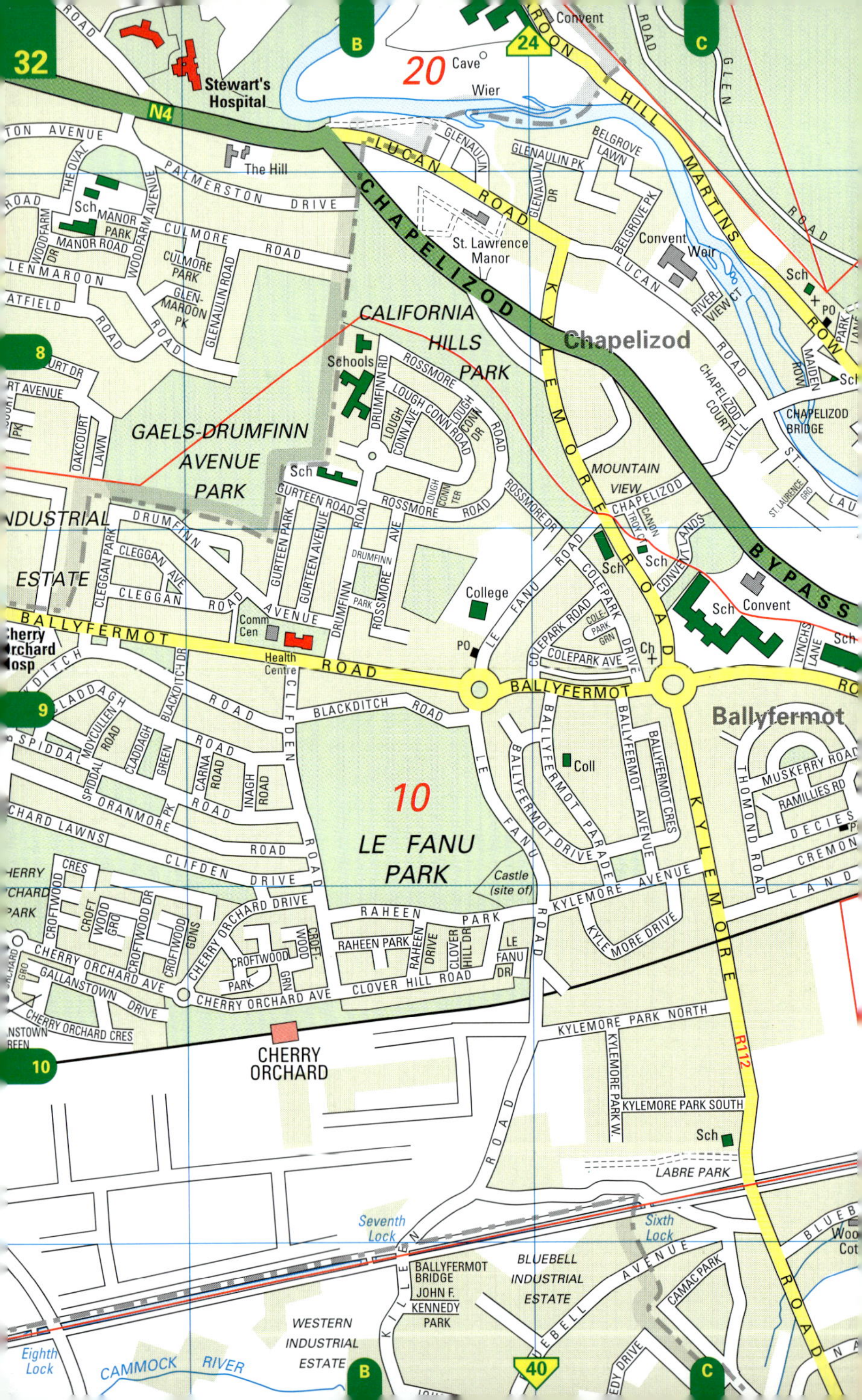

B
C
8
9
10
24
40
20
10
Stewart's Hospital
N4
Cave
Wier
Convent
ROAD
GLEN
HILL
MARTINS
ROW
LUCAN ROAD
CHAPELIZOD BYPASS
The Hill
PALMERSTON DRIVE
TON AVENUE
THE OVAL
Sch
MANOR PARK
MANOR ROAD
WOODFARM DR
WOODFARM AVENUE
CULMORE ROAD
CULMORE PARK
GLENMAROON PK
GLENAULIN ROAD
LENMAROON
ATFIELD
GLENAULIN
GLENAULIN PK
GLENAULIN DR
BELGROVE LAWN
BELGROVE PK
St. Lawrence Manor
Convent
Weir
RIVERVIEW CT
PO
PARK LANE
MAIDEN ROW
CHAPELIZOD COURT
CHAPELIZOD HILL ROAD
CHAPELIZOD BRIDGE
ST. LAURENCE GRO
Chapelizod
CALIFORNIA HILLS PARK
Schools
ROSSMORE ROAD
DRUMFINN RD
LOUGH CONN AVE
LOUGH CONN ROAD
LOUGH CONN DR
LOUGH CONN TER
ROSSMORE DR
GAELS-DRUMFINN AVENUE PARK
OAKCOURT LAWN
RT AVENUE
URT DR
INDUSTRIAL ESTATE
DRUMFINN ROAD
GURTEEN ROAD
GURTEEN PARK
GURTEEN AVENUE
DRUMFINN AVENUE
DRUMFINN PARK
ROSSMORE AVE
CLEGGAN PARK
CLEGGAN AVE
CLEGGAN ROAD
Comm Cen
Health Centre
College
PO
LE FANU ROAD
MOUNTAIN VIEW
CHAPELIZOD
TROY CT
CANON
Sch
CONVENT LANDS
COLEPARK ROAD
COLEPARK GRN
COLEPARK DRIVE
COLEPARK AVE
Ch
KYLEMORE ROAD
BYPASS
Sch
Convent
LYNCHS LANE
Sch
BALLYFERMOT ROAD
Cherry Orchard Hosp
BLACKDITCH DR
BLACKDITCH ROAD
CLIFDEN ROAD
CLADDAGH ROAD
CLADDAGH GREEN
MOYCULLEN ROAD
SPIDDAL ROAD
SPIDDAL PK
CARNA ROAD
INAGH ROAD
ORANMORE ROAD
CHARD LAWNS
CLIFDEN DRIVE
LE FANU PARK
Castle (site of)
BALLYFERMOT
Coll
BALLYFERMOT DRIVE
BALLYFERMOT PARADE
BALLYFERMOT AVENUE
BALLYFERMOT CRES
Ballyfermot
THOMOND ROAD
MUSKERRY ROAD
RAMILLIES RD
DECIES
CREMON
LAND
KYLEMORE AVENUE
KYLEMORE DRIVE
CHERRY ORCHARD PARK
CROFTWOOD CRES
CROFTWOOD GRO
CROFTWOOD DR
CROFTWOOD GDNS
CHERRY ORCHARD DRIVE
CROFTWOOD PARK
CROFTWOOD GRN
RAHEEN PARK
RAHEEN DRIVE
CLOVER HILL DR
CLOVER HILL ROAD
LE FANU DR
CHERRY ORCHARD AVE
GALLANSTOWN DRIVE
CHERRY ORCHARD CRES
CHERRY ORCHARD
KYLEMORE PARK NORTH
KYLEMORE PARK W.
KYLEMORE PARK SOUTH
R112
Sch
LABRE PARK
Seventh Lock
Sixth Lock
KILLEEN ROAD
BALLYFERMOT BRIDGE
JOHN F. KENNEDY PARK
BLUEBELL INDUSTRIAL ESTATE
BLUEBELL AVENUE
CAMAC PARK
WESTERN INDUSTRIAL ESTATE
Eighth Lock
CAMMOCK RIVER

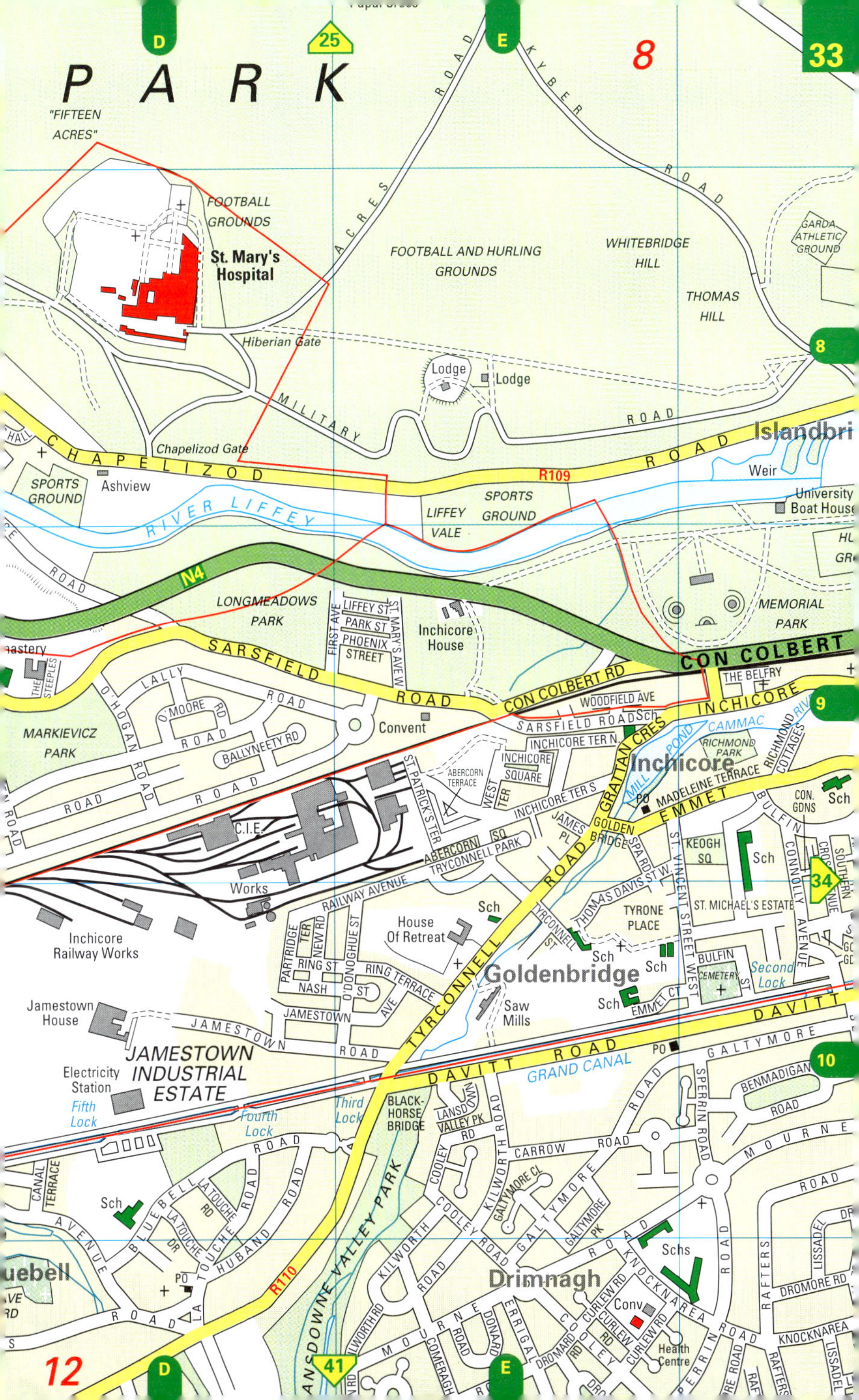
D
25
E
8
PARK
"FIFTEEN ACRES"
FOOTBALL GROUNDS
St. Mary's Hospital
ACRES ROAD
KYBER ROAD
FOOTBALL AND HURLING GROUNDS
WHITEBRIDGE HILL
THOMAS HILL
GARDA ATHLETIC GROUND
Hiberian Gate
Lodge
Lodge
MILITARY ROAD
Chapelizod Gate
CHAPELIZOD ROAD
R109
Islandbri
SPORTS GROUND
Ashview
RIVER LIFFEY
LIFFEY VALE
SPORTS GROUND
Weir
University Boat House
N4
LONGMEADOWS PARK
FIRST AVE
LIFFEY ST
PARK ST
PHOENIX STREET
ST. MARY'S AVE W
Inchicore House
MEMORIAL PARK
CON COLBERT
THE STEEPLES
SARSFIELD ROAD
CON COLBERT RD
THE BELFRY
WOODFIELD AVE
LALLY ROAD
O'MOORE RD
O'HOGAN ROAD
BALLYNEETY RD
Convent
MARKIEVICZ PARK
SARSFIELD ROAD
INCHICORE
CAMMAC
MILL POND
RICHMOND PARK
RICHMOND COTTAGES
INCHICORE TER N
INCHICORE SQUARE
ABERCORN TERRACE
WEST TER
Inchicore
MADELEINE TERRACE
GRATTAN CRES
ST PATRICK'S TER
C.I.E.
Works
INCHICORE TER S
JAMES PL
GOLDEN BRIDGE
EMMET
CON. GDNS
Sch
BULFIN
KEOGH SQ
Sch
CONNOLLY AVENUE
SOUTHERN
34
ABERCORN SQ
TRYCONNELL PARK
SPA RD
ST. VINCENT STREET WEST
THOMAS DAVIS ST W.
RAILWAY AVENUE
Sch
TYRONE PLACE
ST. MICHAEL'S ESTATE
Inchicore Railway Works
PARTRIDGE TER
NEW RD
O'DONOGHUE ST
House Of Retreat
TYRCONNELL ST
Sch
Sch
BULFIN ST
CEMETERY
Second Lock
RING ST
RING TERRACE
NASH ST
Goldenbridge
Sch
EMMET CT
Jamestown House
JAMESTOWN AVE
JAMESTOWN ROAD
TYRCONNELL ROAD
Saw Mills
DAVITT ROAD
PO
GALTYMORE
10
JAMESTOWN INDUSTRIAL ESTATE
Electricity Station
Fifth Lock
Fourth Lock
Third Lock
BLACK-HORSE BRIDGE
LANSDOWN VALLEY PK RD
GRAND CANAL
BENMADIGAN ROAD
SPERRIN ROAD
MOURNE
CANAL TERRACE
ROAD
KILWORTH ROAD
CARROW ROAD
GALTYMORE CL
Sch
BLUEBELL
LA TOUCHE RD
LA TOUCHE DR
LA TOUCHE ROAD
HUBAND ROAD
COOLEY
COOLEY ROAD
GALTYMORE
GALTYMORE PK
Schs
KNOCKNAREA
LISSADEL
DR
AVENUE
LANSDOWNE VALLEY PARK
KILWORTH
Drimnagh
ROAD
RAFTERS
DROMORE RD
uebell
R110
PO
ROAD
MOURNE ROAD
DONARD
ERRIGAL
DROMARD
COOLEY RD
CURLEW RD
CURLEW RD
Conv
Health Centre
KNOCKNAREA
12
D
41
E
COMERAGH

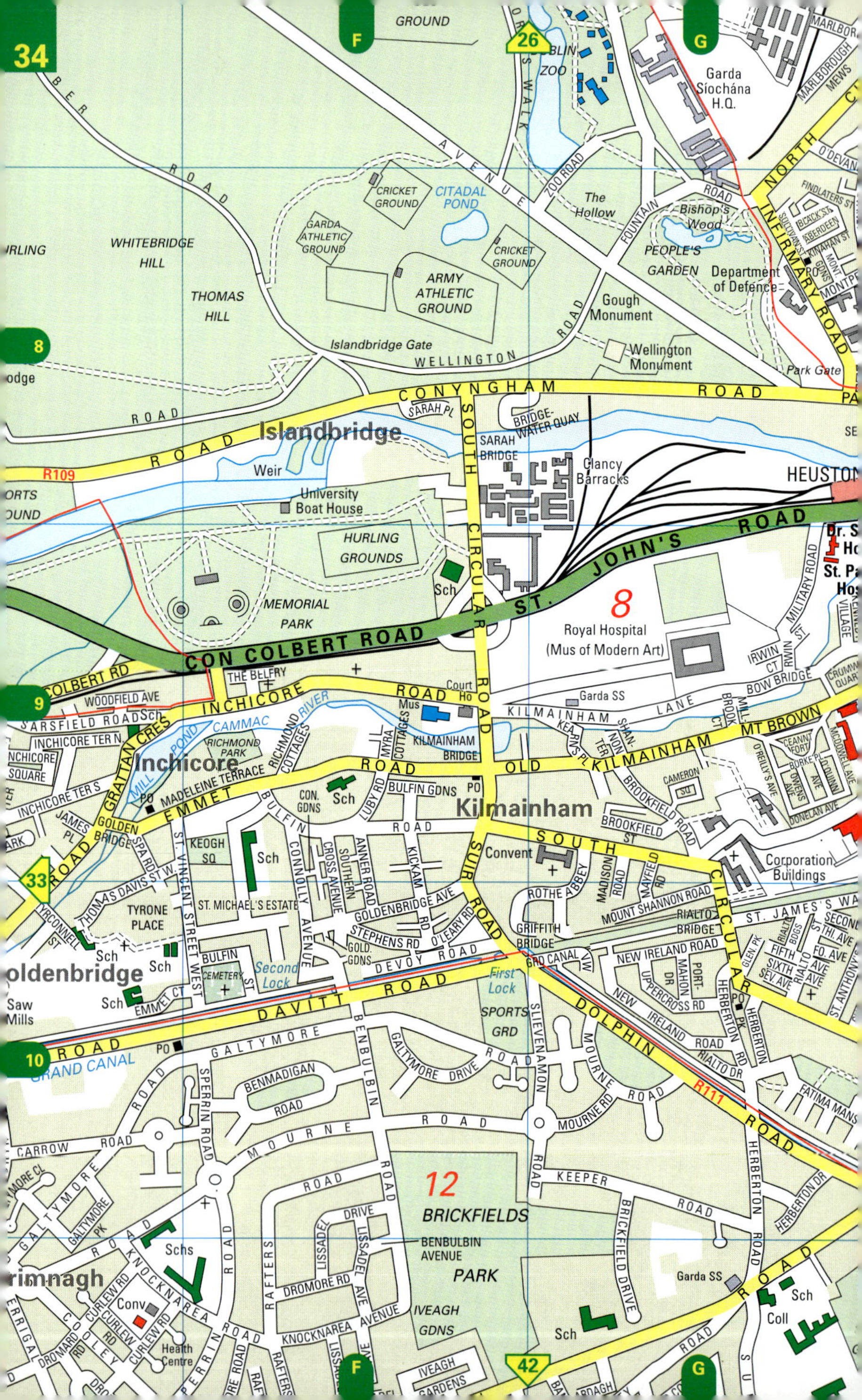
F
G
26
42
33
8
9
10
Garda Síochána H.Q.
Islandbridge
Inchicore
Kilmainham
Goldenbridge
Crimnagh
HEUSTON
CITADAL POND
CRICKET GROUND
GARDA ATHLETIC GROUND
ARMY ATHLETIC GROUND
WHITEBRIDGE HILL
THOMAS HILL
The Hollow
Bishop's Wood
PEOPLE'S GARDEN
Department of Defence
Gough Monument
Wellington Monument
Islandbridge Gate
WELLINGTON ROAD
CONYNGHAM ROAD
Park Gate
INFIRMARY ROAD
NORTH CIRCULAR
ZOO ROAD
FOUNTAIN ROAD
CHESTERFIELD AVENUE
Clancy Barracks
SARAH BRIDGE
BRIDGEWATER QUAY
SARAH PL
University Boat House
Weir
R109
HURLING GROUNDS
MEMORIAL PARK
Sch
CON COLBERT ROAD
ST. JOHN'S ROAD
SOUTH CIRCULAR ROAD
Royal Hospital (Mus of Modern Art)
MILITARY ROAD
IRWIN CT
IRWIN ST
BOW BRIDGE
Garda SS
KILMAINHAM LANE
INCHICORE ROAD
THE BELFRY
Court Ho
Mus
KILMAINHAM BRIDGE
CAMMAC RIVER
MILL POND
RICHMOND PARK
RICHMOND COTTAGES
MYRA COTTAGES
MADELEINE TERRACE
WOODFIELD AVE
SARSFIELD ROAD
INCHICORE TER N
INCHICORE SQUARE
INCHICORE TER S
GRATTAN CRES
EMMET ROAD
OLD KILMAINHAM
MT BROWN
BROOKFIELD ROAD
BROOKFIELD ST
CAMERON SQ
O'REILLY'S AVE
DONELAN AVE
Convent
SUIR ROAD
ROTHE ABBEY
MADISON ROAD
MAYFIELD RD
MOUNT SHANNON ROAD
RIALTO BRIDGE
ST. JAMES'S WALK
Corporation Buildings
BULFIN GDNS
BULFIN ROAD
CON. GDNS
LUBY RD
KEOGH SQ
ST. MICHAEL'S ESTATE
TYRONE PLACE
ST. VINCENT STREET WEST
CONNOLLY AVENUE
CROSS AVENUE
SOUTHERN
ANNER ROAD
KICKAM RD
GOLDENBRIDGE AVE
STEPHENS RD
O'LEARY RD
GOLD. GDNS
DEVOY ROAD
GRIFFITH BRIDGE
GRD CANAL VW
NEW IRELAND ROAD
UPPERCROSS RD
HERBERTON RD
THOMAS DAVIS ST W.
TYRCONNELL ST
JAMES PL
GOLDEN BRIDGE
Second Lock
First Lock
CEMETERY
EMMET CT
Saw Mills
DAVITT ROAD
GRAND CANAL
PO
SPORTS GRD
DOLPHIN ROAD
R111
RIALTO DR
FATIMA MANS
GALTYMORE ROAD
GALTYMORE DRIVE
BENMADIGAN ROAD
SPERRIN ROAD
BENBULBIN ROAD
SLIEVENAMON ROAD
MOURNE ROAD
MOURNE RD
KEEPER ROAD
CARROW ROAD
BRICKFIELDS PARK
12
BENBULBIN AVENUE
BRICKFIELD DRIVE
HERBERTON DR
Garda SS
Schs
Conv
Health Centre
KNOCKNAREA AVENUE
DROMORE RD
LISSADEL DRIVE
LISSADEL AVE
RAFTERS ROAD
IVEAGH GDNS
IVEAGH GARDENS
Coll
CURLEW RD
COOLEY RD
DROMARD RD
GALTYMORE PK

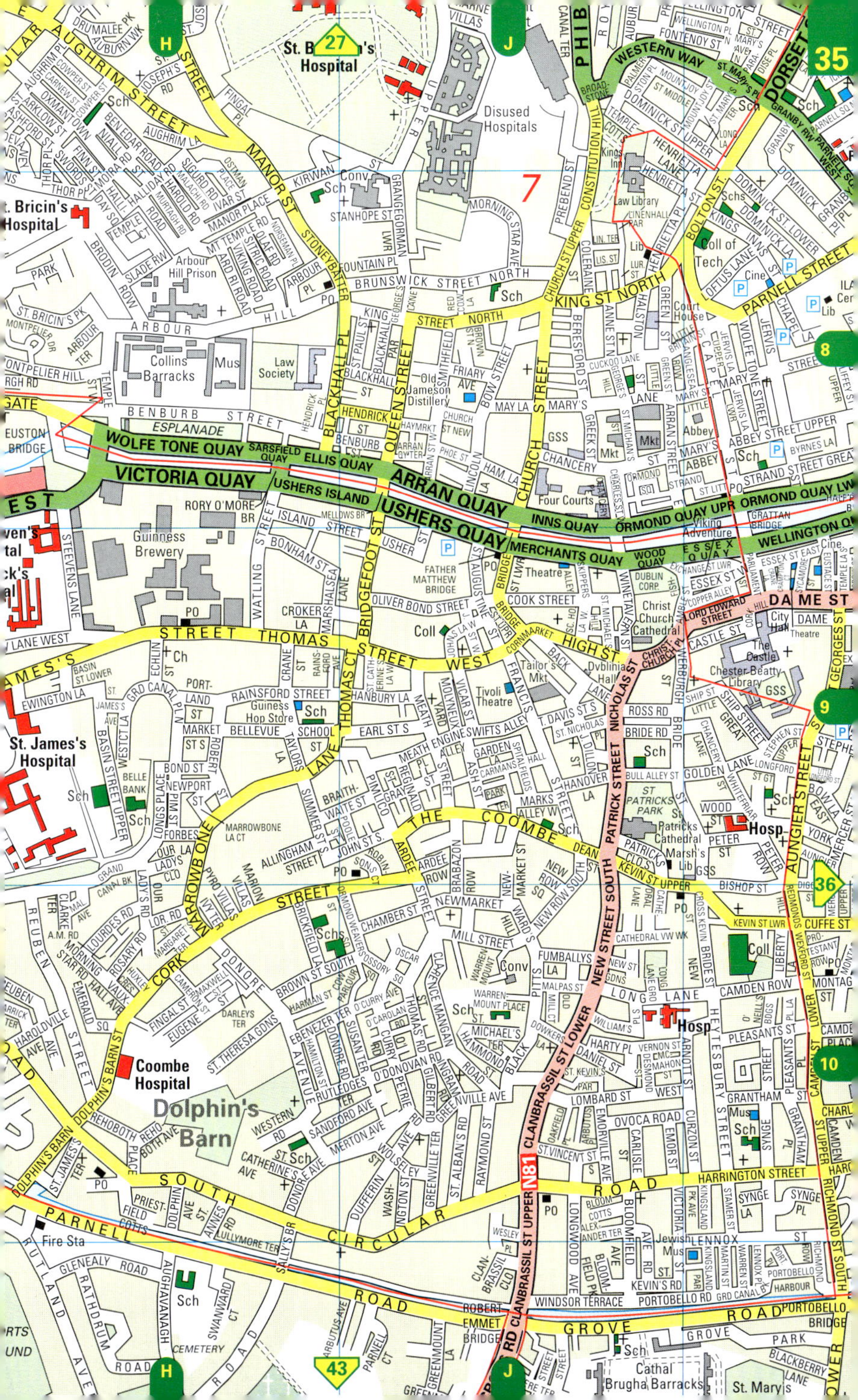

H
J
27
43
36
7
8
9
10
St. Brendan's Hospital
Disused Hospitals
St. Bricin's Hospital
Arbour Hill Prison
Collins Barracks
Mus
Law Society
Old Jameson Distillery
Law Library
Kings Inns
Coll of Tech
Court House
Four Courts
Guinness Brewery
Father Matthew Bridge
Theatre
Christ Church Cathedral
Dvblinia Hall
City Hall
The Castle
Chester Beatty Library
Tailor's Mkt
Tivoli Theatre
Guiness Hop Store
St. James's Hospital
St Patricks Park
St Patricks Cathedral
Marsh's Lib
Hosp
Coll
Coombe Hospital
Dolphin's Barn
Jewish Mus
Fire Sta
Cathal Brugha Barracks
St. Mary's
CEMETERY
Viking Adventure
AUGHRIM STREET
MANOR ST
STONEYBATTER
ARBOUR HILL
BENBURB STREET
ESPLANADE
WOLFE TONE QUAY
SARSFIELD QUAY
ELLIS QUAY
VICTORIA QUAY
USHERS ISLAND
ARRAN QUAY
USHERS QUAY
INNS QUAY
MERCHANTS QUAY
ORMOND QUAY UPR
ORMOND QUAY LWR
WOOD QUAY
ESSEX QUAY
WELLINGTON QUAY
CONSTITUTION HILL
CHURCH ST UPPER
KING ST NORTH
BOLTON ST
DORSET ST
WESTERN WAY
PARNELL STREET
BLACKHALL PL
QUEEN STREET
CHURCH STREET
BRIDGEFOOT ST
THOMAS STREET
STREET WEST
HIGH ST
DAME ST
LORD EDWARD STREET
PATRICK STREET
NICHOLAS ST
NEW STREET SOUTH
CLANBRASSIL ST LOWER
CLANBRASSIL ST UPPER
N81
THE COOMBE
DEAN ST
KEVIN ST UPPER
MARROWBONE LANE
CORK STREET
DOLPHIN'S BARN ST
SOUTH CIRCULAR ROAD
PARNELL ROAD
GROVE ROAD
HARRINGTON STREET
AUNGIER STREET
GEORGES ST
CAMDEN ST
RICHMOND ST SOUTH
LONG LANE
HEYTESBURY STREET
EUSTON BRIDGE
ROBERT EMMET BRIDGE
PORTOBELLO BRIDGE

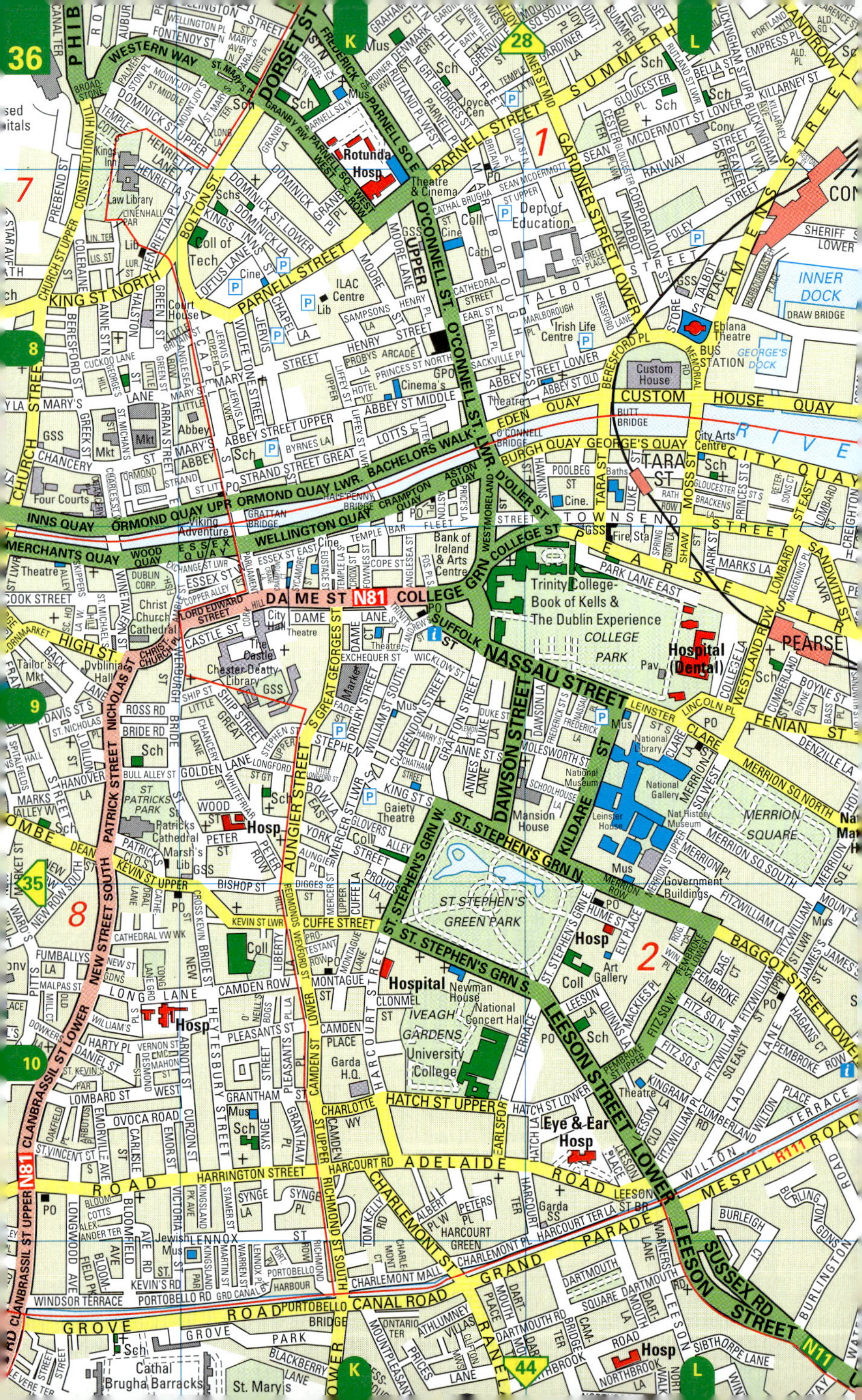
K
L
28
44
7
8
9
10
35
1
2
WESTERN WAY
PHIBSBOROUGH
DORSET ST
FREDERICK ST N
PARNELL SQ E
PARNELL SQ WEST
PARNELL STREET
Rotunda Hosp
Theatre & Cinema
O'CONNELL ST. UPPER
O'CONNELL ST. LWR.
SUMMERHILL
GARDINER STREET LOWER
SEAN MCDERMOTT ST LOWER
MARLBOROUGH ST
Dept of Education
TALBOT STREET
Irish Life Centre
HENRY STREET
ILAC Centre
GPO
ABBEY STREET LOWER
ABBEY ST MIDDLE
ABBEY STREET UPPER
MOORE LANE
KING ST NORTH
BOLTON ST.
Coll of Tech
Kings Inn
Law Library
HENRIETTA ST
CHURCH STREET
CONSTITUTION HILL
DOMINICK ST. LOWER
CAPEL STREET
JERVIS ST
Custom House
CUSTOM HOUSE QUAY
BUS STATION
Eblana Theatre
INNER DOCK
GEORGE'S DOCK
SHERIFF ST LOWER
AMIENS STREET
CON
EDEN QUAY
BURGH QUAY
GEORGE'S QUAY
CITY QUAY
RIVER LIFFEY
TARA ST
BUTT BRIDGE
City Arts Centre
D'OLIER ST
TOWNSEND STREET
PEARSE STREET
PEARSE
INNS QUAY
ORMOND QUAY UPR
ORMOND QUAY LWR.
BACHELORS WALK
WELLINGTON QUAY
ASTON QUAY
MERCHANTS QUAY
WOOD QUAY
ESSEX QUAY
Four Courts
Mkt
Viking Adventure
GRATTAN BRIDGE
HALFPENNY BRIDGE
Bank of Ireland & Arts Centre
COLLEGE GRN
DAME ST
N81
COLLEGE
Trinity College
Book of Kells & The Dublin Experience
COLLEGE PARK
Hospital (Dental)
PARK LANE EAST
WESTLAND ROW
City Hall
The Castle
Chester Beatty Library
Christ Church Cathedral
HIGH ST
CHRIST CHURCH PL
LORD EDWARD STREET
CASTLE ST
Tailor's Mkt
Dvblinia
NASSAU STREET
SUFFOLK ST
GRAFTON STREET
DAWSON STREET
KILDARE ST
National Library
National Museum
National Gallery
Leinster House
Nat History Museum
Government Buildings
MERRION SQUARE
MERRION SQ NORTH
MERRION SQ SOUTH
FENIAN ST
CLARE ST
LINCOLN PL
Mansion House
Gaiety Theatre
ST. STEPHEN'S GRN N
ST. STEPHEN'S GRN W.
ST. STEPHEN'S GRN S
ST STEPHEN'S GREEN PARK
ST PATRICKS PARK
St Patricks Cathedral
Marsh's Lib
PATRICK STREET
NICHOLAS ST
NEW STREET SOUTH
CLANBRASSIL ST LOWER
CLANBRASSIL ST UPPER
KEVIN ST UPPER
KEVIN ST LWR
CUFFE STREET
AUNGIER STREET
GOLDEN LANE
BRIDE ST
Hosp
Hospital
Newman House
National Concert Hall
IVEAGH GARDENS
University College
HARCOURT STREET
CAMDEN ST LOWER
CAMDEN ST UPPER
CAMDEN ROW
CHARLOTTE WY
HATCH ST UPPER
LEESON STREET LOWER
BAGGOT STREET LOWER
FITZWILLIAM SQ
Eye & Ear Hosp
ADELAIDE ROAD
HARRINGTON STREET
SOUTH CIRCULAR ROAD
CHARLEMONT ST
CHARLEMONT MALL
GRAND PARADE
CANAL ROAD
PORTOBELLO
GROVE ROAD
MESPIL ROAD
R111
SUSSEX RD
LEESON STREET
N11
RANELAGH
NORTHBROOK
Cathal Brugha Barracks
St. Mary's
WILTON TERRACE
PEMBROKE ST UPPER
HEYTESBURY STREET
SYNGE ST
LONG LANE
Garda H.Q.
Jewish Mus
WINDSOR TERRACE

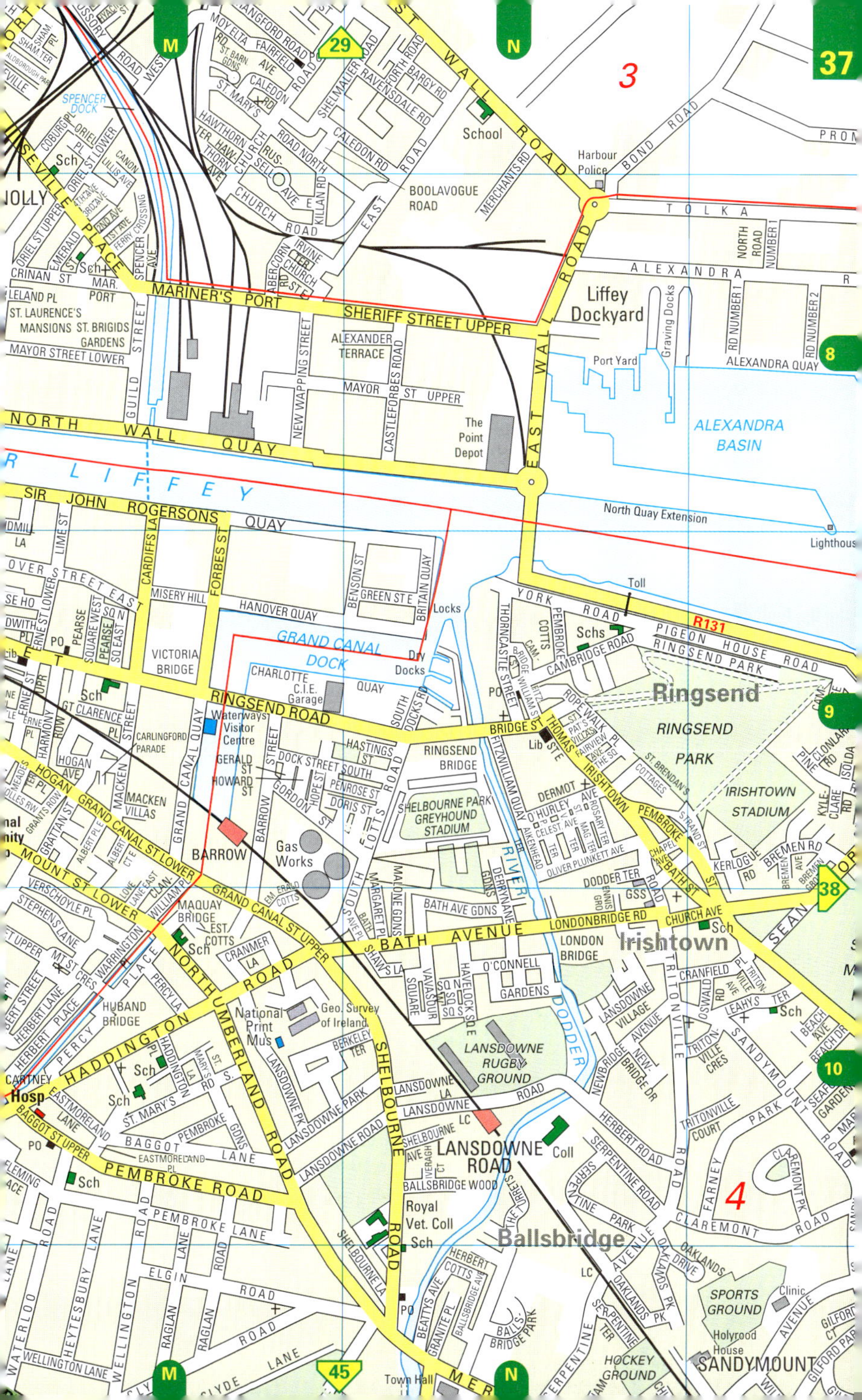

M
N
29
45
3
4
8
9
10
38
East Wall Road
Harbour Police
Bond Road
School
Merchants Rd
Boolavogue Road
Tolka
Alexandra Road
North Road Number 1
Rd Number 1
Rd Number 2
Alexandra Quay
Liffey Dockyard
Graving Docks
Port Yard
Alexandra Basin
North Quay Extension
Lighthouse
Spencer Dock
Seville Place
Mariner's Port
Sheriff Street Upper
Alexander Terrace
Mayor St Upper
Castleforbes Road
New Wapping Street
The Point Depot
Guild Street
Mayor Street Lower
St. Laurence's Mansions
St. Brigids Gardens
Crinan St
North Wall Quay
River Liffey
Sir John Rogersons Quay
Misery Hill
Hanover Quay
Benson St
Green St E
Britain Quay
Locks
Dry Docks
Grand Canal Dock
Charlotte Quay
C.I.E. Garage
Cardiffs La
Forbes St
Lime St
Pearse Street
Pearse Square
Victoria Bridge
Ringsend Road
Waterways Visitor Centre
Grand Canal Quay
Carlingford Parade
Gerald St
Howard St
Dock Street South
Hastings St
Penrose St
Doris St
Gordon St
Hope St
Barrow Street
Barrow
Gas Works
South Lotts Road
South Docks Rd
Ringsend Bridge
Shelbourne Park Greyhound Stadium
York Road
Pigeon House Road
Ringsend Park
R131
Toll
Schs
Cambridge Road
Thorncastle Street
Pembroke Cotts
Bridge St
Thomas St
Lib
PO
Ropewalk Pl
Fitzwilliam Quay
Ringsend
Ringsend Park
Irishtown Stadium
Irishtown Road
Dermot O'Hurley Ave
Oliver Plunkett Ave
Rosary Ter
Dodder Ter
GSS
Pembroke Cottages
St. Brendan's Cottages
Strand St
Chapel Ave
Bath St
Kerlogue Rd
Bremen Rd
Seán Moore Road
Church Ave
Sch
Irishtown
London Bridge
Londonbridge Rd
Bath Avenue
Bath Ave Gdns
River Dodder
O'Connell Gardens
Havelock Sq
Vavasour Square
Shaws La
Malone Gdns
Margaret Pl
Derrynane Gdns
Lansdowne Village
Newbridge Avenue
New Bridge Dr
Tritonville Road
Cranfield Pl
Oswald Rd
Leahys Ter
Sandymount Road
Beach Ave
Tritonville Cres
Tritonville Court
Lansdowne Rugby Ground
Lansdowne Road
Lansdowne Park
Lansdowne La
Coll
Herbert Road
Serpentine Road
Serpentine Park
Serpentine Ave
Claremont Road
Claremont Pk
Farney Park
Ballsbridge
Oaklands Drive
Oaklands Pk
Sports Ground
Clinic
Holyrood House
Sandymount
Hockey Ground
Gilford Rd
Grand Canal St Lower
Grand Canal St Upper
Hogan Pl
Hogan Ave
Macken Street
Macken Villas
Gt Clarence Pl
Grattan St
Albert Pl E
Mount St Lower
Verschoyle Pl
Stephens Lane
Herbert Street
Herbert Lane
Herbert Place
Warrington Place
Mt St Cres
Percy Pl
Percy La
Huband Bridge
Maquay Bridge
Clanwilliam Pl
Northumberland Road
Haddington Road
Cranmer La
National Print Mus
Geo. Survey of Ireland
Berkeley Ter
Shelbourne Road
Lansdowne Pk
Lansdowne Road
Hosp
Cartney
Baggot St Upper
Eastmoreland Lane
Eastmoreland Pl
St. Mary's Rd
Pembroke Gdns
Baggot Lane
Pembroke Road
Pembroke Lane
Royal Vet. Coll
Ballsbridge Wood
Shelbourne La
Herbert Cotts
Ballsbridge Ave
Beattys Ave
Granite Pl
Balls Bridge Park
Town Hall
Elgin Road
Raglan Lane
Raglan Road
Wellington Lane
Heytesbury Lane
Waterloo Lane
Clyde Lane
Clyde Road
Fleming Pl
LC

P
Q
30
3
PROMENADE ROAD
BOND ROAD
Harbour Police
BOND DRIVE
BRANCH ROAD NORTH EXTENSION
TOLKA QUAY
TOLKA QUAY ROAD
NORTH ROAD NUMBER 1
BRANCH ROAD NORTH
ALEXANDRA ROAD
EAST WALL ROAD
Liffey Dockyard
Graving Docks
RD NUMBER 1
RD NUMBER 2
RD NUMBER 3
BRANCH ROAD SOUTH
1
BREAKWATER RD SOUTH
8
Port Yard
ALEXANDRA QUAY
ALEXANDRA BASIN
JETTY ROAD
Timber Quay
Ocean Pier
PETROLEUM BASIN
EASTERN BREAKWATER
North Quay Extension
Lighthouse
West Oil Jetty
East Oil Jetty
Lighthouse
Toll
YORK ROAD
R131
PEMBROKE COTTS
Schs
CAMBRIDGE ROAD
PIGEON HOUSE ROAD
RINGSEND PARK
Ringsend
RINGSEND PARK
CAMBRIDGE AVE
9
ROPEWALK PL
ST. PAT'S VILLAS
FAIRVIEW AVE
THE SQ
Lib
THOMAS STE
IRISHTOWN ROAD
ST. BRENDAN'S COTTAGES
IRISHTOWN STADIUM
PINE RD
CLONLARA RD
ISOLDA RD
LEUKOS RD
KYLE-CLARE RD
CYMRIC RD
SOUTH BANK ROAD
WHITEBANK ROAD
E.S.B. Power Station
SHELLYSBANKS RD
DERMOT O'HURLEY AVE
ST. JOHN'S CELEST. AVE
AIKENHEAD TER
ROSARY TER
MAG. TER
RIVER PLUNKETT AVE
PEMBROKE ST
STRAND ST
CHAPEL AVE
BATH ST
KERLOGUE RD
BREMEN RD
BREMEN AVE
BREMEN GRO
SEAN MORE ROAD
37
DODDER TER
ENNIS GRO
GSS
LONDONBRIDGE RD
CHURCH AVE
Sch
LONDON BRIDGE
Irishtown
SEAN MOORE PARK
IRISH PA
DODDER
LANSDOWNE VILLAGE
AVENUE
TRITONVILLE ROAD
CRANFIELD PL
OSWALD RD
TRITONVILLE AVE
LEAHYS TER
Sch
BEACH AVE
BEACH DR
10
NEWBRIDGE AVENUE
NEWBRIDGE DR
TRITONVILLE CRES
SANDYMOUNT ROAD
SEAFORT GARDENS
MARINE DRIVE
BEACH ROAD
HERBERT ROAD
Coll
SERPENTINE ROAD
TRITONVILLE COURT
PARK
CLAREMONT PK
PO
SEAFORT AVENUE
Rehab. Inst.
Sandymount
Sandymount Strand
SERPENTINE PARK
FARNEY PARK
4
CLAREMONT ROAD
SANDYMOUNT GREEN
NEWGROVE AVENUE
MARTELLO VW
STRAND
allsbridge
AVENUE
OAKLANDS DRIVE
OAKLANDS CRES
LC
OAKLANDS PK
SPORTS GROUND
Clinic
AVENUE
SANDYMOUNT CASTLE RD
SANDYMOUNT CASTLE DR
DURHAM ROAD
LEA RD
LEA CRES
SERPENTINE TER
SERPENTINE AVE
GILFORD CT
GILFORD PARK
GILFORD ROAD
GILFORD AVE
HOCKEY GROUND
Holyrood House
SANDYMOUNT
Sch
46

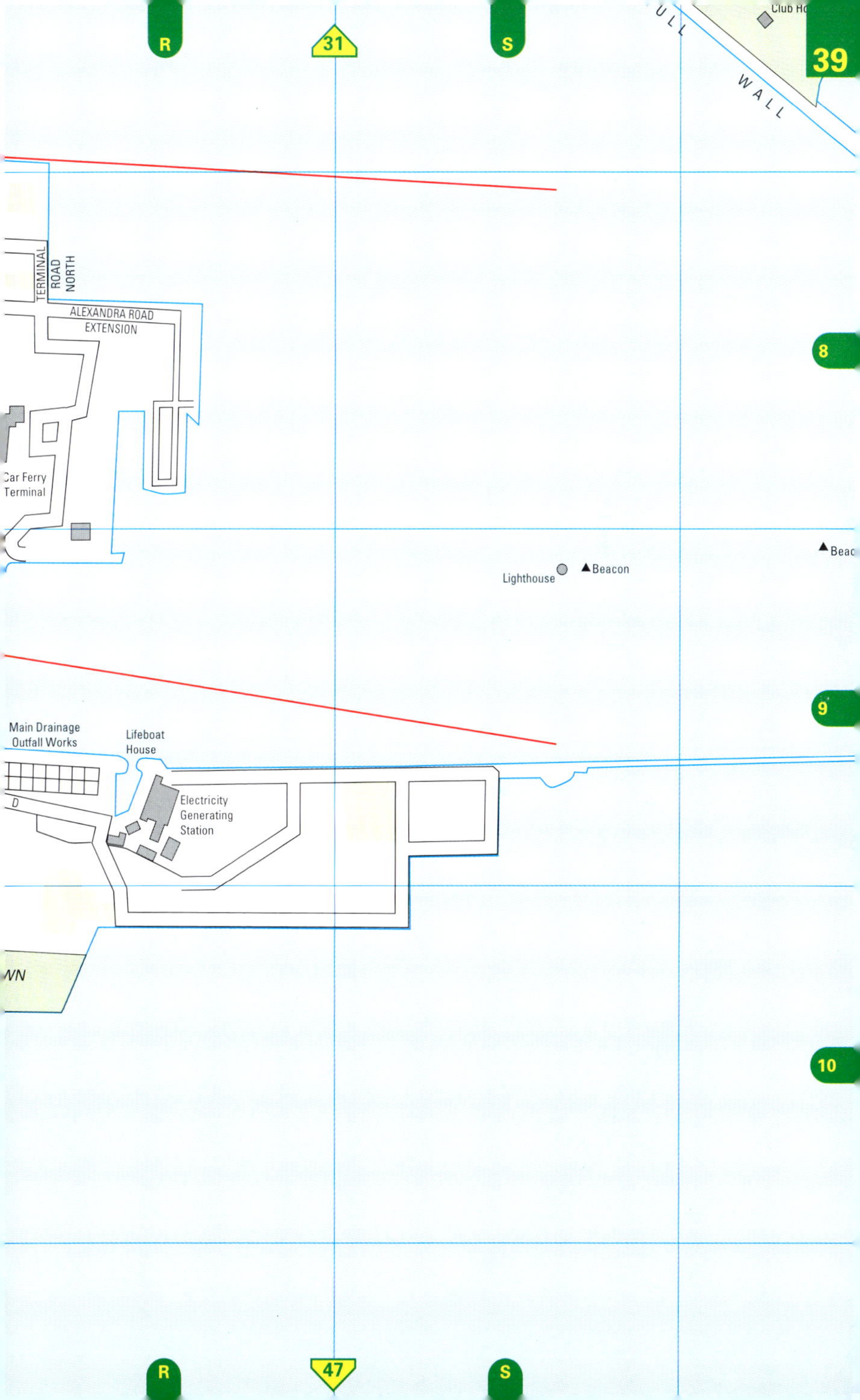
R
31
S
Club Ho
ULL
WALL
TERMINAL ROAD NORTH
ALEXANDRA ROAD EXTENSION
Car Ferry Terminal
8
Lighthouse
Beacon
Beac
9
Main Drainage Outfall Works
Lifeboat House
Electricity Generating Station
D
WN
10
R
47
S

10
B
32
C
KYLEMORE PARK SOUTH
Sch
LABRE PARK
Seventh Lock
Sixth Lock
Eighth Lock
BALLYFERMOT BRIDGE
JOHN F. KENNEDY PARK
BLUEBELL INDUSTRIAL ESTATE
BLUEBELL AVENUE
CAMAC PARK
WESTERN INDUSTRIAL ESTATE
CAMMOCK RIVER
KILLEEN ROAD
JOHN F. KENNEDY ROAD
JOHN F. KENNEDY DRIVE
11
NANGOR ROAD
OAK ROAD
WILLOW ROAD
KNOCKMITTEN CLO
KNOCKMITTEN LA NORTH
KNOCKMITTEN LANE
HAWTHORN RD
CHESTNUT RD
ELM ROAD
INDUSTRIAL ESTATE
SYCAMORE RD
BEECH RD
HOLLY ROAD
UPPER KILLEEN ROAD
Fox & Geese
NAAS ROAD
OLD ROAD
AVONBEG INDUSTRIAL ESTATE
LONG
CLUB ROAD
ROBINHOOD ROAD
PROPOSED ROAD
Walkinstown
ROBINHOOD INDUSTRIAL ESTATE
12
Junction 9
TURNPIKE ROAD
22
INDUSTRIAL ESTATE
LOWER
BALLYMOUNT ROAD
UNDER CONST
13
WESTERN PARKWAY
BALLYMOUNT
BUSINESS PARK
PROPOSED ROAD
UPPER
KINGSWOOD
CASTLE ROAD
DUNMORE PARK
DUNMORE GRO
DUNMORE LAWN
ASHFIELD AVE
ASHFIELD PK
ASHFIELD DR
ASHFIELD CLO
BALLYMOUNT AVE
WALNUT CLO
CHESTNUT GRO
SYLVAN ROAD
FOREST LAWN
FOREST CLOSE
FOREST PARK
KEADEEN AVE
TIBRADDEN
LUGNAQUILLA AVE
48
24

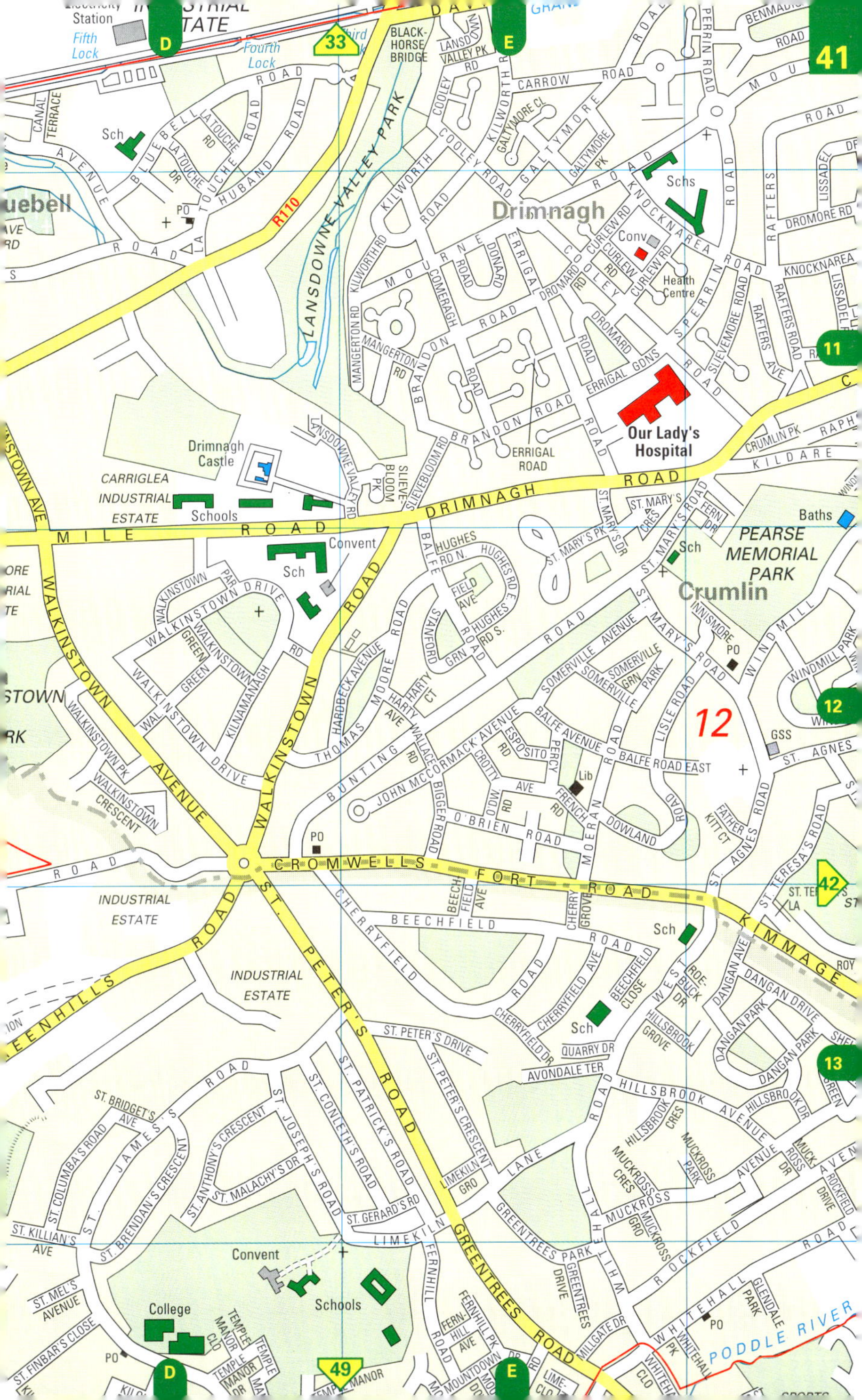
Station
Fifth Lock
Fourth Lock
33
D
E
BLACK-HORSE BRIDGE
LANSDOWNE VALLEY PK
COOLEY RD
KILWORTH ROAD
CARROW ROAD
GALTYMORE CL
GALTYMORE
GALTYMORE PK
PERRIN ROAD
BENMADIGAN ROAD
MOUNT
CANAL TERRACE
Sch
BLUEBELL
LATOUCHE RD
LATOUCHE DR
LA TOUCHE ROAD
HUBAND ROAD
AVENUE
uebell
PO
R110
LANSDOWNE VALLEY PARK
KILWORTH
COOLEY ROAD
Drimnagh
KNOCKNAREA
Schs
Conv
CURLEW RD
Health Centre
RAFTERS
LISSADEL
DROMORE RD
KNOCKNAREA
LISSADEL RD
RAFTERS ROAD
RAFTERS AVE
SLIEVEMORE ROAD
SPERRIN ROAD
MOURNE ROAD
DONARD
ERRIGAL
COOLEY
DROMARD
KILWORTH RD
MANGERTON RD
COMERAGH
BRANDON ROAD
MANGERTON RD
ERRIGAL GDNS
11
Our Lady's Hospital
CRUMLIN PK
RAPH
KILDARE
ERRIGAL ROAD
SLIEVEBLOOM RD
SLIEVE-BLOOM PK
LANSDOWNE VALLEY RD
Drimnagh Castle
CARRIGLEA INDUSTRIAL ESTATE
Schools
DRIMNAGH ROAD
MILE ROAD
ST. MARY'S PK
ST. MARY'S CRES
ST. MARY'S DR
ST. MARY'S ROAD
FERN DR
Baths
PEARSE MEMORIAL PARK
Crumlin
WALKINSTOWN AVE
Convent
Sch
WALKINSTOWN PAR
WALKINSTOWN DRIVE
WALKINSTOWN GREEN
KILNAMANAGH RD
WALKINSTOWN ROAD
BALFE
HUGHES RD N.
HUGHES RD E.
HUGHES RD S.
FIELD AVE
STANFORD GRN
HARDBECK AVENUE
MOORE ROAD
HARTY AVE
HARTY CT
THOMAS
SOMERVILLE AVENUE
SOMERVILLE GRN
SOMERVILLE PARK
INNISMORE
WINDMILL
WINDMILL PARK
12
GSS
ST. AGNES ROAD
LISLE ROAD
BALFE AVENUE
BALFE ROAD EAST
ESPOSITO RD
PERCY FRENCH RD
CROTTY AVE
O'BRIEN ROAD
Lib
MOERAN ROAD
DOWLAND ROAD
FATHER KITT CT
JOHN McCORMACK AVENUE
BUNTING RD
WALLACE RD
BIGGER ROAD
WALKINSTOWN PK
WALKINSTOWN CRESCENT
WALKINSTOWN AVENUE
STOWN
RK
PO
CROMWELLS FORT ROAD
KIMMAGE
ST. TERESA'S ROAD
42
ST. TERESA'S LA
ROY
INDUSTRIAL ESTATE
BEECHFIELD AVE
CHERRY GROVE
BEECHFIELD ROAD
CHERRYFIELD ROAD
CHERRYFIELD AVE
BEECHFIELD CLOSE
CHERRYFIELD DR
Sch
WEST
ROEBUCK DR
DANGAN AVE
DANGAN DRIVE
DANGAN PARK
HILLSBROOK GROVE
QUARRY DR
13
AVONDALE TER
HILLSBROOK AVENUE
HILLSBROOK DR
HILLSBROOK CRES
MUCKROSS CRES
MUCKROSS PARK
MUCKROSS DR
MUCKROSS GRO
GREENHILLS ROAD
ST. PETER'S ROAD
ST. PETER'S DRIVE
ST. PETER'S CRESCENT
ST. PATRICK'S ROAD
ST. CONLETH'S ROAD
ST. JOSEPH'S ROAD
ST. ANTHONY'S CRESCENT
ST. MALACHY'S DR
ST. BRIDGET'S AVE
ST. JAMES'S ROAD
ST. COLUMBA'S ROAD
ST. BRENDAN'S CRESCENT
ST. KILLIAN'S AVE
ST. MEL'S AVENUE
ST. FINBAR'S CLOSE
ST. GERARD'S RD
LIMEKILN GRO
LIMEKILN LANE
GREENTREES PARK
GREENTREES DRIVE
GREENTREES ROAD
WHITEHALL ROAD
ROCKFIELD AVENUE
ROCKFIELD DRIVE
ROCKFIELD ROAD
Convent
Schools
College
TEMPLE MANOR CLO
TEMPLE MANOR DR
FERNHILL ROAD
FERN-HILL AVE
FERNHILL PK
MOUNTDOWN
MILLGATE DR
WHITEHALL PK
GLENDALE PARK
PO
PODDLE RIVER
49
D
E

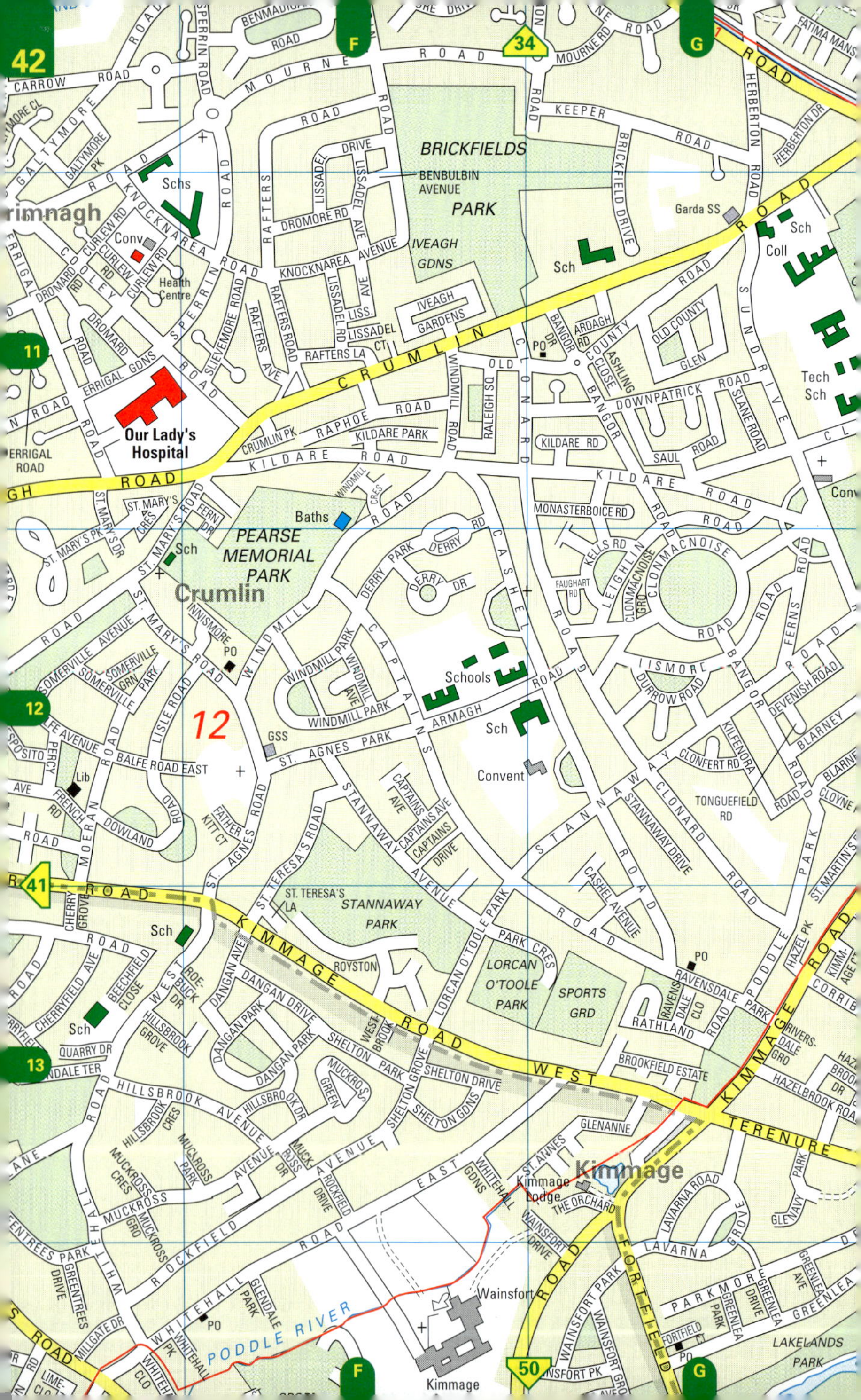
F
34
G
CARROW ROAD
BENMADIGAN ROAD
SPERRIN ROAD
MOURNE ROAD
MOURNE RD
KEEPER ROAD
HERBERTON ROAD
HERBERTON DR
FATIMA MANS.
GALTYMORE CL
GALTYMORE
GALTYMORE PK
GALTYMORE ROAD
Schs
Crimnagh
KNOCKNAREA
KNOCKNAREA AVENUE
KNOCKNAREA ROAD
Conv
CURLEW RD
CURLEW RD
CURLEW RD
COOLEY RD
DROMARD
DROMARD RD
Health Centre
ERRIGAL
RAFTERS ROAD
RAFTERS AVE
RAFTERS LA
DROMORE RD
LISSADEL DRIVE
LISSADEL AVE
LISSADEL RD
LISS.
LISSADEL CT
BRICKFIELDS
BENBULBIN AVENUE
PARK
IVEAGH GDNS
IVEAGH GARDENS
BRICKFIELD DRIVE
Sch
Garda SS
Sch
Coll
SUNDRIVE ROAD
Tech Sch
SLIEVEMORE ROAD
11
ERRIGAL GDNS
ERRIGAL ROAD
Our Lady's Hospital
CRUMLIN ROAD
CRUMLIN PK
RAPHOE ROAD
KILDARE PARK
KILDARE ROAD
KILDARE RD
WINDMILL ROAD
RALEIGH SQ.
OLD COUNTY ROAD
OLD COUNTY GLEN
CLONARD
BANGOR DR
ARDAGH
PO
ASHLING CLOSE
BANGOR
DOWNPATRICK ROAD
SLANE ROAD
SAUL ROAD
CL
Conv
ST. MARY'S ROAD
ST. MARY'S CRES
FERN DR
ST. MARY'S PK
ST. MARY'S DR
Baths
WINDMILL CRES
PEARSE MEMORIAL PARK
Sch
Crumlin
DERRY PARK
DERRY RD
DERRY DR
CASHEL
MONASTERBOICE RD
KELLS RD
FAUGHART RD
LEIGHLIN
CLONMACNOISE GRO
CLONMACNOISE ROAD
FERNS ROAD
BANGOR ROAD
LISMORE
DURROW ROAD
DEVENISH ROAD
INNISMORE
PO
SOMERVILLE AVENUE
SOMERVILLE GRN
SOMERVILLE PARK
12
WINDMILL
WINDMILL PARK
WINDMILL AVE
CAPTAINS ROAD
Schools
ARMAGH ROAD
Sch
KILFENORA ROAD
CLONFERT RD
BLARNEY PARK
TONGUEFIELD RD
BLARNEY
CLOYNE
LISLE ROAD
12
GSS
ST. AGNES PARK
Convent
PERCY
ESPOSITO
BALFE AVENUE
BALFE ROAD EAST
Lib
FRENCH RD
DOWLAND ROAD
FATHER KITT CT
ST. AGNES ROAD
ST. TERESA'S ROAD
STANNAWAY AVENUE
CAPTAINS AVE
CAPTAINS AVE
CAPTAINS DRIVE
STANNAWAY ROAD
STANNAWAY DRIVE
CLONARD ROAD
ST. MARTIN'S
MOERAN ROAD
41
KIMMAGE ROAD
CHERRY GROVE
ST. TERESA'S LA
STANNAWAY PARK
LORCAN O'TOOLE PARK
CASHEL AVENUE
PARK CRES
Sch
CHERRYFIELD AVE
BEECHFIELD CLOSE
ROEBUCK DR
DANGAN AVE
DANGAN DRIVE
DANGAN PARK
ROYSTON
LORCAN O'TOOLE PARK
SPORTS GRD
PO
RAVENSDALE PARK
RAVENSDALE CLO
RATHLAND ROAD
HAZEL PK
KIMMAGE ROAD
KIMMAGE GROVE
CORRIB
Sch
QUARRY DR
HILLSBROOK GROVE
WEST BROOK
SHELTON PARK
SHELTON GROVE
SHELTON DRIVE
SHELTON GDNS
MUCKROSS GREEN
KIMMAGE ROAD WEST
BROOKFIELD ESTATE
RIVERSDALE GRO
HAZELBROOK DR
HAZELBROOK ROAD
13
GLENDALE TER
HILLSBROOK AVENUE
HILLSBROOK CRES
HILLSBROOK DR
MUCKROSS PARK
MUCKROSS CRES
MUCKROSS AVENUE
MUCKROSS DR
MUCKROSS GRO
MUCKROSS
ROCKFIELD AVENUE
ROCKFIELD DRIVE
GLENANNE
ST. AGNES
TERENURE ROAD
KIMMAGE ROAD EAST
WHITEHALL GDNS
Kimmage
Kimmage Lodge
THE ORCHARD
LAVARNA ROAD
LAVARNA GROVE
GLENAVY PARK
WHITEHALL ROAD
GREENTREES PARK
GREENTREES DRIVE
GREENTREES
ROCKFIELD ROAD
WAINSFORT DRIVE
Wainsfort
LAVARNA
PARKMORE DRIVE
GREENLEA PARK
GREENLEA
GREENLEA AVE
GREENLEA ROAD
MILLGATE DR
WHITEHALL PARK
GLENDALE PARK
PO
PODDLE RIVER
WAINSFORT PARK
WAINSFORT ROAD
FORTFIELD ROAD
FORTFIELD
PO
LAKELANDS PARK
WHITEHALL CLO
LIME CLO
F
50
WAINSFORT PK
Kimmage
G

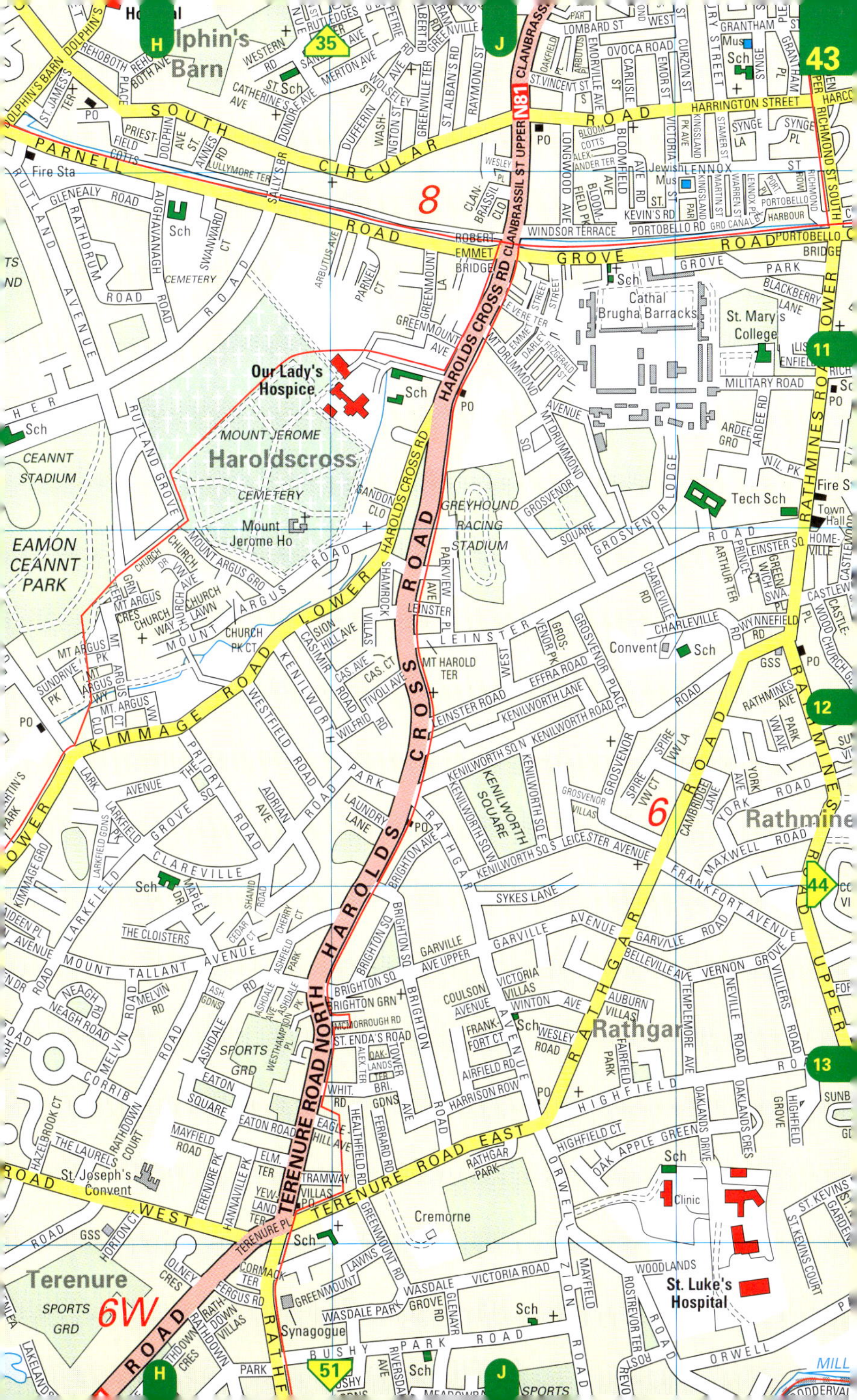
43
Dolphin's Barn
Hospital
35
51
44
11
12
13
H
J
8
6
6W
N81
South Circular Road
Parnell Road
Grove Road
Clanbrassil St Upper
Harrington Street
Harolds Cross Rd
Harolds Cross Road
Kimmage Road Lower
Terenure Road North
Terenure Road East
Terenure Road West
Rathgar Road
Rathmines Road Lower
Rathmines Road Upper
Leinster Road
Leinster Road West
Kenilworth Road
Kenilworth Square
Kenilworth Park
Grosvenor Road
Grosvenor Square
Grosvenor Place
Leicester Avenue
Frankfort Avenue
Garville Avenue
Highfield Road
Orwell Road
Bushy Park Road
Mount Argus Road
Mount Jerome
Haroldscross
Cemetery
Mount Jerome Ho
Our Lady's Hospice
Greyhound Racing Stadium
Cathal Brugha Barracks
St. Mary's College
Military Road
Tech Sch
Town Hall
Fire Sta
Convent
Eamon Ceannt Park
Ceannt Stadium
Rathmines
Rathgar
Terenure
Sports Grd
St. Joseph's Convent
Cremorne
Synagogue
St. Luke's Hospital
Clinic
Jewish Mus
Mount Tallant Avenue
Clareville
Larkfield Avenue
Westfield Road
Kenilworth Lane
Rathgar Park
Victoria Road
Wasdale Park
Woodlands
Portobello Rd
Windsor Terrace
Robert Emmet Bridge
Harbour
Rutland Avenue
Glenealy Road
Aughavanagh Road
Priory Road
Sch
PO
GSS

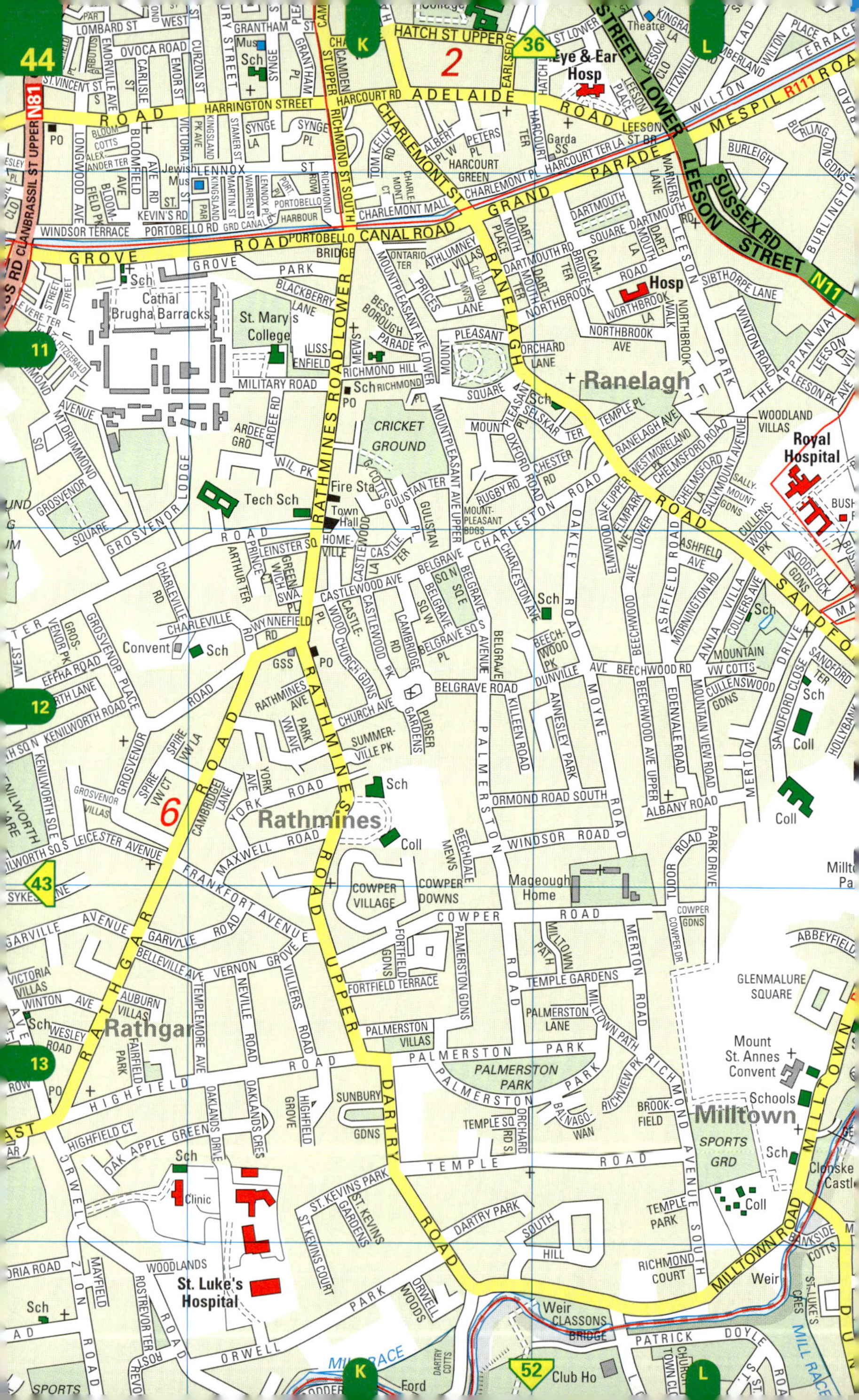
2
6
K
L
36
43
52
11
12
13
N81
N11
R111
HATCH ST UPPER
ADELAIDE ROAD
HARRINGTON STREET
LOMBARD ST
OVOCA ROAD
GRANTHAM ST
SYNGE ST
CLANBRASSIL ST UPPER
LEESON STREET LOWER
LEESON STREET
SUSSEX RD
MESPIL ROAD
Eye & Ear Hosp
Theatre
Garda SS
HARCOURT TER
HARCOURT RD
CHARLEMONT ST
CHARLEMONT MALL
CAMDEN ST UPPER
RICHMOND ST SOUTH
GRAND PARADE
CANAL ROAD
PORTOBELLO
PORTOBELLO RD
Jewish Mus
LENNOX
KEVIN'S RD
WINDSOR TERRACE
GROVE ROAD
GROVE PARK
BURLEIGH CT
BURLINGTON
DARTMOUTH SQUARE
DARTMOUTH RD
NORTHBROOK ROAD
NORTHBROOK AVE
Hosp
SIBTHORPE LANE
WINTON ROAD
THE APPIAN WAY
LEESON PK AVE
Cathal Brugha Barracks
St. Mary's College
RATHMINES ROAD LOWER
RANELAGH
Ranelagh
MILITARY ROAD
RICHMOND HILL
MOUNTPLEASANT AVE LOWER
MOUNTPLEASANT AVE UPPER
MOUNT PLEASANT SQUARE
CRICKET GROUND
Fire Sta
Town Hall
Tech Sch
Sch
PO
GROSVENOR SQUARE
GROSVENOR ROAD
MT DRUMMOND AVENUE
LEINSTER SQ
HOME-VILLE
CASTLEWOOD AVE
CHARLESTON ROAD
CHARLESTON AVE
BELGRAVE SQ
BELGRAVE ROAD
OAKLEY ROAD
WOODLAND VILLAS
Royal Hospital
SANDFORD ROAD
CHELMSFORD ROAD
SALLYMOUNT AVENUE
EDENVALE ROAD
BEECHWOOD AVE UPPER
BEECHWOOD AVE LOWER
BEECHWOOD RD
ASHFIELD ROAD
MORNINGTON RD
MOUNTAIN VIEW ROAD
SANDFORD CLOSE
Convent
CHARLEVILLE ROAD
WYNNEFIELD RD
GSS
EFFRA ROAD
KENILWORTH ROAD
KENILWORTH SQ
LEICESTER AVENUE
RATHMINES ROAD UPPER
Rathmines
Coll
MOYNE ROAD
PALMERSTON ROAD
ORMOND ROAD SOUTH
WINDSOR ROAD
ALBANY ROAD
MERTON ROAD
MERTON DRIVE
PARK DRIVE
TUDOR ROAD
Mageough Home
COWPER VILLAGE
COWPER DOWNS
COWPER ROAD
FRANKFORT AVENUE
MAXWELL ROAD
YORK ROAD
GARVILLE AVENUE
GARVILLE ROAD
VERNON GROVE
BELLEVILLE AVE
RATHGAR ROAD
Rathgar
AUBURN VILLAS
WINTON AVE
VICTORIA VILLAS
ABBEYFIELD
GLENMALURE SQUARE
FORTFIELD TERRACE
PALMERSTON GDNS
PALMERSTON VILLAS
PALMERSTON PARK
TEMPLE GARDENS
MILLTOWN PATH
Mount St. Annes Convent
Schools
Milltown
SPORTS GRD
HIGHFIELD ROAD
OAKLANDS DRIVE
OAK APPLE GREEN
HIGHFIELD CT
DARTRY ROAD
TEMPLE ROAD
RICHMOND AVENUE SOUTH
Clinic
St. Luke's Hospital
WOODLANDS
ORWELL PARK
ORWELL ROAD
ST. KEVINS PARK
DARTRY PARK
SOUTH HILL
TEMPLE PARK
RICHMOND COURT
MILLTOWN ROAD
Weir
CLASSONS BRIDGE
PATRICK DOYLE ROAD
MILL RACE
Club Ho
Ford
Clonskea Castle

37
M
N
4
LANSDOWNE ROAD
Ballsbridge
SANDYMOUNT
Royal Vet. Coll
PEMBROKE ROAD
BAGGOT ST UPPER
EASTMORELAND LANE
PEMBROKE LANE
ELGIN ROAD
CLYDE ROAD
CLYDE LANE
WELLINGTON LANE
WELLINGTON PL
HEYTESBURY LANE
SHELBOURNE ROAD
HERBERT PARK
MORHAMPTON ROAD
MERRION ROAD
Town Hall
Royal Dublin Society's Showgrounds
JUMPING GROUND
SIMMONSCOURT ROAD
Masonic Sch
Agiculture Inst.
Simmonscourt Castle
SERPENTINE AVENUE
HOCKEY GROUND
SPORTS GROUND
Holyrood House
CLAREMONT ROAD
11
SHREWSBURY ROAD
ANGLESEA ROAD
RUGBY GROUND
Muckross College
Donnybrook
Convent
Fire Sta.
DONNYBROOK RD
ANGLESEA BRIDGE
AILESBURY DRIVE
AILESBURY ROAD
12
EGLINTON ROAD
CLONSKEAGH ROAD
Vergemount Hospital
Weir
Clonskeagh
RIVER DODDER
CLONSKEAGH BRIDGE
STILLORGAN ROAD
N11
Television Studios
NUTLEY ROAD
NUTLEY AVENUE
NUTLEY LANE
NUTLEY PARK
Beechmount
Club House
46
13
Dept of Horticulture
RICHVIEW OFFICE PARK
University Lodge
Faculty of Architecture
WHITEBEAM ROAD
WHITETHORN ROAD
MAPLE ROAD
Woodview
Flyover
Sports Centre
Depts of Physics Botany Zoology Geology and Lecture Rooms
Dept of Industrial Medical Microbiology
Dept of Administration
University College
14
WYNNSWARD PARK
WYNNSWARD DR
NUTGROVE PARK
THE MAPLES
53

46
38
P
Q
11
12
13
45
54
Sandymount
Sandymount Strand
Ballsbridge
SANDYMOUNT
SYDNEY PARADE
Merrion
Booterstown
4
BEACH ROAD
STRAND ROAD
MERRION ROAD
ROAD
HERBERT ROAD
SERPENTINE ROAD
SERPENTINE PARK
SERPENTINE AVENUE
SERPENTINE TER
TRITONVILLE COURT
FARNEY PARK
CLAREMONT PK
CLAREMONT ROAD
SEAFORT AVENUE
SEAFORT GARDENS
SANDYMOUNT GREEN
NEWGROVE AVENUE
MARTELLO VW
LEA RD
LEA CRES
DURHAM ROAD
SANDYMOUNT CASTLE RD
SANDYMOUNT CASTLE DR
SANDYMOUNT AVENUE
GILFORD CT
GILFORD PARK
GILFORD DRIVE
GILFORD ROAD
GILFORD AVE
TRAMWAY TERRACE
OAKLANDS DRIVE
OAKLANDS PK
OAKLANDS TER
SYDENHAM ROAD
SPAFIELD TERRACE
CHURCHILL TERRACE
ADAIR
SANDYMOUNT ROAD
WILFIELD
WILLFIELD PARK
WILLFIELD ROAD
PRINCE OF WALES TER
KIRKWOOD
PARK LANE
PARK AVENUE
WILLOWFIELD
MARTELLO WOOD
SHREWSBURY
SHREWSBURY PARK
SHREWSBURY ROAD
COURT ROAD
MERLYN DRIVE
MERLYN RD
MERLYN PARK
ST. JOHN'S ROAD EAST
ST. JOHN'S
SEABURY
RICHELIEU PK
SYDNEY PARADE AVENUE
ADELAIDE MEWS
MARTELLO MWS
ST. ALBAN'S PARK
MERRION STRAND
WILLOW MWS
AILESBURY ROAD
AILESBURY GARDENS
AILESBURY PK
AILESBURY MWS
SYDNEY PAR AVE
MERRION VW AVE
BROOKLANDS
MERRION VILLAGE
NUTLEY AVENUE
NUTLEY ROAD
NUTLEY LANE
NUTLEY PARK
NUTLEY SQ
SEA VIEW TERRACE
ELM PK
HERBERT AVENUE
ESTATE AVE
STILLORGAN ROAD
N11
GREENFIELD PARK
GREENFIELD CRES
DONNYBROOK GREEN
CRANFORD CT
THE ELMS
BELLEVUE AVENUE
BELLEVUE PK AVE
BELLEVUE PK
BELLEVUE CT
BELLEVUE COPSE
DORNDEN PARK
TRIMLESTON AVE
TRIMLESTON PK
TRIMLESTON RD
TRIMLESTON GARDENS
WOODBINE ROAD
WOODBINE PK
WOODBINE AVENUE
MERRION CRES
GLENOMENA PARK
GLENOMENA GRO
ASHFIELD PARK
SEAFIELD ROAD
SEAFIELD CRES
SEAFIELD PK
SEAFIELD CLO
ST. HELEN'S ROAD
CASTLE COURT
Coll
Rehab. Inst.
PO
SPORTS GROUND
Clinic
Holyrood House
HOCKEY GROUND
LC
Sch
Pav
Martello Tower
Masonic Sch
Agiculture Inst.
Simmonscourt Castle
Ailesbury House
Television Studios
Beechmount
St.Vincent's Hospital
Hospital
ELM PARK GOLF COURSE
Club House
St.Mary's Home for the Blind
Dept of Horticulture
Flyover
Woodview
Depts of Physics Botany Zoology Geology and Lecture Rooms
Dept of Industrial Medical Microbiology
Dept of Administration
Lib
University College
SPORTS GROUND

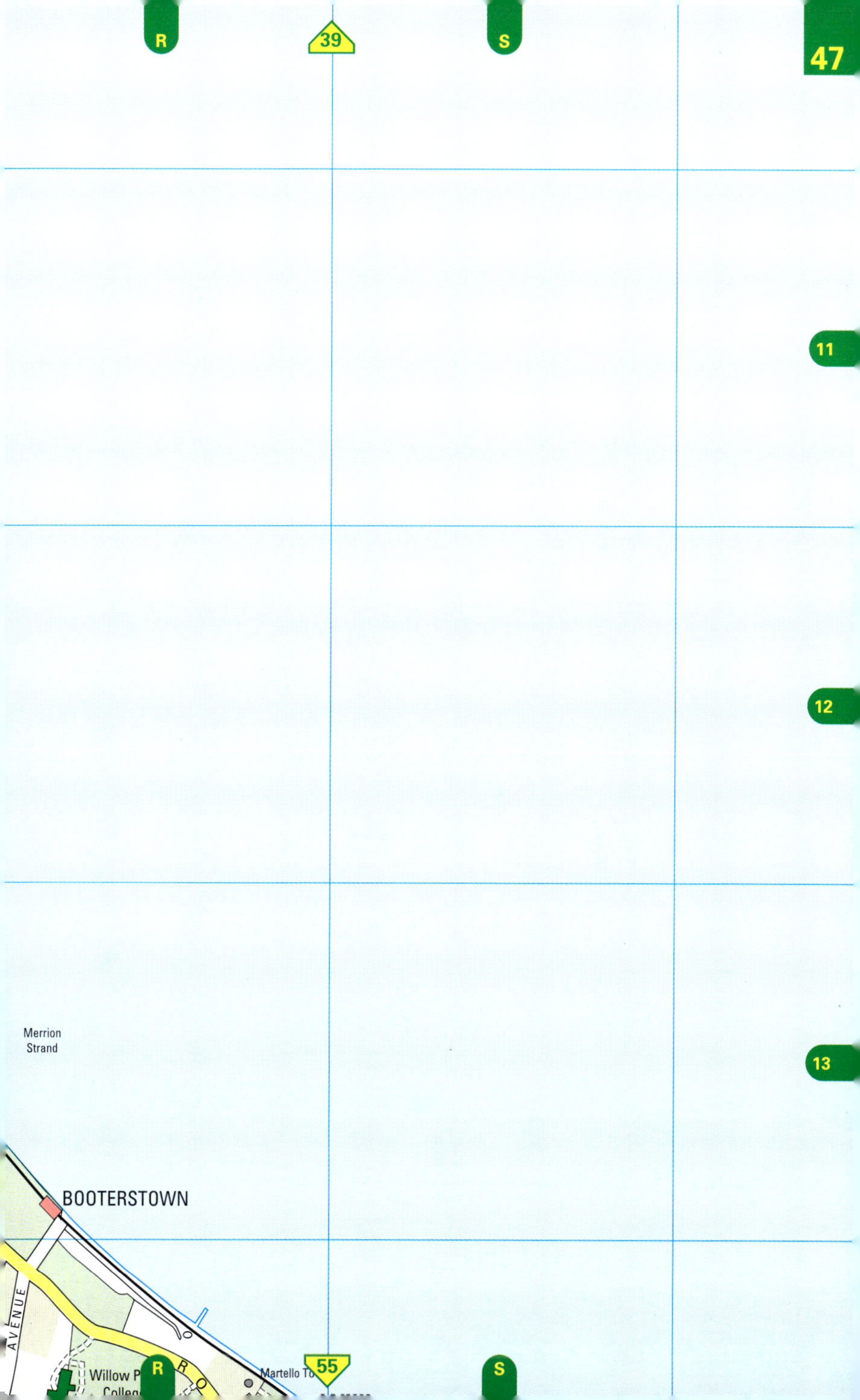

47
R
39
S
11
12
13
Merrion
Strand
BOOTERSTOWN
AVENUE
Willow P
Colleg
Martello To
55
R
S

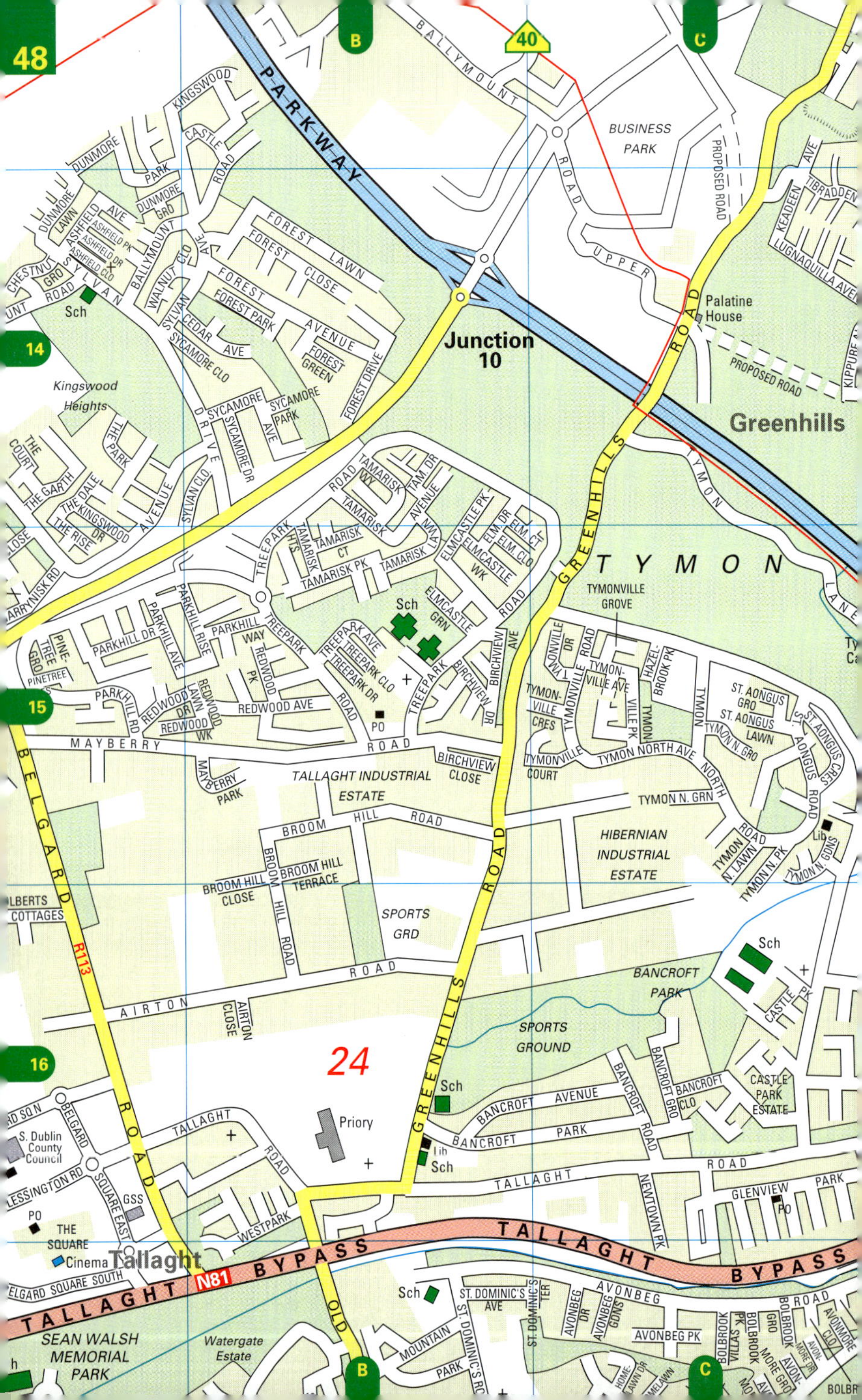
B
40
C
BALLYMOUNT
PARKWAY
KINGSWOOD
CASTLE
ROAD
DUNMORE
PARK
DUNMORE GRO
DUNMORE LAWN
ASHFIELD AVE
ASHFIELD PK
ASHFIELD DR
ASHFIELD CLO
BALLYMOUNT
WALNUT CLO
AVE
CHESTNUT GRO
SYLVAN ROAD
Sch
BUSINESS PARK
ROAD
PROPOSED ROAD
UPPER
FOREST LAWN
FOREST CLOSE
FOREST PARK
FOREST AVENUE
FOREST GREEN
FOREST DRIVE
CEDAR AVE
SYCAMORE CLO
SYLVAN
Junction 10
Palatine House
PROPOSED ROAD
KEADEEN AVE
TIBRADDEN
LUGNAQUILLA AVE
KIPPURE AV
Greenhills
14
Kingswood Heights
THE COURT
THE PARK
THE GARTH
THE DALE
KINGSWOOD DR
THE RISE
AVENUE
SYCAMORE AVE
SYCAMORE PARK
SYCAMORE DR
DRIVE
SYLVAN CLO
CLOSE
TAMARISK WY
TAMARISK
TAM. DR
AVENUE
ROAD
TREEPARK HTS
TAMARISK CT
TAMARISK PK
TAMARISK LAWN
ELMCASTLE PK
ELM DR
ELM CT
ELM CLO
ELMCASTLE WK
ROAD
GREENHILLS
TYMON
LANE
TYMON
CARRYNISK RD
PINE TREE GRO
PINETREE
PARKHILL DR
PARKHILL RISE
PARKHILL AVE
PARKHILL WAY
REDWOOD PK
TREEPARK
Sch
TREEPARK AVE
TREEPARK CLO
TREEPARK DR
TREEPARK
ELMCASTLE GRN
BIRCHVIEW AVE
BIRCHVIEW DR
TYMONVILLE GROVE
TYMONVILLE DR
TYMONVILLE ROAD
TYMONVILLE AVE
HAZELBROOK PK
TYMONVILLE CRES
TYMONVILLE PK
TYMON
TYMON
ST. AONGUS GRO
ST. AONGUS LAWN
ST. AONGUS CRES
TYMON N. GRO
ST. AONGUS ROAD
15
PARKHILL RD
REDWOOD DR
REDWOOD LAWN
REDWOOD WK
REDWOOD AVE
ROAD
PO
MAYBERRY ROAD
BIRCHVIEW CLOSE
TYMONVILLE COURT
TYMON NORTH AVE
NORTH
MAYBERRY PARK
TALLAGHT INDUSTRIAL ESTATE
BROOM HILL ROAD
TYMON N. GRN
ROAD
Lib
HIBERNIAN INDUSTRIAL ESTATE
TYMON N. LAWN
TYMON N. PK
TYMON N. GDNS
BELGARD
BROOM HILL CLOSE
BROOM HILL TERRACE
BROOM HILL ROAD
GILBERTS COTTAGES
SPORTS GRD
R113
ROAD
Sch
BANCROFT PARK
CASTLE PK
AIRTON ROAD
AIRTON CLOSE
SPORTS GROUND
16
24
GREENHILLS
BANCROFT GRO
BANCROFT ROAD
BANCROFT CLO
CASTLE PARK ESTATE
Sch
BANCROFT AVENUE
Priory
BANCROFT PARK
BELGARD SQ N
S. Dublin County Council
TALLAGHT ROAD
Lib
Sch
TALLAGHT ROAD
NEWTOWN PK
GLENVIEW PARK
PO
LESSINGTON RD
SQUARE EAST
GSS
PO
THE SQUARE
WESTPARK
TALLAGHT BYPASS
Cinema
Tallaght
N81
BELGARD SQUARE SOUTH
TALLAGHT BYPASS
OLD
Sch
ST. DOMINIC'S AVE
ST. DOMINIC'S TER
AVONBEG ROAD
AVONBEG DR
AVONBEG GDNS
AVONBEG PK
BOLBROOK VILLAS
BOLBROOK PK
BOLBROOK GRO
AVONMORE CLO
SEAN WALSH MEMORIAL PARK
Watergate Estate
MOUNTAIN PARK
ST. DOMINIC'S RD
B
C

D
E
41
ST. BRIDGET'S AVE
ST. COLUMBA'S ROAD
ST. JAMES
ST. BRENDAN'S CRESCENT
ST. ANTHONY'S CRESCENT
ST. MALACHY'S DR
ST. JOSEPH'S ROAD
PATRICK'S ROAD
ST. GERARD'S RD
ST. KILLIAN'S AVE
ST. MEL'S AVENUE
ST. FINBAR'S CLOSE
KILMASHOGUE DRIVE
GROVE
12
Convent
Schools
College
PO
TEMPLE MANOR CLO
TEMPLE MANOR DR
TEMPLE MANOR GRO
TEMPLE MANOR WY
TEMPLE MANOR AVE
TEMPLE MANOR CT
KILOHAN GROVE
Sch
LIMEKILN
FERNHILL ROAD
FERNHILL PK
FERN-HILL AVE
MOUNTDOWN DR
MOUNTDOWN PARK
MOUNT DOWN DR
MOUNTDOWN RD
LIMEKILN PK
LIMEKILN DR
LIME-KILN CLO
LIMEKILN GRO
GREENTREES ROAD
GREENTREES PARK
GREENTREES DRIVE
HILLSBROOK AVENUE
HILLSBROOK CRES
HILLSBROOK DR
MUCKROSS PARK
MUCKROSS CRES
MUCKROSS GRO
MUCKROSS AVENUE
MUCKROSS DR
ROCKFIELD DRIVE
ROCKFIELD ROAD
WHITEHALL ROAD
WHITEHALL PARK
WHITEHALL PK
WHITEHALL CLO
GLENDALE PARK
MILLGATE DR
PODDLE RIVER
SPORTS GROUND
14
TEMPLEVILLE
R115
GROSVENOR CT
WELLINGTON PK
LIMEKILN GROVE
LIMEKILN ROAD
LIMEKILN LANE
GLENDOWN CRES
GLENDOWN AVENUE
GLENDOWN GRO
GLENDOWN CT
GLENDOWN PK
GLENDOWN LAWN
GLENDOWN ROAD
SPORT GRD
PARK
6W
OSPREY LAWN
OSPREY AVE
OSPREY PK
OSPREY DR
OSPREY RD
WILLINGTON CT
WILLINGTON CRES
WILLINGTON DR
WILLINGTON GRN
WILLINGTON AVE
WILLINGTON GRO
WELLINGTON
RUSH. WY
RUSH. AVE
RUSH. DR
RUSH. PK
RUSH. GRO
RUSH. CT
KENNINGTON ROAD
KENNINGTON CRES
KENNINGTON LAWN
KENNINGTON CLOSE
WILDERWOOD GRO
ORWELL PK GLADE
ORWELL PK GRO
ORWELL PK GLEN
ORWELL PK AVE
ORWELL PK LAWNS
ORWELL PK CLO
ORWELL PK CRES
ORWELL PK DR
ORWELL PK WY
ORWELL PK GRN
ORWELL PK RISE
ORWELL PK VW
ORWELL PARK HEIGHTS
ORWELL PK DALE
ORWELL ROAD
THE HEATH
THE COURT
CYPRESS DR
THE CLOSE
THE AVE
THE WALK
CYPRESS DOWNS
DOMVILLE RD
DOMVILLE DR
15
Alberta
CYPR
TEMPLEOGUE WOOD
ROSSMORE AVE
ROSSMORE ROAD
ROSSMORE DR
ROSSMORE GRO
ROSSMORE CLO
ROSSMORE LAWN
ROSSMORE CRESCENT
ROSSMORE PK
LANE
Golf Range
50
Convalescent Home
TEMPLEOGUE
STLETYMON URT
Tymon Cottage
Tymon Villa
TYMON LANE
M50
National Basketball Arena
CASTLE LAWNS
BROOKMOUNT AVE
TALLAGHT ROAD
N81
GLENVIEW LAWNS
GLENVIEW PARK
Spawell Ho
HILLCREST
UNDER CONSTRUCTION
Cherry Field
16
R11
DODDER VALLEY PARK
Bella Vista
Weir
FIRHOUSE ROAD
PINE GRO
LANSDOWNE PARK
CREMORNE
LODGE
COOLAMBER PARK
GREEN-ACRE CT
KNOCKLYON PK
KNOCKLYON GRN
KNOCKLYON ROAD
KNOCKLYON CT
KNOCKLYON GROVE
KNOCKLYON AVENUE
WESTBOURNE
IDRONE DR
IDRONE CLO
IDRONE PARK
WOODSTOCK PARK
DELAFORD PARK
DELAFORD GROVE
DELAFORD DRIVE
DELAFORD LAWN
DELAFORD AVENUE
MT CARMEL PK
TAOBH NA CHOILLE
PROPOSED ROAD
Firhouse
Conv
MONALEA WD
MONALEA PK
R114
16

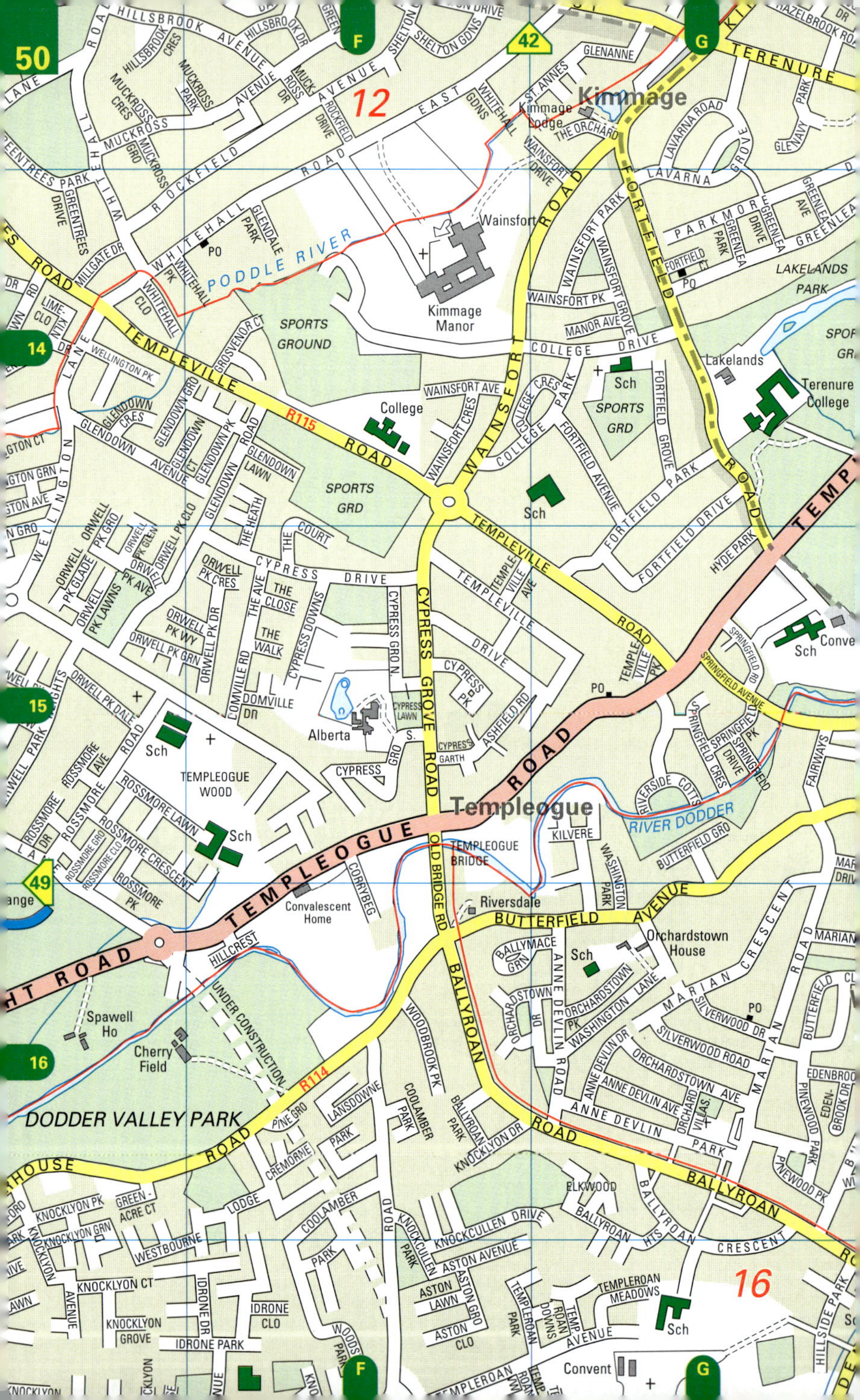

F
G
42
12
Kimmage
Kimmage Lodge
Wainsfort
Kimmage Manor
PODDLE RIVER
TEMPLEVILLE ROAD
R115
SPORTS GROUND
College
SPORTS GRD
Sch
Lakelands
Terenure College
LAKELANDS PARK
TERENURE ROAD
WAINSFORT ROAD
FORTFIELD ROAD
COLLEGE DRIVE
CYPRESS DRIVE
CYPRESS GROVE ROAD
Alberta
TEMPLEOGUE WOOD
Templeogue
RIVER DODDER
TEMPLEOGUE ROAD
TEMPLEOGUE BRIDGE
Riversdale
Convalescent Home
BUTTERFIELD AVENUE
Orchardstown House
BALLYROAN ROAD
OLD BRIDGE RD
Spawell Ho
Cherry Field
UNDER CONSTRUCTION
R114
DODDER VALLEY PARK
WELLINGTON LANE
ROSSMORE ROAD
MARIAN CRESCENT
ANNE DEVLIN ROAD
ANNE DEVLIN PARK
KNOCKLYON AVENUE
TEMPLEROAN AVENUE
Convent
14
15
16
49

H
J
43
6
6W
14
14
15
16
52
Terenure
SPORTS GRD
Rathfarnham
BUSHY PARK
CASTLE GOLF COURSE
BLACK WOOD
Club House
Rathfarnham Castle
MILL POND
St. Luke's Hospital
Mount Carmel Hospital
Clinic
Cremorne
Synagogue
Danum
Loreto Abbey
CEMETERY
Grave Yard
Nutgrove Shopping Centre
LORETO PARK
WHITECHURCH ABBEY
Silveracre
WILLBROOK ESTATE
St. Joseph's Convent
TERENURE ROAD EAST
TERENURE ROAD WEST
TERENURE RD
TERENURE PL
TERENURE PK
RATHFARNHAM ROAD
DODDER PARK ROAD
R112
N81
LOWER DODDER ROAD
BUSHY PARK ROAD
VICTORIA ROAD
ZION ROAD
ORWELL ROAD
HIGHFIELD ROAD
HIGHFIELD CT
OAK APPLE GREEN
OAKLANDS DRIVE
OAKLANDS CRES
RATHGAR PARK
WOODLANDS
ROSTREVOR TER
ROSTREVOR ROAD
MAYFIELD ROAD
MAYFIELD
WASDALE PARK
WASDALE GROVE
GLENAYR RD
GREENMOUNT RD
GREENMOUNT LAWNS
CORMACK TER
FERGUS RD
RATHDOWN VILLAS
RATHDOWN CRES
RATHDOWN DRIVE
RATHDOWN PARK
RATHDOWN AVENUE
LAKELANDS PARK
HORTON CT
OLNEY CRES
HAZELBROOK CT
THE LAURELS
RATHDOWN COURT
EATON SQUARE
EATON ROAD
HANNAVILLE PK
ELM. TER
YEWLAND TER
TRAMWAY VILLAS
HEALTHFIELD RD
FERRARD RD
HILL AVE
WESTBOURNE RD
BIG BRIDGE
BUSHY PK GDNS
RIVERSDALE AVE
LAURELTON
MEADOWBANK
WALDRON'S BRIDGE
DODDER PK DR
DODDER PK GRO
BROOKVALE DOWNS
BROOKVALE ROAD
BALLYTORE ROAD
RATHFARNHAM PARK
CRANNAGH PK
CRANNAGH GROVE
CRANNAGH WAY
CRANNAGH ROAD
CRANNAGH CT
CRANNAGH CASTLE
WOODSIDE
WOODSIDE DRIVE
WOODSIDE GROVE
RIVERSIDE
HILLSIDE DRIVE
BRAEMOR PARK
BRAEMOR DR
BRAEMOR ROAD
REDWOOD CT
LANDSCAPE ROAD
LANDSCAPE AVE
CHURCHTOWN
WHITEBARN
NUGENT ROAD
CASTLE CT
BERWICK HALL
WHITEHALL
CHURCH LANE
MAIN STREET
RATHFARNHAM GATE
WOODVIEW COTTS
RATHFARNHAM MILL
DODDER DALE
THE PARKLANDS
THE COURTYARD
THE CASTLELANDS
CASTLESIDE DRIVE
THE GREENLANDS
THE LAKELANDS
RATHFARNHAM WOOD
THE WOODLANDS
BUTTERFIELD AVENUE
BUTTERFIELD CRES
BUTTERFIELD DRIVE
BUTTERFIELD PARK
BUTTERFIELD ORCHARD
OWENDORE AVE
OWENDORE CRES
ST. MARY'S AVE
GRANGE ROAD
WILLBROOK ROAD
NUTGROVE AVENUE
NUTGROVE WAY
BEAUFORT DOWNS
LORETO TERRACE
DISPENSARY LANE
CONVENT LA
STONEPARK DRIVE
STONEPARK COURT
STONEPARK ABBEY
STONEPARK GREEN
LONGWOOD PARK
LORETO AVENUE
LORETO CT
LORETO PK
LORETO CRES
LORETO ROW
MARIAN GROVE
GLENBROOK PARK
FAIRBROOK LAWN
OWENDOHER RIVER
BODEN WOOD
EDENBROOK CT
WILLBROOK PK
WILLBROOK ST
WILLBROOK LAWN
WILLBROOK GROVE
TARA HILL CRES
TARA HILL GRO
TARA HILL RD
ST. PATRICK'S COTTAGES
WHITECHURCH
FONTHILL PK
FONTHILL ROAD
GRANGE PARK
ST. ENDA'S DRIVE
ST. ENDA'S PARK
ARANLEIGH MT TER
ARANLEIGH MT CT
ARANLEIGH MT PK
ARANLEIGH MT DELL
ARANLEIGH MOUNT AVE
BARTON AVE
BARTON DRIVE
BARTON ROAD WEST
BARTON RD EXTENSION
GRANGE DOWNS
WILLBROOK DOWNS
ST. GAT. RD
WILLOWBANK DRIVE
GLENDOHER RD
GLENDOHER AVE
BODEN DALE
SARAH CURRAN AVE
PROPOSED ROAD
SPORTS
PARK AVE
HERMITAGE
GRANGE MANOR ROAD
GRANGE MANOR CLO
MARLEY CT N
MARLEY CT S
DARGLE VALLEY
DARGLE DRIVE
MEADOW CLOSE
MEADOW PARK AVENUE
CARRICKMOUNT DRIVE
ST. KEVINS COURT
ST. KEVINS GARDENS
HIGHFIELD GROVE
Sch
Coll
PO
GSS

HIGHFIELD
HIGHFIELD CT
OAK APPLE GREEN
OAKLANDS DRIVE
OAKLANDS CRES
HIGHFIELD GROVE
Sch
Clinic
St. Luke's Hospital
6
DARTRY
GDNS
PALMERSTON PARK
44
TEMPLE S
RICHVIEW
BROOKFIELD
Milltown
Schools
SPORTS GRD
Sch
Clonskeagh Castle
Coll
TEMPLE ROAD
DARTRY ROAD
DARTRY PARK
ST. KEVINS PARK
ST. KEVINS GARDENS
ST. KEVINS COURT
SOUTH HILL
TEMPLE PARK
RICHMOND COURT
RICHMOND AVENUE SOUTH
MILLTOWN ROAD
BANKSIDE COTTS
Weir
ST. LUKE'S CRES
MILL RACE
ORWELL ROAD
MAYFIELD ROAD
ZION ROAD
ROSTREVOR ROAD
ROSTREVOR TER
WOODLANDS
ORWELL PARK
ORWELL WOODS
MILL RACE
DARTRY COTTS
Ford
Weir
CLASSONS BRIDGE
PATRICK DOYLE ROAD
Club Ho
CHURCHTOWN CLO
CHURCHTOWN DR
CHURCHTOWN AVE
ST. COLUMBANUS AVE
ST. COLUMBANUS ROAD
ST. GALL GDNS N.
ST. GALL GDNS S.
ST. C. PL
FARRENBOLEY COTTS
FARRENBOLEY PARK
MILLMOUNT GROVE
GLASGOW
SPORTS GRD
Danum
14
DODDERVALE
WALDRON'S BRIDGE
ORWELL GDNS
STIRLING PK
THORNCLIFFE PARK
Mount Carmel Hospital
DODDER ROAD
PARK R112 ROAD
BRAEMOR PARK
EATON BRAE
ORWELL ROAD
GREEN PK
MILLTOWN GOLF COURSE
LOWER CHURCHTOWN ROAD
ROAD
Sch
WESTBROOK RD
PARK
HIGHFIELD
WOODSIDE
WOODSIDE DRIVE
RIVERSIDE DRIVE
WOODSIDE GROVE
BRAEMOR DR
BRAEMOR GROVE
BRAEMOR AVENUE
MILLTOWN GROVE
MILLTOWN DRIVE
BRAEMOR ROAD
REDWOOD CT
LANDSCAPE ROAD
LANDSCAPE AVE
HILLSIDE DRIVE
15
Club House
LANDSCAPE PARK
LANDSCAPE CRESCENT
Churchtown
WOODLAWN GRO
WOODLAWN CRES
WOODLAWN PARK
FRANKFORT
LANDSCAPE GARDENS
BLACK WOOD
CASTLE GOLF COURSE
Sch
CHURCHTOWN ROAD
MAYOLA CT
CHARLEVILLE
HENLEY PARK
HENLEY VILLAS
FLEMINGSTOWN PARK
FRANKFORT PK
WHITEBARN ROAD
PO
GLENBOWER PK
ARDTONA AVE
WOODBINE TERRACE
51
NUGENT ROAD
OAKDOWN ROAD
CAMBERLEY OAKS
HEN. CT
CHURCHTOWN ROAD UPPER
WOODLAWN TER
THE OAKS
CASTLE CT
BERWICK HALL
WHITEHALL ROAD
BEAUMONT DRIVE
Sch
GROVE AVENUE
HEADFORD GRO
WESTON TER
FINSBURY PARK
WALDEMAR TER
Grave Yard
16
LORETO AVENUE
LORETO CT
LORETO PK
LORETO CRES
LORETO ROW
LORETO PARK
NUTGROVE WAY
Nutgrove Shopping Centre
MEADOW PARK AVENUE
MOUNTAIN VIEW PARK
BEAUMONT AVENUE
WESTON ROAD
WESTON GRO
WESTON PARK
SWEETMOUNT AVENUE
THE LAURELS
BEAUMONT CLOSE
WESTON AVE
MT ALBION RD
MT ALBION TER
WESTON CLOSE
LAUREL AVENUE
SWEETMOUNT DRIVE
SWEETMOUNT PARK
CARRICKMOUNT AVENUE
MOUNTAIN VIEW DRIVE
CARRICKMOUNT DR
CARRICKMOUNT PK
PO
MEADOW PARK
LAUREL ROAD
LAUREL DRIVE
Dundrum
GRANGE DOWNS
ON RD EXTENSION
BARTON ROAD EAST
AILSBURY GROVE
MARLEY CT N
MARLEY CT S
MEADOW GROVE
MEADOW VILLAS
MEADOW CLOSE
MEADOW AVE
WILLOW
Hosp
DUNDRUM WOOD
AILSBURY LAWN
GRANGE MANOR ROAD
GRANGE MANOR DR
G.M. AVE
G.M. GRO
HERMITAGE
DARGLE VALLEY
DARGLE DRIVE
CLOSE
LAWN
BEECH
SYCAMORE
16
K
L

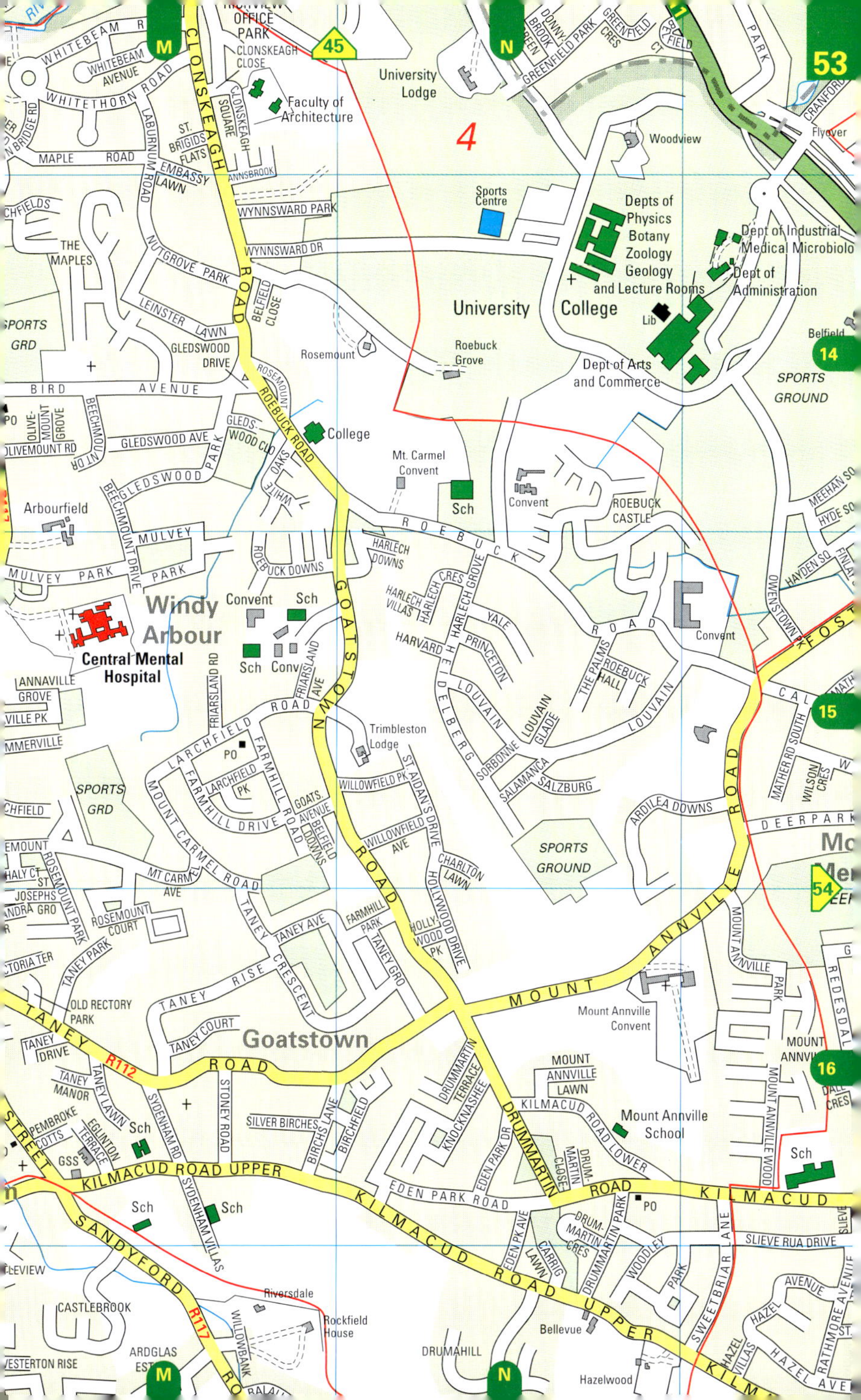

OFFICE PARK
45
M
N
WHITEBEAM RD
WHITEBEAM AVENUE
WHITETHORN ROAD
CLONSKEAGH CLOSE
CLONSKEAGH SQUARE
Faculty of Architecture
University Lodge
DONNYBROOK GREEN
GREENFIELD PARK
GREENFIELD CRES
PARK
CRANFORD
Flyover
4
Woodview
MAPLE ROAD
LABURNUM ROAD
ST. BRIGIDS FLATS
EMBASSY LAWN
ANNSBROOK
CLONSKEAGH ROAD
Sports Centre
WYNNSWARD PARK
WYNNSWARD DR
Depts of Physics Botany Zoology Geology and Lecture Rooms
Dept of Industrial Medical Microbiolo
Dept of Administration
THE MAPLES
NUTGROVE PARK
LEINSTER LAWN
BELFIELD CLOSE
University College
Lib
SPORTS GRD
GLEDSWOOD DRIVE
Rosemount
Roebuck Grove
Dept of Arts and Commerce
Belfield
14
SPORTS GROUND
BIRD AVENUE
ROSEMOUNT
ROEBUCK ROAD
OLIVEMOUNT GROVE
OLIVEMOUNT RD
BEECHMOUNT DR
GLEDSWOOD AVE
GLEDSWOOD PARK
GLEDSWOOD CLO
WHITE OAKS
College
Mt. Carmel Convent
Sch
Convent
ROEBUCK CASTLE
MEEHAN SQ
HYDE SQ
Arbourfield
BEECHMOUNT DRIVE
MULVEY PARK
ROEBUCK
HARLECH DOWNS
ROEBUCK DOWNS
HAYDEN SQ
FINLAY
OWENSTOWN PK
Windy Arbour
Convent
Sch
GOATSTOWN ROAD
HARLECH VILLAS
HARLECH CRES
HARLECH GROVE
YALE
PRINCETON
ROAD
Convent
FOSTERS
Central Mental Hospital
Sch
Conv
FRIARSLAND AVE
HARVARD
HEIDELBERG
THE PALMS
ROEBUCK HALL
ANNAVILLE GROVE
ANNAVILLE PK
SUMMERVILLE
FRIARSLAND RD
ROAD
LOUVAIN
LOUVAIN GLADE
CALLARY
15
LARCHFIELD
PO
Trimbleston Lodge
SORBONNE
SALAMANCA
SALZBURG
MATHER RD SOUTH
WILSON CRES
LARCHFIELD PK
FARMHILL DRIVE
FARMHILL ROAD
GOATS. AVENUE
BELFIELD DOWNS
WILLOWFIELD PK
ST. AIDAN'S DRIVE
WILLOWFIELD AVE
ARDILEA DOWNS
DEERPARK
SPORTS GRD
SPORTS GROUND
ROSEMOUNT
HALY CT
ST JOSEPHS
ALEXANDRA GRO
MT CARMEL AVE
MOUNT CARMEL ROAD
CHARLTON LAWN
HOLLYWOOD DRIVE
54
ROSEMOUNT PARK
ROSEMOUNT COURT
TANEY AVE
FARMHILL PARK
HOLLYWOOD PK
MOUNT ANNVILLE ROAD
MOUNT ANNVILLE PARK
VICTORIA TER
TANEY PARK
TANEY RISE
TANEY CRESCENT
TANEY GRO
REDESDALE
OLD RECTORY PARK
TANEY COURT
Goatstown
Mount Annville Convent
MOUNT ANNVILLE
TANEY DRIVE
TANEY ROAD
R112
ROAD
DRUMMARTIN TERRACE
MOUNT ANNVILLE LAWN
16
TANEY MANOR
TANEY LAWN
SYDENHAM RD
STONEY ROAD
SILVER BIRCHES
BIRCHES LANE
BIRCHFIELD
KNOCKNASHEE
DRUMMARTIN
KILMACUD ROAD LOWER
Mount Annville School
MOUNT ANNVILLE WOOD
CRES
PEMBROKE COTTS
EGLINTON TERRACE
Sch
GSS
STREET
KILMACUD ROAD UPPER
EDEN PARK DR
DRUMMARTIN CLOSE
Sch
EDEN PARK ROAD
ROAD
PO
KILMACUD
Sch
Sch
SYDENHAM VILLAS
SANDYFORD
DRUMMARTIN CRES
DRUMMARTIN PARK
SLIEVE RUA DRIVE
EDEN PK AVE
CARRIG LAWN
WOODLEY PARK
SWEETBRIAR LANE
KILMACUD ROAD UPPER
AVENUE
R117
Riversdale
HAZEL AVENUE
RATHMORE AVENUE
CASTLEBROOK
Rockfield House
Bellevue
WILLOWBANK
ARDGLAS EST
DRUMAHILL
WESTERTON RISE
Hazelwood
HAZEL VILLAS

P
Q
46
14
15
16
53
4
14
Woodview
Flyover
Cranford Ct
The Elms
Bellevue Ave
Bellevue Ct
Bellevue Pk
PO
Bellevue Copse
Pk Ave
Woodbine Road
Woodbine Pk
Woodbine Avenue
Glenomena Park
Dornden Park
Trimleston Ave
Trimleston Pk
Trimleston Rd
Trimleston Gardens
Trimleston Dr
Merrion Cres
Ashfield Park
Glenomena Gro
Seafield Road
Seafield Pk
Seafield Cres
Seafield Clo
Seafield Dr
St. Helen's Road
Castle Court
Sch
Depts of Physics Botany Zoology Geology and Lecture Rooms
Dept of Industrial Medical Microbiology
Dept of Administration
Lib
College
Dept of Arts and Commerce
Sports Ground
Belfield
Stillorgan Road
Fosterbrook
Booterstown
Rosemount Ter
Pembroke Cotts
St.Helens
McCabe Villas
The Stables
Rosemount Ct
Sans Souci Pk
Hampton Cres
Hampton Pk
Helens Wood
Merrion Grove
Depts of Biochemistry Pharmacology
Convent
Roebuck Castle
Meehan Sq
Hyde Sq
Hayden Sq
Finlay Sq
Hopkins Sq
The Fosters
R112
Fosters Avenue
St. Thomas Mead
St. Thomas' Road
Iris Grove
Owenstown Pk
North Avenue
Greygates
Booterstown Avenue
Cherbury Mews
Cherbury Gdns
Cherbury Ct
Booterstown Pk
South Hill Pk
South Hill Avenue
Beechlawn
Merrion Park
Roebuck Road
The Palms
Roebuck Hall
Louvain
Glade
Mather Road North
Cypress Road
Callary Road
The Close
Roebuck Ave
Chestnut Rd
Greenfield Road
Mount Merrion Avenue
Salamanca
Salzburg
Mather Rd South
Wilson Cres
Wilson Road
Ardilea Downs
Deerpark Road
Mount Anville Road
Sports Ground
Mount Merrion
Deer Park
Sycamore Cres
Sycamore Road
The Rise
Woodlands Park
Priory Hall
Priory Drive
Priory
South Avenue
Mount Merrion
Glenabbey Road
Trees Ave
Trees Road
Mount Anville Park
Mount Road
Cedar Mount
Redesdale Road
Redesdale Cres
Mount Anville
Mount Anville Convent
Mount Anville Lawn
Mount Anville Wood
Mount Anville School
Kilmacud Road Lower
Drummartin Close
Drummartin Road
Clonmore Rd
Thornhill Road
Oatlands
Cherry Garth
Woodlands Ave
Woodlands Drive
Beaufield
Beaufield Manor
Beaufield Park
Stillorgan Road
Dublin Road
St.
Stillorgan
Kilmacud Road
Kilmacud Park
Lower
PO
Drummartin Park
Drummartin Cres
Slieve Rua Drive
Dale Drive
Dale Clo
Dale Dr
Dale Road
Woodley Park
Sweetbriar Lane
Eden Pk Ave
Carrig Lawn
Kilmacud Road Upper
Bellevue
Hazelwood
Hazel Villas
Hazel Avenue
Rathmore Avenue
Annville Drive
St. Kevin's Park
Dale Gdns
Marsham Court
Upper
Convent Ct
Coolnevaun
Allen Park Road
Allen Pk Dr
Glen Albyn
Merville Avenue
Wesbury
Carmelite
Lind

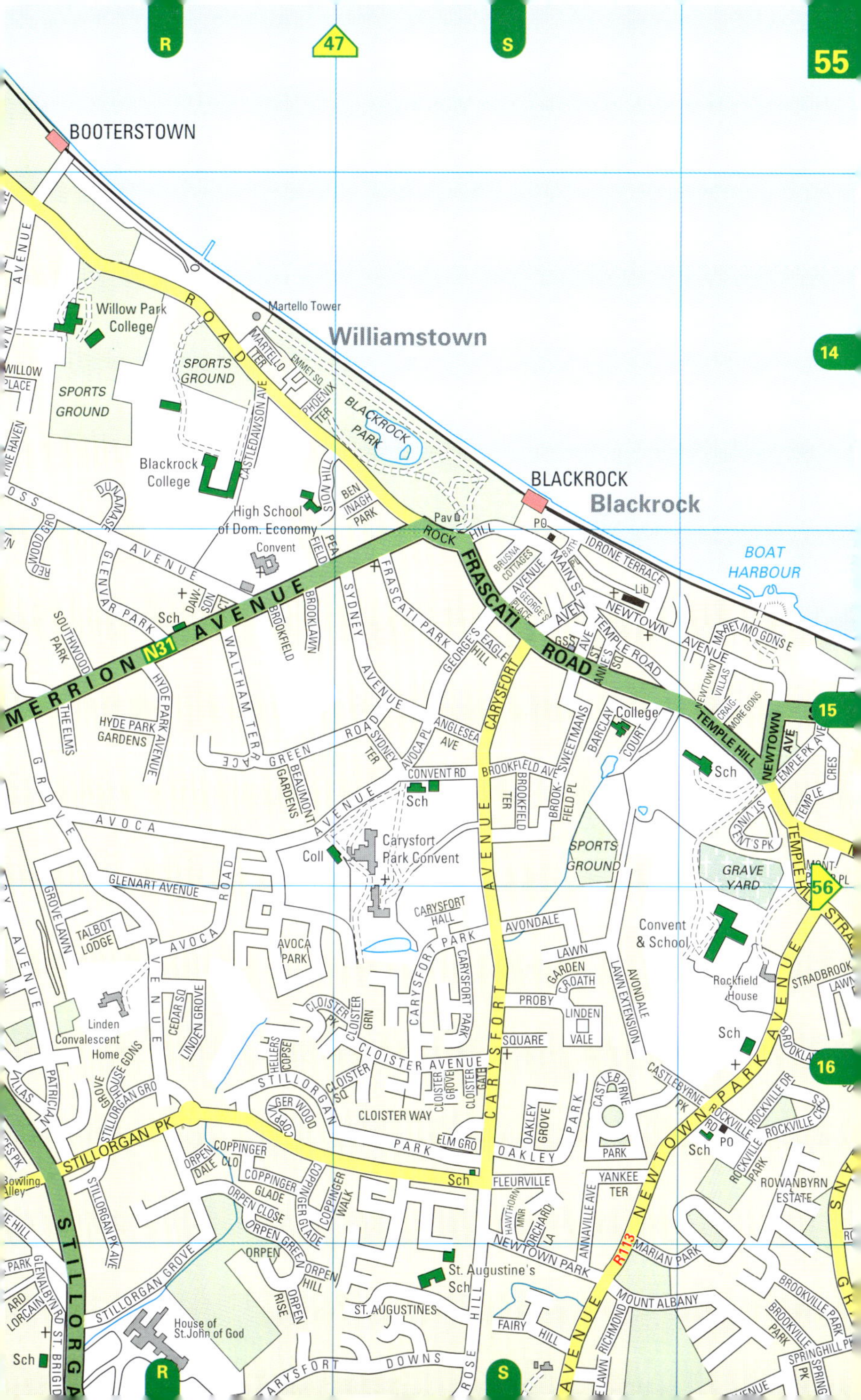
R
47
S
14
15
16
56
BOOTERSTOWN
Willow Park College
SPORTS GROUND
Blackrock College
Martello Tower
Williamstown
MARTELLO TER
EMMET SQ
PHOENIX TER
BLACKROCK PARK
SION HILL
BEN INAGH PARK
High School of Dom. Economy
Convent
BLACKROCK
Blackrock
Pav
PO
ROCK HILL
FRASCATI ROAD
IDRONE TERRACE
BOAT HARBOUR
Lib
NEWTOWN AVENUE
MAIN ST
BATH PL
BRUSNA COTTAGES
GEORGE'S PLACE
TEMPLE ROAD
MARETIMO GDNS E
NEWTOWN VILLAS
CRAIGMORE GDNS
TEMPLE HILL
NEWTOWN AVE
TEMPLE PK AVE
TEMPLE CRES
ST. VINCENT'S PK
GRAVE YARD
MONT PL
STRADBROOK
Convent & School
Rockfield House
STRADBROOK LAWN
BROOKLAWN
MERRION AVENUE
N31
WILLOW PLACE
AVENUE
PINE HAVEN
DUNAMASE
REDWOOD GRO
GLENVAR PARK
DAWSON CT
CASTLEDAWSON AVE
PEAFIELD
SOUTHWOOD PARK
THE ELMS
HYDE PARK GARDENS
HYDE PARK AVENUE
WALTHAM TERRACE
BROOKFIELD
BROOKLAWN
SYDNEY AVENUE
FRASCATI PARK
GEORGE'S AVENUE
EAGLE HILL
CARYSFORT AVENUE
ST. ANNE'S SQ
GREEN ROAD
SYDNEY TER
BEAUMONT GARDENS
AVOCA PL
ANGLESEA AVE
CONVENT RD
BROOKFIELD AVE
BROOKFIELD TER
BROOKFIELD
SWEETMANS
BROOKFIELD PL
BARCLAY COURT
College
Sch
GROVE AVENUE
AVOCA AVENUE
Coll
Carysfort Park Convent
GLENART AVENUE
AVOCA ROAD
GROVE LAWN
TALBOT LODGE
AVOCA PARK
CARYSFORT HALL
CARYSFORT PARK
AVONDALE LAWN
GARDEN CROATH
PROBY
LINDEN VALE
AVONDALE LAWN EXTENSION
Linden Convalescent Home
CEDAR SQ
LINDEN GROVE
CLOISTER PK
CLOISTER GRN
SQUARE
CLOISTER AVENUE
HELLERS COPSE
STILLORGAN PARK
CLOISTER SQ
CLOISTER WAY
CLOISTER GROVE
CLOISTER GATE
CASTLEBYRNE PARK
CASTLEBYRNE PK
OAKLEY GROVE
OAKLEY PARK
ELM GRO
VILLAS
PATRICIAN
GROVE HOUSE GDNS
STILLORGAN GRO
STILLORGAN PK
COPPINGER WOOD
ORPEN DALE
COPPINGER CLO
COPPINGER GLADE
COPPINGER WALK
ORPEN CLOSE
ORPEN GREEN
ORPEN HILL
ORPEN RISE
Bowling Alley
STILLORGAN PK AVE
STILLORGAN GROVE
STILLORGAN
FLEURVILLE
HAWTHORN MNR
ORCHARD LA
ANNAVILLE AVE
YANKEE TER
NEWTOWN PARK
NEWTOWN PARK AVENUE
R113
MARIAN PARK
ROCKVILLE RD
ROCKVILLE DR
ROCKVILLE CRES
ROCKVILLE PARK
ROWANBYRN ESTATE
St. Augustine's Sch
ST. AUGUSTINES
CARYSFORT DOWNS
ROSE HILL
FAIRY HILL
MOUNT ALBANY
RICHMOND LAWN
BROOKVILLE PARK
SPRINGHILL PK
SPRINGHILL PARK
House of St.John of God
GLENALBYN RD
LORCAIN
ST. BRIGID
PARK

T
U
14
15
55
16
BLACKROCK
Blackrock
BOAT HARBOUR
SEAPOINT
Martello Tower
SALTHILL & MONKSTOWN
IDRONE TERRACE
MAIN ST
NEWTOWN AVENUE
TEMPLE ROAD
TEMPLE HILL
NEWTOWN AVE
SEAPOINT AVENUE
N31
MONKSTOWN ROAD
CLIFTON TER
LONGFORD TE
SALTHILL GARDENS
BRIGHTON VALE
TRAFALGAR TER
TRAFALGAR LA
BELGRAVE ROAD
BELGRAVE SQUARE
EATON SQUARE
ALMA ROAD
ARDENZA TER
TEMPLE PK AVE
TEMPLE CRES
ST VINCENT'S PK
MONTPELIER PL
MONTPELIER PAR
SHANDON PARK
SEAFIELD AVE
ALBANY AVE
BRIGHTON AVE
CLIFTON LA
CLIFTON AVE
MONKSTOWN CR
CARRICKBRENNAN ROAD
ALMA PL
RICHMOND GREEN
HEATHFIELD
DRAYTON CLO
SOUTHDENE
Monkstown
RICHMOND HILL
RICHMOND PARK
RICHMOND AVENUE
CARRICK BRENNAN LAWN
ARUNDEL
THE BEECHES
MONKSTOWN VALLEY
THE POPLARS
THE WILLOWS
THE MAPLES
THE CEDARS
THE ALDERS
QUEENS PARK
GLEANN NA SMOL
Stradbrook
SPORTS GROUND
WYNBERG PARK
BROOK PARK CT
ASHTON PARK
ASHTON PK
RICHMOND GROVE
WINDSOR PARK
WINDSOR DRIVE
MONKSTOWN AVENUE
Monkstown House
Dunedin
Swimming Pool
DUNEDIN PK
DUNEDIN CLO
DUNEDIN DR
DUNEDIN TERR
ST. PATRICK'S CLO
MONKSTOWN GRO
MONKSTOWN FARM
LANESVILLE
OLIVER PLUNKETT VILLAS
ABBEY PK
STRADBROOK ROAD
STRADBROOK LAWN
STRADBROOK PK
STRAD-BROOK GDNS
GREENVILLE RD
BROOKLAWN AVE
BROOKLAWN WOOD
DEANS GRANGE
ROWAN PK AVE
ROCKFORD PK
ROCKFORD PARK
ROCKFORD GRN
Convent
GRANGE GRO
SPRINGHILL PK
SPRING
NEWTOWN PARK AVENUE
R113
ROCKVILLE DR
ROCKVILLE CR
ROCKVILLE RD
ROCKVILLE PARK
ROWANBYRN ESTATE
CASTLEBYRNE PK
CASTLEBYRNE PARK
OAKLEY GROVE
OAKLEY
YANKEE TER
ANNAVILLE AVE
MARIAN PARK
MOUNT ALBANY
BROOKVILLE PARK
RICHMOND LAWN
FAIRY HILL
NEWTOWN PARK
ORCHARD LA
HAWTHORN MNR
LEURVILLE
GRAVE YARD
Convent & School
Rockfield House
SPORTS GROUND
AVONDALE LAWN
AVONDALE LAWN EXTENSION
GARDEN CROATH
PROBY SQUARE
LINDEN VALE
BROOKFIELD TER
BROOKFIELD PL
SWEETMANS AVE
BARCLAY COURT
College
GEORGE'S AVE
ST ANNE'S SQ
CRAIGMORE GDNS
NEWTOWN VILLAS
MAREtIMO GDNS E
Lib
PO
Sch

V
W
14
15
16
DUN LAOGHAIRE HARBOUR
(DUNLEARY)
WEST PIER
EAST PIER
Captain Boyds
Memorial
Traders
Wharf
Dunleary
Pier
Jetties
OLD
HARBOUR
HARBOUR TER
Coastguard
Station
Yacht
Club
Car Ferry
Terminal
Mail
Boat Pier
Band
Stand
DUN
LAOGHAIRE
Geographical
Pointer
Swimming
Pool
SCOTSMAN
BAY
OLD DUNLEARY RD
DUNLEARY RD
CROFTON ROAD
Fire Sta
CROFTON TER
GEORGE'S PLACE
KELLY'S AVE
CROFTON AVE
CHARLEMONT AVE
WELLINGTON ST
Town Hall
St.Michael's
Hospital
LONGFORD PL
DUNLEARY HILL
CUMBERLAND
DE VESCI GARDENS
DE VESCI TER
Sch
BARRETT ST
SMITHS VILLAS
YORK TERRACE
Lib
LIBRARY ROAD
GEORGE'S STREET LOWER
GEORGE'S STREET UPPER
EBLANA AVE
SUSSEX ST
ROYAL MARINE RD
MORAN PARK
RESERVOIR
HADDINGTON TER
VICTORIA TER
Shopping
Centre
Maritime
Museum
ADELAIDE ST
HAIGH TER
QUEENS ROAD
MELLIFONT AVE
MARINE TER
STONEVIEW PL
PARK RD
PEOPLES
PARK
MARTELLO AVE
WINDSOR TER
NEWTOWNSMITH
SUMMERHILL PAR
ISLINGTON AVE
LOPERTON
PACKENHAM
WILLOW BANK
ROSARY GDNS W
ROSARY GDNS E
THE SLOPES
VESEY GARDENS
VESEY PLACE
VESEY MEWS
ST. MARY'S ST
NORTHCOTE AVE
DOMINICK ST
NORTHCOTE PL
CROSS AVENUE
CONVENT ROAD
STREET
MULGRAVE STREET
MONKSTOWN GATE
GROSVENOR RD
Dun Laoghaire
(Dunleary)
MONKSTOWN PARK
KNAPTON ROAD
YORK ROAD
Coll
Sch
TIVOLI TERRACE NORTH
TIVOLI TERRACE EAST
DESMOND AVE
WOLFE TONE AVE
PATRICK
MULGRAVE TERRACE
NORTHUMBERLAND AVE
ANGLESEA LA
SYDENHAM MEWS
AVENUE
GSS
CORRIG AVENUE
CLARINDA PARK NORTH
CLARINDA PARK WEST
CLARINDA PARK EAST
CLARINDA MANOR
CLARINDA PARK
CROSTHWAITE TER
NORTHUMBERLAND PARK
CORRIG PK
TIVOLI TERRACE SOUTH
MONKSTOWN UPPER
Monkstown Castle
ST. JOHN'S PK
TIVOLI ROAD
PRIMROSE HILL
EGLINTON PK
Convent
Club House
CORRIG ROAD
LOWER ROAD
R118
ROSMEEN GDNS
ROSMEEN PK
SUMMERHILL ROAD
GLASTHULE RD
LINK ROAD
MARINE
GRANITE HALL
SANDYCOVE
GLASTULE
EDEN PK
Coll
O'DONNELL GDNS
MAGENTA PL
EDEN ROAD UPPER
EDEN ROAD LOWER
EDEN TER
FINDLATER ST
COLDWELL ST
CATHERINE'S PK
ST. PAUL'S TER
ST. PETER'S
HUDSON ROAD
SPORTS
BEAUFORT
CONGRESS GDNS
GLASTHULE BLDGS
SEABANK
ST HELENS
WILLMONT AVE
GLANDORE PK
WOODLAWN PARK
TIVOLI CLOSE
MOUNT TOWN PK
MOUNTWOOD
MOUNT TOWN LOWER
GOLF
ROYAL TERRACE LANE
ROYAL TERRACE W
ROYAL TERRACE
ROYAL TER EAST
NORTH
MYRTLE AVE
CROSTHWAITE PARK WEST
CROSTHWAITE PARK EAST
CROSTHWAITE PARK
SARA CLO
GLENG

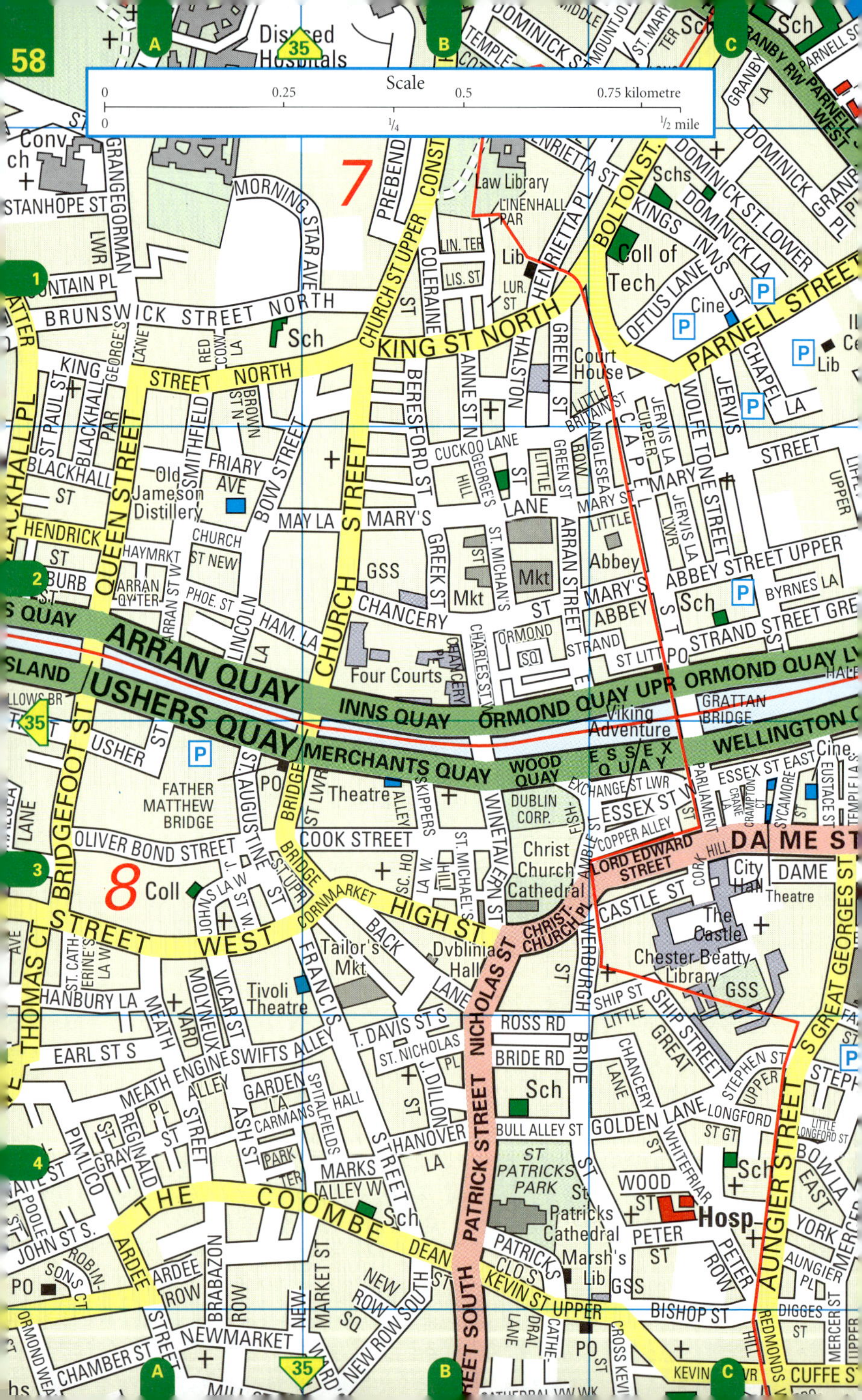
Scale
0
0.25
0.5
0.75 kilometre
0
1/4
1/2 mile
A
B
C
1
2
3
4
7
8
35
Disused Hospitals
DOMINICK ST
TEMPLE
MOUNTJOY
ST. MARY
Sch
GRANBY RW
PARNELL ST
PARNELL WEST
Conv
STANHOPE ST
GRANGEGORMAN LWR
MORNING STAR AVE
PREBEND
CHURCH ST UPPER
CONSTITUTION
Law Library
LINENHALL PAR
HENRIETTA ST
HENRIETTA PL
BOLTON ST
Schs
KINGS INNS ST
DOMINICK ST. LOWER
DOMINICK LA
GRANBY LA
DOMINICK PL
Coll of Tech
LOFTUS LANE
Cine
PARNELL STREET
FOUNTAIN PL
BRUNSWICK STREET NORTH
GEORGE'S LANE
RED COW LA
Sch
COLERAINE ST
LIN. TER
LIS. ST
Lib
LUR. ST
KING ST NORTH
HALSTON
GREEN ST
Court House
CHAPEL LA
JERVIS ST
WOLFE TONE STREET
BLACKHALL PL
KING STREET NORTH
ST PAUL ST
BLACKHALL PAR
QUEEN STREET
SMITHFIELD
BROWN ST N
BOW STREET
CHURCH STREET
BERESFORD ST
ANNE ST N
CUCKOO LANE
LITTLE BRITAIN ST
CAPEL ST
JERVIS LA UPPER
MARY STREET
UPPER
BLACKHALL ST
Old Jameson Distillery
FRIARY AVE
MAY LA
MARY'S LANE
GEORGE'S HILL
LITTLE GREEN ST
ANGLESEA ROW
MARY ST LITTLE
HENDRICK ST
HAYMRKT
CHURCH ST NEW
ST. MICHAN'S ST
ARRAN STREET
Abbey
JERVIS LA LWR
ABBEY STREET UPPER
BURGH QUAY
ARRAN ST W
ARRAN QY TER
PHOE. ST
LINCOLN LA
HAM. LA
GSS
CHANCERY ST
GREEK ST
Mkt
MARY'S ABBEY
BYRNES LA
ARRAN QUAY
CHANCERY PL
CHARLES ST.W
ORMOND SQ
STRAND ST LITT
STRAND STREET GREAT
Four Courts
ORMOND QUAY UPR
ORMOND QUAY LWR
USHERS ISLAND
USHERS QUAY
INNS QUAY
GRATTAN BRIDGE
Viking Adventure
WELLINGTON QUAY
USHER ST
MERCHANTS QUAY
WOOD QUAY
ESSEX QUAY
FATHER MATTHEW BRIDGE
ST. AUGUSTINE ST
BRIDGE ST LWR
Theatre
SKIPPERS ALLEY
EXCHANGE ST LWR
ESSEX ST EAST
SYCAMORE ST
EUSTACE ST
TEMPLE LA S
DUBLIN CORP.
FISHAMBLE ST
ESSEX ST W
PARLIAMENT ST
CRANE LA
CRAMPTON CT
Cine
BRIDGEFOOT ST
LANE
OLIVER BOND STREET
COOK STREET
WINETAVERN ST
Christ Church Cathedral
COPPER ALLEY
LORD EDWARD STREET
CORK HILL
DAME ST
DAME
City Hall
Theatre
Coll
JOHNS LA W
BRIDGE ST UPR
CORNMARKET
HIGH ST
SC. HO
LA. W.
ST. MICHAEL'S HILL
CASTLE ST
The Castle
THOMAS CT
THOMAS STREET WEST
ST. CATHERINE'S LA W
BACK LANE
Tailor's Mkt
Dvblinia Hall
CHRIST CHURCH PL
NICHOLAS ST
WERBURGH ST
Chester Beatty Library
GSS
GEORGES ST S GREAT
HANBURY LA
MEATH
MOLYNEUX YARD
VICAR ST
Tivoli Theatre
FRANCIS
T. DAVIS ST S
ROSS RD
BRIDE ST
SHIP ST LITTLE
SHIP STREET GREAT
EARL ST S
MEATH PL
ENGINE ALLEY
SWIFTS ALLEY
ST. NICHOLAS PL
BRIDE RD
CHANCERY LANE
STEPHEN ST UPPER
STEPHEN
GARDEN LA
CARMANS HALL
SPITALFIELDS
J. DILLON ST
Sch
GOLDEN LANE
LONGFORD ST GT
LITTLE LONGFORD ST
PIMLICO
GRAY ST
REGINALD ST
ASH ST
PARK TER
HANOVER LA
BULL ALLEY ST
ST PATRICKS PARK
WHITEFRIAR ST
BOW LA EAST
JOHN ST S.
POOLE ST
THE COOMBE
MARKS ALLEY W
PATRICK STREET
St Patricks Cathedral
WOOD ST
Hosp
AUNGIER STREET
YORK
MERCER
ARDEE ST
ROBINSONS CT
ARDEE ROW
BRABAZON ROW
NEW MARKET
MARKET ST
NEW ROW SQ
NEW ROW SOUTH
DEAN ST
PATRICKS CLOS
Marsh's Lib
PETER ST
PETER ROW
AUNGIER PL
PO
KEVIN ST UPPER
GSS
BISHOP ST
DIGGES ST
MERCER ST
ORMOND WAY
CHAMBER ST
NEWMARKET
WARD'S HILL
PATRICK STREET SOUTH
CATHEDRAL LANE
CROSS KEVIN ST
KEVIN ST LWR
REDMONDS HILL
CUFFE ST

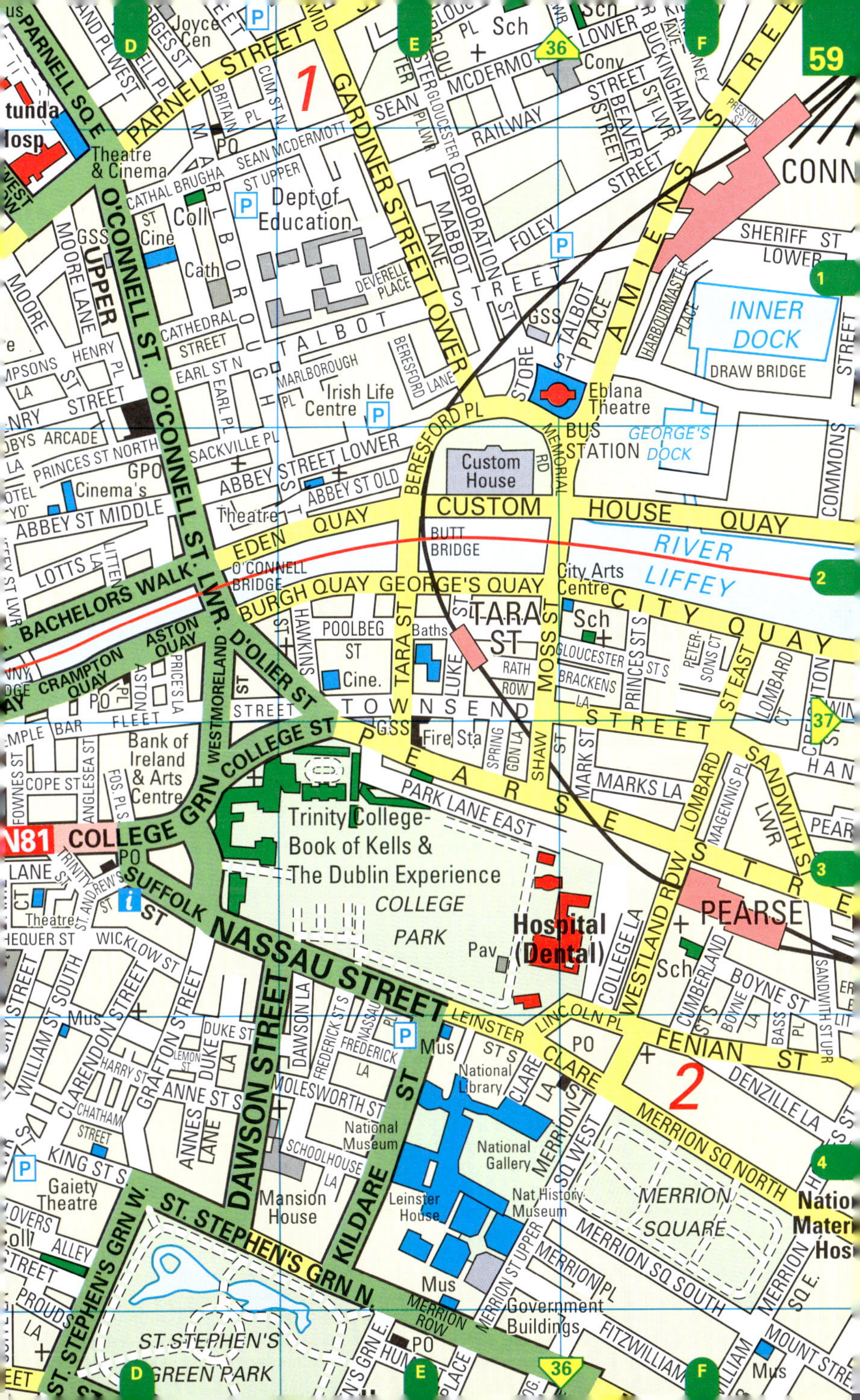

PARNELL STREET
PARNELL SQ E
Joyce Cen
Theatre & Cinema
GARDINER STREET LOWER
SEAN McDERMOTT ST UPPER
GLOUCESTER PL
Sch
36
LOWER
Cony
BUCKINGHAM STREET
RAILWAY STREET
BEAVER STREET
CONN
O'CONNELL ST. UPPER
CATHAL BRUGHA ST
Coll
Cine
Dept of Education
MARLBOROUGH
MOORE LANE
MOORE ST
Cath
CATHEDRAL STREET
TALBOT
DEVERELL PLACE
MABBOT LANE
CORPORATION ST
FOLEY STREET
AMIENS STREET
SHERIFF ST LOWER
HARBOURMASTER PLACE
INNER DOCK
DRAW BRIDGE
EARL ST N
HENRY STREET
MARLBOROUGH PL
Irish Life Centre
BERESFORD LANE
BERESFORD PL
STORE ST
TALBOT PLACE
GSS
Eblana Theatre
BUS STATION
GEORGE'S DOCK
COMMONS
ARCADE
PRINCES ST NORTH
GPO
Cinema's
SACKVILLE PL
ABBEY STREET LOWER
ABBEY ST OLD
ABBEY ST MIDDLE
Theatre
Custom House
MEMORIAL RD
CUSTOM HOUSE QUAY
EDEN QUAY
BUTT BRIDGE
RIVER LIFFEY
LOTTS
BACHELORS WALK
O'CONNELL BRIDGE
O'CONNELL ST. LWR.
BURGH QUAY
GEORGE'S QUAY
City Arts Centre
CITY QUAY
ASTON QUAY
CRAMPTON QUAY
D'OLIER ST
HAWKINS ST
POOLBEG ST
TARA ST
Baths
LUKE ST
TARA ST
MOSS ST
Sch
GLOUCESTER ST S
BRACKENS LA
PRINCES ST S
PETERSONS CT
ST EAST
LOMBARD CT
RATH ROW
TOWNSEND STREET
Cine.
WESTMORELAND ST
PRICE'S LA
FLEET STREET
BAR
PO
Bank of Ireland & Arts Centre
COLLEGE ST
GSS
Fire Sta
SPRING GDN LA
SHAW ST
MARK ST
MARKS LA
LOMBARD ST
MAGENNIS PL
SANDWITH ST LWR
PEARSE STREET
37
COPE ST
ANGLESEA ST
FOWNES ST
FOS PL
N81
COLLEGE GRN
PARK LANE EAST
Trinity College-
Book of Kells &
The Dublin Experience
COLLEGE PARK
Pav
Hospital (Dental)
PEARSE
WESTLAND ROW
COLLEGE LA
CUMBERLAND ST S
BOYNE ST
BASS PL
SANDWITH ST UPR
Sch
TRINITY ST
ST ANDREW'S ST
SUFFOLK ST
NASSAU STREET
Theatre
WICKLOW ST
EXCHEQUER ST
WILLIAM ST SOUTH
CLARENDON STREET
Mus
GRAFTON STREET
DUKE ST
DUKE LA
LEMON ST
HARRY ST
CHATHAM STREET
ANNE ST S
ANNES LANE
DAWSON STREET
DAWSON LA
FREDERICK ST S
NASSAU PL
FREDERICK LA
MOLESWORTH ST
LEINSTER ST S
LINCOLN PL
PO
CLARE ST
CLARE LA
FENIAN ST
DENZILLE LA
Mus
National Library
National Museum
SCHOOLHOUSE LA
KILDARE ST
National Gallery
MERRION SQ WEST
MERRION SQ NORTH
MERRION SQUARE
KING ST S
Gaiety Theatre
Mansion House
Leinster House
Nat History Museum
ALLEY
ST. STEPHEN'S GRN W.
ST. STEPHEN'S GRN N.
MERRION ST UPPER
MERRION PL
MERRION SQ SOUTH
MERRION SQ E.
Mus
MERRION ROW
Government Buildings
FITZWILLIAM
MOUNT STREET
ST. STEPHEN'S GREEN PARK
PO
HUME ST
36
D
E
F
1
2
3
4

History

The ford over the River Liffey has been important since Celtic times and there was a thriving Christian community here from the 5thC, following their conversion by St Patrick in AD448. Marauding Vikings landed here in AD840, established a garrison port by the Dark Pool or Dubbh Linn, and within a few years had built a fortified town on the high ground above the estuary. Originally a base for raiding sorties, Dublin soon became a flourishing trading port as well, until Viking dominance was curtailed following a defeat by Brian Boru at the Battle of Clontarf in 1014.

Many of the Vikings had inter-married with the Irish and converted to Christianity but they were finally driven out by the Anglo-Normans under Strongbow, who took Dublin by storm and executed the Viking leader Hasculf. In 1170 Henry II arrived in Dublin, defeated Strongbow and received the submission of the Irish chieftains on the site of College Green. Henry granted the city by charter to the citizens of Bristol, thereby establishing English authority in Ireland.

The city and surrounding area, established as the seat of English government and protected by an enclosing wall and strategic castles, was known as The Pale. Frequently attacked during the 12thC and 13thC by the Irish clans based in the Wicklow Mountains, it was assaulted unsuccessfully by Edward Bruce in 1316. The city witnessed the crowning of Lambert Simnel, pretender to the English throne, in Christ Church in 1486. Unmoved by the rebellion of 'Silken' Thomas Fitzgerald in 1534, the inhabitants remained loyal to the English crown, supporting King Charles during the Civil Wars. Parliamentarians captured Dublin in 1647 and at this time the city was in decline. Following the Restoration of Charles I, however, Dublin underwent a great economic and architectural expansion.

By the end of the 17thC Dublin had become a flourishing commercial centre and during the following century the city was transformed into one of the most beautiful Georgian cities in Europe. The 'Wide Streets Commission' was established in 1757 and in 1773 the Paving Board was formed. New, elegantly spacious streets and squares were planned and palatial town houses built. In 1783 the Irish Parliament led by Henry Grattan was granted a short-lived autonomy but there was growing political unrest, which erupted in the unsuccessful uprising of 1798. Lord Edward Fitzgerald died of wounds sustained resisting arrest and in 1800 the detested Act of Union was established and the fortunes of the city began to wane.

With government now in London, few of the noblemen required their fine mansions and many returned to their country estates or left for London. Bitterness increased; in 1803 the Lord Chief Justice was assassinated and Robert Emmet, the leader of an abortive insurrection, was hanged. The newspaper The Nation was established by Charles Gavan Duffy in 1842, the heyday of the Repeal Movement. Daniel O'Connell was elected Lord Mayor in 1841 but only three years later he was interned in Richmond Gaol for campaigning for the repeal of the Union and the restoration of Grattan's 'Irish Parliament'. In 1873 the first great Home Rule Conference was held and in 1879 the Land League was formed, whose leaders, including Parnell and Davitt, were imprisoned as a consequence. In 1882 the new Chief Secretary, Lord Frederick Cavendish, and his Under-Secretary were assassinated in Phoenix Park by the Invincibles, a new terrorist organisation.

As the campaign for Home Rule gathered momentum, the Gaelic League, which started the Irish literary renaissance, was established by Douglas Hyde and Eóin MacNeill in 1893. Conceived as a means of reviving interest in the Irish language and traditional Irish life, the Gaelic League was also responsible for a remarkable literary revival resulting in the formation of the Abbey Theatre in 1904, where plays by J M Synge, Sean O'Casey and W B Yeats, amongst others, were performed.

In 1905 the Sinn Fein movement was formed, in 1909 the Irish Transport and General Workers Union was set up under the leadership of James Connolly, and in 1913 there was a massive strike, paralysing the city. The Irish Volunteers came into being in 1914, largely to combat the Ulster Volunteers who had been raised by Edward Carson in January 1913 to defend the right of Ulster to remain united with Great Britain. In 1916 the Irish Volunteers seized the General Post Office in Lower O'Connell Street as their headquarters and the Easter Rising had begun. It was quickly crushed, but so brutally that public conscience, clearly appalled, overwhelmingly elected Sinn Fein at the general election of December 1918 with Eamon de Valera as the new president.

Whilst the Dublin faction was openly in support of the guerrilla bands operating across the country, the Ulster Unionists set up their own provisional government, and the ambushes and assassinations which characterised the Anglo-Irish War, featuring the notorious Black and Tans, began in bloody earnest. The war ended in the truce of July 1921. Despite the ratification of the Irish Free State in January 1922, a large and dissatisfied faction of leaders in the Irish movement took up arms against their former comrades and seized the Four Courts, which they held for two months. The subsequent shelling ordered by the new Dublin Government destroyed much of O'Connell Street but by the 1930s Dublin was emerging as a modern capital city and most of the public buildings had been restored.

Visiting Dublin

Passports

Citizens of the European Union need either a valid national identity card or passport to enter the Republic of Ireland. It is recommended that visitors from the UK bring a passport as a means of identification. Nationals of other countries require a passport and may require a visa. Enquiries should be made with a travel agent or Irish Embassy before travelling. The address of the Irish Embassy in London is 17 Grosvenor Place.

Tel: 020 7235 2171

Web: www.irlgov.ie

Banks

The unit of currency in use is the Irish Punt (IEP) or pound, which is divided into one hundred pence. Euro notes and coins are also legal tender and are expected to be in circulation by 2002.

Banks open Monday–Friday from 10.00–16.00 and in Dublin most branches remain open until 17.00 on Thursdays. Major banks have 24 hour ATM machines which accept Plus and Cirrus symbols. Most credit cards, including all those with the Eurocard symbol, are widely accepted in shops, petrol stations, restaurants and hotels. Personal cheques from banks outside the Republic of Ireland are not accepted in the country without prior arrangement.

Bureaux de Change

Banks and Bureaux de Change generally offer the best exchange rates, although post offices, hotels, travel agents and some department stores offer exchange facilities.

There is a Bureau de Change at Dublin Airport and Dún Laoghaire ferry terminal. Dublin Airport also has a 24 hour Bank of Ireland foreign currency note exchanger and multi-currency Pass machines. Foreign exchange facilities are also to be found at the central bus station (Bus Áras) and Connolly railway station.

Language

English is spoken by everyone in Ireland. The country is officially bilingual with Irish (Gaelic) also spoken.

Customs and Excise

The Republic of Ireland is a member of the European Union and, in accordance with EU regulations, travellers within the Community can import 90 litres of wine, 110 litres of duty paid beer and 800 cigarettes without question. Duty free sales of goods amongst European community members are now abolished. There are restrictions on taking certain food items into Ireland and checks should be made beforehand with the Irish Embassy or travel agent. Pets may not be brought into the country unless travelling from the UK, all other animals entering the country have to undergo quarantine.

Emergency

If you are involved in an emergency and require the services of the Police, Fire Brigade, Ambulance Service, or Coastguard, dial 999.

Medical Treatment

Visitors to Ireland from European Community countries are entitled to free treatment by a general practitioner, medicines on prescription and treatment on a public ward in a hospital. British citizens need only show some form of identification such as a passport or driving licence to the doctor or hospital and request treatment under the EU health agreement. Visitors from other EU countries need to present form EIII (available from social security offices prior to departure). Health Insurance is recommended for visitors from outside the EU. No inoculations are required for travellers to Ireland.

Disabled Visitors

The Irish Wheelchair association can offer advice and can arrange wheelchair hire. Tel: 01 833 8241 (Mon–Fri 09.00–17.00).

Irish Rail publishes a 'Guide for Mobility Impaired Passengers' which details the accessibility of all railway and DART stations. Obtainable at all manned stations or from the Access and Liaison officer, tel: 01 703 2634. Most of the Dublin Bus fleet is low floor easy access, and the buses run by Irish Bus are largely wheelchair accessible. Discounts on many ferry sailings from Britain are available to disabled drivers who wish to take their own car to Ireland. Drivers should contact the Disabled Drivers' Association or Motor Club in Britain to obtain the relevant form. This form should then be sent to the ferry company.

Phones

Most calls are dialled direct with cheaper call charge rates between 18.00 and 08.00 Mon–Fri and all day Saturday, Sunday and bank holidays. The dialling code for Dublin is 01 and so for calls within Dublin omit 01 at the beginning of a number. To dial Dublin from abroad dial the access code for Ireland (00353) plus the area code for Dublin but omitting the zero (1) and then the number. For directory enquiries, including Northern Ireland, dial 1190; 1197 for UK numbers; 1198 for international numbers. For operator assistance dial 10 (Ireland and UK) or 114 for the international operator. Card phones are cheaper than payphones and are widely available. Callcards are obtainable at post offices, newsagents and supermarkets. Mobile phones can be brought into Ireland but visitors need to ensure their phone company has a roaming agreement with the Irish network operators.

Transport

Driving

Driving is on the left-hand side of the road in Ireland as in the UK; at roundabouts give way to traffic from the right. All drivers and front seat passengers must wear seat belts, and rear belts if they are fitted. Children under twelve must have a suitable restraint. Helmets are compulsory for motorcyclists. The maximum speed limit is 97kph (60mph) outside urban areas and the motorway speed limit is 110kph (70mph). In urban areas the limit is usually 50kph (30mph). There are on-the-spot fines for speeding and drink driving laws are strict. Parking infringements are taken seriously and illegally parked cars in Dublin City are liable to be clamped or towed away to the Corporation pound with a recovery charge payable.

Distances on the green and white road signs are in kilometres while the older black and white fingerpost signs are in miles. Place names are generally in English and Irish. Unleaded petrol and diesel are widely available. Recorded weather information is available for Dublin by calling the Meteorological Service Tel: 1550 123 854. There is a charge for this call.

Car Hire

Car hire is readily available in Dublin, although in July and August there is a high demand and it is best to book in advance. You must have held a full licence for 2 years and be under 70 and over 23. Some companies make exceptions to this but charges may be higher. A full valid driving licence of your country of residence (which you must have held for at least two years without endorsements) must be presented at the time of hiring.

Most international car rental companies have offices in Dublin and cars can also be hired at the airport and Dún Laoghaire ferry terminal. The cost of hire will depend on the type of car and time of year and it is worthwhile shopping around. It is important, however, to check the insurance details and ensure Collision Damage Waiver is included. A deposit is usually payable at the time of booking or before you drive away. Fly-drive or rail-sail-drive packages arranged by travel agents or the air and ferry companies can be an economical and easy way of hiring a car.

Public Transport

Dublin is linked with the cities and towns of Ireland by a network of rail and bus services overseen by Córas Iompair Éireann (CIE), which is Ireland's National Transport Authority. All information regarding rail and bus services can be obtained from CIE, 59 O'Connell Street Upper, Dublin 1. Tel: 01 830 2222. Bus and rail timetables can be bought at most newsagents. Unlimited use period tickets are available for use on rail and/or bus services.

Bus and Coach Travel

Dublin Bus (Bus Átha Cliath) operates the public bus services in Dublin and the surrounding area. Pre-paid tickets can be bought for periods of time ranging from one day to one month and are good value for money. They can be bought at any of the many bus ticket agencies in the city, from the CIE information desk at Dublin Airport or at Dublin Bus head office at 59 O'Connell Street Upper. Dublin Bus also operates late night services (Nitelink) to most suburban areas on Thursdays, Fridays and Saturdays, links to the ferry ports and railway stations, and also sightseeing tours.

Open Mon–Sat 09.00–18.00.

Tel: 01 872 0000 or 01 873 4222

Web: www.dublinbus.ie has details of routes, timetables, and special tickets.

National bus services between Dublin, Dublin Airport and other major cities and towns are provided by Irish Bus (Bus Éireann) and many private companies. Bus Éireann also operate combined bus and ferry services between Britain and Ireland.

Irish Bus Booking Office, Store Street.

Tel: 01 836 6111

Web: www.buseireann.ie

Scheduled daily hop-on hop-off city sightseeing tours operated by Gray Line Tours depart every 15 minutes from 10.00–17.00; also available are seasonal half and full day excursions further afield including to Malahide Castle, the Boyne Valley, Enniskerry, Wicklow Mountains and Ballykissangel. Information and tickets from the

Gray Line desk at the Dublin Tourism Centre, Suffolk Street.
Tel: 01 605 7705
Email: grayline@tlp.ie

Taxis

Taxis are available at taxi ranks or by phoning one of the many radio-linked taxi companies. There are numerous taxi ranks including ones on O'Connell Street, Dame Street, and St. Stephen's Green West.
Taxi companies are listed in the Golden Pages classified telephone directory.

Rail Travel

Dublin Connolly and Dublin Heuston are the two mainline railway stations and Irish Rail (Iarnród Éireann) operates an excellent service to most towns and cities in Ireland. Irish rail also operates the suburban rail network in Dublin and DART (Dublin Area Rapid Transit) with 26 stations between Howth on the north of Dublin Bay to Bray in the south.
Tel: 01 836 6222
Web: www.irishrail.ie

Bike Hire

Tracks Bikes, Botanic Road, Glasnevin.
Tel: 01 850 0252
Mike's Bikes, Patrick Street, Dún Laoghaire.
Tel: 01 280 0417

Lost Property

Enquire at the nearest police station or:
Dublin Airport. Open Mon–Fri 09.30-16.00.
Tel: 01 814 4481
Dublin Bus. Open Mon–Fri 08.45–17.00.
Tel: 01 703 3055
Irish Bus. Open Mon–Thurs 09.00–17.00, Fri 09.00–16.00. **Tel: 01 703 2489**
Irish Rail (Connolly Station). Open Mon–Fri 09.00–17.00. **Tel: 01 703 2365**
Irish Rail (Heuston Station). Open Mon–Fri 09.00–17.30. **Tel: 01 703 2102**

Places of Interest

Arbour Hill Cemetery.

The leaders of the Easter Rising are buried here.

Bank of Ireland, College Green.

Designed by Sir Edward Lovett Pearce in 1729, it was later enlarged by James Gandon and Robert Parke between 1785–1794. Originally the Parliament House, the first of a series of great public buildings erected in 18thC Dublin, it was taken over by the Bank of Ireland in 1804. A statue of Henry Grattan, leader of the Irish parliament of 1782, stands outside on the lawn of College Green. Two huge 18thC tapestries commemorating the Siege of Londonderry and the Battle of the Boyne hang in the oak-panelled chamber of the former House of Lords.
There are guided tours of the House of Lords on Tuesdays at 10.30, 11.30, and 13.45. Admission free. Disabled access.
Tel: 01 671 1488

Bank of Ireland Arts Centre, Foster Place.

An arts centre which presents classical concerts and recitals and houses an interactive museum. The museum illustrates the history of the adjoining College Green buildings where many of the dramatic events of Irish history were played out in the Irish parliament. The museum also reflects the role played by the Bank of Ireland in the economic and social development of Ireland.
Open Tues-Fri 10.00–16.00. Disabled access.
Tel: 01 671 1488

Belvedere House, North Great George's Street.

One of the best 18thC mansions in Dublin. Taken over by Jesuit Belvedere College in 1841; James Joyce went to school here between 1893–1898.

Casino, off Malahide Road, Marino.

A miniature 18thC neo-classical masterpiece designed by Sir William Chambers and recently restored. Casino means 'small house'. It was built as a pleasure house beside Marino House (now demolished), Lord Charlemont's country residence, for the enormous sum of £60,000. It is a compact building, remarkably containing 16 rooms, with many interesting architectural features. The interior circular hall, ringed by columns, is crowned by a coffered dome. The graceful roof urns disguise chimneys while the columns conceal drainpipes.
Open daily Jun–Sept 10.00–18.00; May & Oct 10.00–17.00; (Feb, March, November) Sun & Thurs only 12.00–16.00; (Apr) Sun & Thurs only 12.00–17.00. Last admission 45 minutes before closing. Closed December & January. Access by guided tour only. Access to interior by stairway.
Tel: 01 833 1618

Ceol, Irish Traditional Music Centre, Smithfield Village.

An interactive museum which explores and celebrates the history and personalities of traditional Irish music, song and dance. Ceol – the Irish word for music – shows how important traditional music has been to the cultural life of Ireland, and its relevance to the social and political history of the country. Among the displays are musical instruments of the Irish tradition including Uilleann pipe, fiddle, flute, and button accordion. The highlight of the centre is a film about present day musicians

from various parts of Ireland, shown in an 180 degree widescreen auditorium. There is also a dedicated area for children to experience and enjoy Irish Music. Smithfield Village is located between Arran Quay and King Street North.
Open Mon–Sat 10.00–18.00, Sun 11.00–18.00.
Tel: 01 817 3820
Web: www.ceol.ie
Email: info@ceol.ie

City Hall, Lord Edward Street.
Completed in 1779, this fine building was designed as The Royal Exchange. Subsequent use included a prison and corn exchange before being taken over by the city in 1852. It features a beautiful Corinthian coffered dome and portico. The archives include the original charter of 1171 in which Henry II granted Dublin to the citizens of Bristol.

Custom House Visitor Centre, Custom House Quay.
The Custom House, with a magnificent long river frontage, is an architectural masterpiece designed by James Gandon and completed in 1791. Exhibits relate to James Gandon and the history of the Custom House itself, with illustrations of how the building was restored after it was gutted by fire in 1921. The building is best viewed from the south bank of the River Liffey.
Open: Mon–Fri 10.00–12.30, Sat & Sun 14.00–17.00. Disabled access by prior arrangement.
Tel: 01 878 7660

Drimnagh Castle, Long Mile Road.
Ireland's only castle with a flooded moat. This Norman castle has a fully restored Great Hall, medieval undercroft and 17thC style formal garden.
Open (Apr–Sept) Wed, Sat, Sun 12.00–17.00; (Oct–March) Wed, Sun 12.00–17.00. Last tour 16.45. Open at other times by appointment.
Tel: 01 450 2530

Dublin Castle, off Dame Street.
The Castle was originally built between 1204–1228 as part of Dublin's defensive system. The Record Tower is the principal remnant of the 13thC Anglo-Norman fortress and has walls 5 metres (16ft) thick but what remains today is largely the result of 18thC and 19thC re-building. The 15thC Bermingham Tower was once the state prison where Red Hugh O'Donnell was interned in the 16thC; it was rebuilt in the 18thC. The State Apartments, Undercroft and ornate Chapel Royal are open to the public. The State Apartments, dating from the British Administration, were once the residence of the English Viceroys and are now used for Presidential Inaugurations and state receptions. Within these apartments are the magnificent throne room and St Patrick's Hall, 25 metres (82ft) long with a high panelled and decorated ceiling. In the undercroft can be seen the remains of a Viking fortress, part of the original moat, and part of the old city wall.
Open: Mon–Fri 10.00–17.00, Sat & Sun & bank holidays 14.00–17.00. Closed 24–26 Dec & Good Friday. Access by guided tour only. Disabled access/toilets.
Tel: 01 677 7129

Dublin Civic Museum, South William Street.
Housed in the former Georgian City Assembly House, the museum illustrates the history of Dublin and has a large collection of maps, prints and newspapers. Among the artefacts is the head of the statue of Lord Nelson, blown off its pillar in O'Connell Street in an IRA explosion in 1966.
Open Tues–Sat 10.00–18.00, Sun 11.00–14.00. Admission free.
Tel: 01 679 4260

Dublin Experience, Trinity College.
A film about the story of Dublin which is shown every hour in the Trinity College Arts Building.
Open daily from mid May–30th Sept 10.00–17.00.
Tel: 01 608 1688

Dublin's Viking Adventure, Essex Street West.
A reconstruction of the sights, sounds and smells of life in Viking Dublin 1,000 years ago, along with a fascinating exhibition of Viking artefacts discovered in the area. A Viking guide leads visitors through the narrow streets of the Viking town of Dyflin to observe daily life and work; there is even the opportunity to talk to the people who live there. The museum is located close to Wood Quay which was the centre of Viking settlement from 9thC–10thC.
Open Tues–Sat 10.00–16.30; closed 13.00–14.00 Nov–Feb only.
Tel: 01 679 6040
Email: viking@dublintourism.ie

Dublin Writers Museum, Parnell Square.
Tracing the history of Irish literature from its earliest times to the 20thC, this museum is a celebration of this literary heritage. Writers and playwrights including Jonathan Swift, George Bernard Shaw, Oscar Wilde, W B Yeats, James Joyce and Samuel Beckett are brought to life through personal items, portraits, their books and letters. There is also a room dedicated to children's authors. The museum is housed in a restored 18thC Georgian mansion with decorative stained-glass windows and ornate plaster-work.
Open Mon–Sat 10.00–17.00, Sun & bank

holidays 11.00–17.00. Disabled access to ground floor.

Tel: 01 872 2077

Email: writers@dublintourism.ie

Dublinia, Christ Church, St. Michael's Hill.

A multi-media recreation of Dublin life in medieval times from the Anglo-Norman arrival in 1170 to the dissolution of the monasteries in 1540. There is a scale model of the medieval city, a life size reconstruction of a merchant's house, and numerous Viking and Norman artefacts from excavations at nearby Wood Quay. The building is the old Synod Hall and is linked to Christ Church Cathedral by an ornate Victorian pedestrian bridge which spans the road.

Open daily 10.00–17.00; 11.00–16.00 Oct–March. Disabled access.

Tel: 01 679 4611

Dublin Zoo, Phoenix Park.

The Zoo is well known for its captive-breeding programme and is committed to the conservation and protection of endangered species. The 'big cats', living in enclosures which simulate their natural habitats, include lions, tigers, jaguars and snow leopards. Attractive gardens surround two natural lakes where pelicans, flamingos, ducks and geese abound, while the islands in the lakes are home to chimps, gibbons, spider monkeys and orang-utans. A recent development 'Fringes of the Arctic' has provided a state of the art enclosure for the polar bears and is home to wolves, arctic foxes and snowy owls. After the acquisition of more land, the zoo doubled in size in 2000 and an African Plains area has been developed providing greater space and freedom for giraffe, hippo, rhino and other African animals and birds. The city farm and pets' corner provide encounters with Irish domestic animals. Other attractions include a zoo train, discovery centre, and 'meet the keeper' programme.

Open: Mon–Sat 09.30–18.00, Sun 10.30–18.00. Last admission 17.00. Closes 1 hour earlier in winter.

Tel: 01 677 1425

Web: www.dublinzoo.ie

Email: info@dublinzoo.ie

Dunsink Observatory, Castleknock, Dublin 15.

Founded in 1783, it is one of the oldest observatories in the world and houses the astronomy section of the School of Cosmic Physics. Public open nights are held on the first and third Wednesdays of each month from September to March inclusive at 20.00. Requests for tickets for the open nights must be made by post to the Observatory.

Tel: 01 838 7911

Web: www.dunsink.dias.ie

Four Courts, Inns Quay.

Originally designed by James Gandon in 1785, it was partially destroyed by a fire in 1922 in the struggle for Irish independence but restored again by 1932. The Four Courts has a 137 metre (450ft) river frontage and the building is fronted by a Corinthian portico with six columns. The square central block with circular hall is crowned by a copper-covered lantern-dome. Housed here are the Irish Law Courts and Law Library.

Tel: 01 872 5555

Fry Model Railway, Malahide.

Covering 233 square metres (2,500sq.ft) this is one of the world's largest working miniature railways and is a delight for children and adults alike. Besides the track, the railway has stations, bridges, trams, buses and barges and includes the Dublin landmarks of Heuston station and O'Connell Bridge. On display are the hand constructed models of Irish trains by Cyril Fry, draughtsman and railway engineer, who made them from the 1930s until his death in 1974. Perfectly engineered, the models represent the earliest trains to those of more modern times. Situated in the grounds of Malahide Castle, 13km (8 miles) north of Dublin city centre.

Open (Apr–Oct) Mon–Sat 10.00–17.00, Sun & public holidays 14.00–18.00; (Nov–March) daily 14.00–17.00. Closed all year 13.00–14.00.

Tel: 01 846 3779

Email: fryrailway@dublintourism.ie

GAA Museum, Croke Park.

The Gaelic Athletic Association (GAA) is Ireland's largest sporting and cultural organisation and is dedicated to promoting the games of hurling, Gaelic football, handball, rounders and camogie. The museum is at Croke Park, home of Irish hurling and football, and traces the history of Gaelic sports and their place in Irish culture right up to the present day. Interactive exhibits allow visitors the chance to try out the skills of the games for themselves. National trophies and sports equipment are also on display.

Open (May–Sept) daily 09.30–17.00; (Oct–Apr) Tues–Sat 10.00–17.00, Sun 12.00–17.00. Last admission 1 hour before closing.

Tel: 01 855 8176

Web: www.gaa.ie

Heraldic Museum, Kildare Street.

Part of the National Library of Ireland, the museum illustrates the uses of heraldry with displays of coat of arms and banners and a collection of heraldic glass, seals, stamps, and

coins.
Open Mon–Fri 10.00–12.30, 14.00–16.30.
Admission is free.
Tel: 01 603 0200

General Post Office, O'Connell Street.
Designed by Francis Johnston and completed in 1818. A century later the GPO became the headquarters of the 1916 Easter Rising and the Proclamation of the Irish Republic was read from the steps by Patrick Pearse. Bullet marks can still be seen on the pillars. Badly damaged in 1922 in the fight for independence, it was restored in 1929. A bronze sculpture, The Death of Cúchulainn by Oliver Sheppard, stands within the building.

Guinness Hopstore Visitors' Centre,
St. Jame's Gate Brewery, Crane Street.
Established in 1759, the Guinness Brewery is now the largest exporting brewery in the world. The converted hopstore features an audio-visual show documenting the company's development, displays of vats and casks and other artefacts used in the brewing process, and an advertising gallery.
Open (Apr–Sept) Mon–Sat 09.30–17.00, Sun 10.30–16.30; (Oct–Mar) Mon–Sat 09.30–16.00, Sun 12.00–16.00. Disabled access.
Tel: 01 408 4800

Ha'penny Bridge, Crampton Quay.
An elegant arching narrow cast-iron pedestrian bridge spanning the Liffey; it was first opened in 1816 and the name derives from the toll once charged.

Hot Press Irish Music Hall of Fame, Abbey Street Middle.
The Hall of Fame Tour is an interactive multimedia tour through the history of Irish music with particular emphasis on 20thC rock music including U2. The building is also used as a concert venue.
Open daily May–Sept 10.00–18.00; Oct–April 11.00–17.00. Disabled access/toilet.
Tel: 01 878 3345

Icon @ the Baileys Centre, Leopardstown Racecourse.
Bars and restaurants on five floors with an audio-visual display on Ireland.
Open daily 10.00–11.30.
Tel: 01 289 1000
Web: www.baileys.com

Irish Jewish Museum, Walworth Road
Opened by President Herzog of Israel in 1985, exhibits relate to the Jewish community in Ireland including synagogue fittings and the reconstruction of a typical Dublin Jewish kitchen of 100 years ago.
Open (May–Sept) Sun, Tues, Thurs 11.00–15.30; (Oct–Apr) Sun 10.30–14.30. Admission is free.
Tel: 01 453 1797

Irish Museum of Modern Art, Military Road, Kilmainham.
Opened in the 17thC Royal Hospital building and grounds in 1991, the museum is an important institution for the collection of modern and contemporary art. A wide variety of work by major established 20thC figures and that of younger contemporary artists is presented in an ever changing programme of exhibitions, drawn from the museum's own collection and from public and private collections world-wide.
Open Tues–Sat 10.00–17.30, Sun & bank holidays 12.00–17.30. Admission is free.
Tel: 01 612 9900
Web: www.modernart.ie
Email: info@modernart.ie

James Joyce Centre, North Great George's Street.
A museum in a restored Georgian town house, built in 1784, devoted to the great novelist and run by members of his family. Dennis J Maginni, dancing master in Joyce's novel Ulysses, ran his dancing school from this house. The library contains editions of Joyce's work and that of other Irish writers as well as biographical and critical writing. There is a set of biographies of real Dublin people fictionalised in Ulysses, and also the door from the house occupied by the central character of the novel, Leopold Bloom and his wife Molly. The centre hosts readings, lectures and debates on all aspects of Joyce and his literature and conducts guided city tours.
Open Mon–Sat 09.30–17.00, Sun 12.30–17.00.
Tel: 01 878 8547
Web: www.jamesjoyce.ie
Email: jamesjoyce@adnet.ie

James Joyce Museum, Sandycove.
The museum is housed in the Martello Tower which Joyce used as the setting for the opening chapter of Ulysses, his great work of fiction which immortalised Dublin. Joyce stayed here briefly in 1904 and the living room and view from the gun platform remains much as he described it in the novel. The museum collection includes personal possessions, letters, photographs, first editions and items that reflect the Dublin of Joyce. Situated 13km (8 miles) south of Dublin city centre, the tower was one of 15 defensive towers built along Dublin Bay in 1804 to withstand a threatened invasion from Napoleon.
Open (Apr–Oct) Mon–Sat 10.00–17.00, Sun & bank holidays 14.00–18.00. Closed 13.00–14.00.
Tel: 01 280 9265
Email: joycetower@dublintourism.ie

Kilmainham Gaol, Inchicore Road, Kilmainham.
Built as a gaol in 1796, Kilmainham is now dedicated to the Irish patriots imprisoned there from 1792–1924, including Emmet and his United Irishmen colleagues, the Fenians, the Invincibles and the Irish Volunteers of the Easter Rising. Patrick Pearse and James Connolly were executed in the prison yard and Eamon de Valera, later Prime Minister and then President of Ireland, was one of the last inmates. After its closure in 1924 Kilmainham re-opened as a museum in 1966. It is one of the largest unoccupied gaols in Europe with tiers of cells and overhead catwalks. Access is by guided tour only and features an exhibition and audio-visual show on the political and penal history of the gaol.
Open daily (Apr–Sept) 09.30–18.00; (Oct–Mar) Mon–Fri 09.30–17.00, Sun 10.00–18.00 (closed Sat). Last admission 1 hour 15 minutes before closing. Disabled toilets. Tours for visitors with special needs by prior arrangement.
Tel: 01 453 5984

King's Inns, Henrietta Street.
The Dublin Inns of Court is a glorious classical building, partly built to the plans of James Gandon at the end of the 19thC. The library was founded in 1787 and contains a large legal collection with about 100,000 books. The courtyard opens into Henrietta Street, where Dublin's earliest Georgian mansions remain.

Leinster House, Kildare Street.
Originally a handsome town mansion designed by Richard Castle for the Duke of Leinster in 1745; it has been a Parliament House since 1922. The Dáil Éireann (House of Representatives) and Seanad Éireann (Senate) sit here. The house has two contrasting facades: an imposing formal side facing Kildare Street while from Merrion Square the building has more of the appearance of a country residence. The public may be admitted when the parliament is not sitting and advance notice is required.
Tel: 01 618 3000

Malahide Castle, Malahide.
Originally built in 1185, it was the seat of the Talbot family until 1973 when the last Lord Talbot died; the history of the family is detailed in the Great Hall alongside many family portraits. Malahide also has a large collection of Irish portrait paintings, mainly from the National Gallery, and is furnished with fine period furniture. Within the 100 hectares (250 acres) of parkland surrounding the castle is the Talbot Botanic Gardens, largely created by Lord Milo Talbot between 1948 and 1973. The grounds include walled gardens and a shrubbery with a collection of southern hemisphere plants. Malahide is situated 13km (8 miles) north of Dublin city centre.
Open Mon–Sat 10.00–17.30, Sun & bank holidays 11.00–18.00. Nov–March opens later on Sundays and bank holidays at 14.00. Gardens open 1st May–30th Sept 14.00–17.00. Disabled access.
Tel: 01 846 2184 (castle),
Tel: 01 846 2456 (botanic gardens)
Email: malahidecastle@dublintourism.ie

Mansion House, Dawson Street.
Built in 1705, this Queen Anne style house has been the official residence of the Lord Mayor of Dublin since 1715. The first Irish parliament assembled here in 1919 to adopt Ireland's declaration of Independence and ratify the 1916 proclamation of the Irish Republic. Not open to the public.

National Maritime Museum, Haigh Terrace, Dún Laoghaire.
A former Mariner's Church is home to the museum which features a French Longboat sent to Bantry Bay in support of the United Irishmen in 1796. There are models of the Irish Fleet, a lifeboat display and an exhibit about Robert Halpin, captain of the Great Eastern steamship which laid the first transatlantic telegraph cable in 1866.
Open (Easter–Oct) Tues–Sun 13.00–17.00 (only Sundays in October).
Tel: 01 280 0969

National Museum of Ireland, Archaeology and History, Kildare Street.
Houses a fabulous collection of national antiquities including prehistoric gold ornaments, and outstanding examples of Celtic and medieval art. The 8thC Ardagh Chalice and Tara Brooch are amongst the treasures. The entire history of Ireland is reflected in the museum with 'The Road to Independence Exhibition' illustrating Irish history from 1916–1921. Additionally, there is an Ancient Egypt exhibition.
Open Tues–Sat 10.00–17.00, Sun 14.00–17.00. Admission is free. A Museumlink bus linking the 3 sites of the National Museum operates regularly throughout the day.
Tel: 01 677 7444

National Museum of Ireland, Decorative Arts and History (Collins Barracks), Benburb Street.
Ireland's museum of decorative arts and economic, social, political and military history, based in the oldest military barracks in Europe. Major collections include Irish silver, Irish country furniture, and costume jewellery and

accessories. The work of museum restoration and conservation is explained and the Out of Storage gallery provides visitors with a view of artefacts in storage.

Open Tues–Sat 10.00–17.00; Sun 14.00–17.00. Admission is free. Full disabled access. A Museumlink bus linking the 3 sites of the National Museum operates regularly throughout the day.

Tel: 01 677 7444

National Museum of Ireland, Natural History, Merrion Street.

First opened in 1857 and hardly changed since then, the museum houses a large collection of stuffed animals and the skeletons of mammals and birds from both Ireland and the rest of the world. The exhibits include three examples of the Irish Great Elk which became extinct over 10,000 years ago and the skeleton of a Basking Shark. Fascinating glass reproductions of marine specimens, known as the Blaschka Collection, are found on the upper gallery.

Open Tues–Sat 10.00–17.00; Sun 14.00–17.00. Admission is free. A Museumlink bus linking the 3 sites of the National Museum operates regularly throughout the day.

Tel: 01 677 7444

National Print Museum, Haddington Road.

Situated in the former Garrison Chapel in Beggars Bush Barracks, the museum illustrates the development of printing from the advent of printing to the use of computer technology with a unique collection of implements and machines from Ireland's printing industry.

Open (May–Sept) Mon–Fri 10.00–17.00, Sat & Sun 12.00–17.00; (Oct–Apr) Tues, Thurs, Sat & Sun 14.00–17.00.

Tel: 01 660 3770

National Sea Life Centre, Bray.

Features marine life from the seas around Ireland including stingrays, conger eels, and sharks; also freshwater fish from Irish rivers and streams. A touch pool gives children the opportunity to pick up small creatures such as starfish, crabs and sea anemones. By way of contrast is the fascinating 'Danger in the Depths' tank with many sea creatures from around the world which have proved harmful or fatal to humans.

Open daily 10.00–17.00.

Tel: 01 286 6939

National Transport Museum, Howth Castle.

A collection of buses, trams, trucks, tractors and fire engines, some dating back to 1880, along with other memorabilia from the transport industry.

Open (Jun–Aug) Mon–Fri 10.00–17.00, Sat & Sun 12.00–17.00; (Oct–Apr) Sat & Sun only 14.00–17.00. Bank holidays 14.00–17.00.

Tel: 01 848 0831

National Wax Museum, Granby Row.

Over 300 life-size wax figures of well-known people and personalities from the past and present ranging from Eamon De Valera to Elvis Presley. Also a dimly lit Chamber of Horrors.

Open: Mon–Sat 10.00–17.30, Sun 12.00–17.30.

Tel: 01 872 6340

Newbridge House, Donabate.

Built in 1737 for Archbishop Charles Cobbe, and still the residence of his descendants, Newbridge has one of the most beautiful period manor house interiors in Ireland and is set within 142 hectares (350 acres) of parkland. A fully restored 18thC farm lies on the estate together with dairy, forge, tack room, and estate worker's house. Situated 19km (12 miles) north of Dublin.

Open (Apr–Sept) Tues–Sat 10.00–17.00, Sun & bank holidays 14.00–18.00; (Oct–Mar) Sat, Sun & bank holidays 14.00–17.00.

Tel: 01 843 6534

Newman House, St Stephen's Green.

Newman House is made up of two splendid Georgian mansions, No 85 and No 86, which were once part of the buildings of the Catholic University of Ireland and named after Cardinal Newman, the first rector of the university. They are now owned by University College Dublin. No 86 was built in 1765 for Richard Whaley MP with marvellous stucco by Robert West, the house has also been owned by the celebrated gambler Buck Whaley. The smaller house, No 85, was designed by Richard Castle in 1739 with beautiful plasterwork by the Swiss La Franchini brothers and includes the Apollo Room with a figure of the god above the mantle. Gerald Manley Hopkins was Professor of Classics here at the end of the 19thC and his study is on view. Also open to the public is a classroom furnished as it would have been when James Joyce was a pupil here from 1899–1902. A guided tour explains the history and heritage of the house and how it was restored.

Open (Jun, Jul, Aug) Tues–Fri 12.00–17.00, Sat 14.00–17.00, Sun 11.00–14.00.

Tel: 01 706 7422

Number 29, Lower Fitzwilliam Street.

This elegant four-storey house has been restored and furnished exactly as it would have been between 1790–1820 by any well-to-do middle class family. Everything in the house is authentic with period items from the National Museum. The wallpaper was hand-made for Number 29 using 18thC methods. Among the

rooms in the house are a kitchen, pantry, governess' room, nursery and boudoir.
Open Tues–Sat 10.00–17.00, Sun 14.00–17.00. Closed for 2 weeks preceding Christmas.
Tel: 01 702 6165

Old Jameson Distillery, Bow Street, Smithfield Village.
The art of Irish Whiskey making shown through an audio-visual presentation, working models of the distilling process, and guided tour of the old distillery which was in use between 1780–1971.
Open daily 09.30–17.30 (tours only). Disabled access.
Tel: 01 807 2355

Pearse Museum, St. Enda's Park, Grange Road, Rathfarnham.
Housed in the former school run by nationalist Patrick Pearse from 1910–1916, it includes an audio-visual presentation and a nature study room with displays on Irish flora and fauna. Pearse was executed in 1916 for his part in the Easter Rising.
Open daily from 10.00–17.00, closing 13.00–14.00 for lunch, and closing at 16.00 Nov–Jan. Admission is free. Disabled access to ground floor/toilet.
Tel: 01 493 4208

Powerscourt Centre, South William Street.
A lively three storey centre of craft shops, galleries, boutiques and cafés, converted from Powerscourt Townhouse, a classical style mansion designed by Robert Mack and built between 1771–74. It features the original grand wooden staircase and finely detailed plasterwork.

Powerscourt House & Gardens, County Wicklow.
First laid out in the 1740s, the 18 hectare (45 acre) gardens, perhaps the finest in Ireland, include sweeping terraces cut into a steep hillside, statues and ornamental lakes. A spectacular Italian style stairway leading down to the main lake was added in 1874. Secluded Japanese gardens with bamboo and walled gardens are also notable and there is a huge variety of trees and shrubs. The house suffered a serious fire in 1974 and is no longer lived in. Visitors may walk through the old ballroom, and an exhibition area illustrates the history of the construction of the house and there are models of some of the rooms as they would have been before the fire. The house dates back to the 18thC when in 1731 architect Richard Castle was commissioned by Richard Wingfield to transform the medieval Powerscourt Castle into a grand Pallladian style mansion; the castle walls were used to form the main structure and the central courtyard was converted into an entrance hall. Powerscourt is in the foothills of the Wicklow mountains, 19km (12 miles) south of Dublin.
Open daily 09.30–17.30.
Tel: 01 204 6000
Web: www.powerscourt.ie

Phoenix Park Visitor Centre, Phoenix Park.
The visitor centre illustrates the history and wildlife of the park with an audio-visual display, a variety of fascinating exhibits and temporary exhibitions. Adjoining the centre is a restored medieval tower house, Ashtown Castle. On Saturdays there are free guided tours to the Irish President's House which is situated in the Park.
Open: (Apr–Oct) daily 10.00–18.00; (Nov–Mar) Sat & Sun only 09.30–16.30. Last admission 45 minutes before closing. Toilet for people with disabilities.
Tel: 01 677 0095

Rathfarnham Castle, Rathfarnham.
Dating from around 1583, this castle has 18thC interiors by Sir William Chambers and James Stuart and is presented to visitors as a castle undergoing conservation. There is a toilet for people with disabilities but restricted access to the castle.
Open daily from May–Oct 09.30–17.30 (last tour 16.30).
Tel: 01 493 9462

Royal Hospital, Military Road, Kilmainham.
The Royal Hospital was built as a home for army pensioners and invalids by Charles I, and continued in use for almost 250 years. Designed by Sir William Robinson in 1684, it has a formal facade and large courtyard and bears similarities to Les Invalides in Paris and The Royal Hospital in Chelsea. The restored building has one of Dublin's finest interiors and houses the Irish Museum of Modern Art in which there is an audio-visual presentation "The Story of the Royal Hospital Kilmainham". The grounds, including a formal garden, are open to the public.
Tel: 01 612 9900

Shaw Birthplace, Synge Street.
This delightful Victorian terrace home was the birthplace of one of Ireland's four Nobel prize-winners for literature, George Bernard Shaw. Restored to give the feeling that the Shaw family is still in residence, the home provides an insight into the domestic life of Victorian Dubliners.
Open (1st May–31st Oct) Mon–Sat 10.00–17.00, Sun & bank holidays 11.00–17.00. Closed

13.00–14.00.
Tel: 01 475 0854
Email: shawhouse@dublintourism.ie

Tara's Palace – Dolls House, Malahide.
The centrepiece of this museum is the one-twelfth size scale model house reflecting the splendour of 18thC Irish mansions. Conceived by Ronald and Doreen McDonnell in 1980, it was ten years in the making. Irish craftsmen paid meticulous attention to detail, with unique miniature furniture and paintings adorning the walls. The museum also has rare pieces of porcelain, miniature glass and silver. Dolls houses of the 18thC and 19thC are displayed, together with dolls and antique toys.
Open (Apr–Sept) Mon–Sat 10.00–17.00, Sun and bank holidays 14.00–18.00; (Oct–Mar) Sat, Sun and bank holidays 14.00–17.00. Closed all year 13.00–14.00.
Tel: 01 846 3779

Temple Bar
Named after a 17thC landowner, Sir William Temple, this charming neighbourhood is Dublin's cultural quarter. With its narrow cobbled streets running close to the Liffey, Temple Bar is full of character and home to many artists and musicians. The area has been regenerated in recent years and boasts a wide variety of cultural venues and events and an eclectic mix of studios, galleries, shops, markets and eating-places. Modern architecture now blends with the historic. Many free open-air events take place in summer at Meeting House Square and Temple Bar Square, including circus acts, concerts and the outdoor screening of films. Temple Bar is bounded by the south quays of the Liffey, Dame Street, Westmoreland Street and Fishamble Street.
Temple Bar Information Centre, 18 Eustace Street.
Temple Bar Cultural Information Line
Tel: 01 671 5717
Web: www.temple-bar.ie

The Chimney, Smithfield Village.
Originally built in 1895, this 53 metre (175ft) chimney which belonged to the Jameson Whiskey Distillery now provides a 360 degree panoramic viewpoint over the city. A glass walled lift takes visitors up the side of the chimney to two viewing galleries at the top.
Open daily 10.00–18.00.
Tel: 01 817 3800

Trinity College, College Green.
The original Elizabethan college was founded in 1592 but the present building was largely built between 1755–1759. The cruciform complex surrounding cobbled quadrangles and peaceful gardens has an impressive 91 metre (300ft) Palladian facade designed by Henry Keene and John Sanderford. One of the most notable features within the main college square is the 30 metre (98ft) Campanile or bell tower built in 1853 by Sir Charles Lanyon. The oldest surviving part of the college is the red brick apartment building from 1700 known as The Rubrics. Originally a Protestant College, Catholics did not start entering Trinity until the 1970s. The Library has over a million books and a magnificent collection of early illuminated manuscripts, including the famous Book of Kells; areas open to the public include the Colonnades, the Treasury, and the Long Room Library. Edmund Burke, Oliver Goldsmith and Samuel Beckett are among famous former Trinity College students.
Web: www.tcd.ie

Waterways Visitor Centre, Grand Canal Quay.
A modern centre built on piers over the Grand Canal, housing an exhibition about Ireland's inland waterways. Working models of various engineering features are displayed and there is an interactive multimedia presentation.
Open (Jun–Sept) daily 09.30–17.30; (Oct–May) Wed–Sun 12.30–17.00. Last admission 45 minutes before closing. Access to ground floor for people with disabilities.
Tel: 01 677 7510

Cathedrals and Churches

Augustinian Church, Thomas Street.
Designed by E W Pugin and G C Ashlin in 1862, it has a mountainous exterior with lofty side aisles to the nave and a 49 metre (160ft) high tower crowned by a spire.

Christ Church Cathedral, Christchurch Place.
The Cathedral was established by Strongbow and Archbishop Laurence O'Toole in 1173 on the site of the cathedral founded around 1030 by the Norse King Sitric Silkenbeard. Lambert Simnel, pretender to the English throne, was crowned here as Edward VI in 1487. It was extensively restored between 1871–78 by George Edmund Street and is one of the best examples in Ireland of early Gothic architecture. The medieval crypt is one of the oldest and largest in Ireland.
Open usually 10.00–17.00.
Tel: 01 677 8099.
Web: www.cccdub.ie
Email: cccdub@indigo.ie

Franciscan Church, Merchant's Quay.
Designed by Patrick Byrne in 1830.

St. Anne's Church, Dawson Street.
Designed by Isaac Wells in 1720 with a Romanesque-style facade added by Sir Thomas Deane in 1868. Much of the colourful stained glass dates back to the mid 19thC. Wooden shelves behind the altar were once used to take bread for distribution to the poor. Music recitals are held in the church.
Tel: 01 676 7727

St. Audoen's Church, High Street.
Dublin's only surviving medieval parish church, with a 12thC font and portal. The bell tower, restored in the 19thC, has three 15thC bells. The guild chapel has an exhibition on the importance of the church in the life of the medieval city. Dublin's only surviving city gate, known as St. Audoen's Arch, stands nearby.
Open Jun–Sept 09.30 (10.15 on Sun)–16.45. Toilet for people with disabilities and church partly accessible.
Tel: 01 677 0088

St. Audoen's RC Church, High Street.
Designed by Patrick Byrne in 1841–47, it has a monumental, cliff-like exterior with a huge Corinthian portico added by Stephen Ashlin in 1898.

St. George's, Temple Street.
This neo-classical church was designed by Francis Johnston in 1802 and has a 61 metre (200ft) high steeple modelled on St. Martin-in-the-Fields, London.

St. Mary's Church, Mary Street.
A handsome galleried church designed by Thomas Burgh in 1627. Wolfe Tone, leader of the United Irishmen, was baptised here in 1763 and Sean O'Casey in 1880.

St. Mary's Abbey, Meetinghouse Lane.
Established originally as a Benedictine foundation in 1139, it became Cistercian eight years later. Until the 16thC it was one of the largest and most important monasteries in Ireland. The remains include a fine vaulted Chapter House of 1190 and there is an interesting exhibition about the history of the abbey.
Open mid June–mid Sept, Wed and Sun 10.00–17.00. Last admission 45 minutes before closing.
Tel: 01 872 1490

St. Mary's Pro-Cathedral, Marlborough Street.
A Greek Doric style building with the interior modelled on the Church of St. Philippe de Roule in Paris, designed by John Sweetman and built between 1815–1825. St. Mary's is Dublin's most important Catholic Church and is used on State occasions. Tenor John McCormack was once a member of the Palestrina choir that sings a Latin mass every Sunday at 11.00.
Tel: 01 874 5441
Web: www.procathedral.ie

St. Michan's Church, Church Street.
Founded in 1095 as a Viking parish church, largely rebuilt in 1685 and restored in 1828. Famous for the 17thC mummified bodies in the crypt which are preserved with skin and hair because of the dry atmosphere created by the limestone walls. Handel is thought to have played on the organ which dates from 1724.
Open (Apr–Oct) Mon–Fri 10.00–17.00; (Nov–March) Mon–Fri 12.30–15.30; all Saturdays 10.00–13.00. Vaults closed on Sundays.
Tel: 01 872 4154

St. Patrick's Cathedral, Patrick Street.
The National Cathedral of the Church of Ireland, it was built in the late 12thC on the site of the pre-Norman parish church of St. Patrick. It gained and lost cathedral status more than once in its chequered history and Cromwellian soldiers stabled horses here in the Civil War. Architect John Semple added a spire in 1749 and St. Patrick's was fully restored in the 19thC with finance from the Guinness family. The massive west tower houses the largest ringing peel of bells in Ireland. The cathedral is full of memorial brasses, busts and monuments to famous Irishmen. Jonathan Swift was Dean here from 1713–1745; there are memorials to Swift and his beloved Stella (Esther Johnson) and Swift's pulpit contains his writing table and chair, and portrait.
Usually open daily 09.00–17.00. Wheelchair access by arrangement.
Tel: 01 453 9472
Web: www.stpatrickcathedral.ie
Email: stpcath@iol.ie

St. Saviour's, Dominick Street.
Designed by J J McCarthy in 1858, this extravagant French style Gothic edifice has a bold west door under a triangular hood, crowned by a large rose window.

St. Stephen's, Mount Street Crescent.
This handsome neo-classical church, designed by John Bowden in 1824, has a Greek style portico.

St. Werburgh's Church, Werburgh Street.
Originally the site of an Anglo-Norman foundation, the present church was built in 1715–19 and rebuilt in 1759 following a fire. St. Werburgh's was the Chapel Royal until 1790. Lord Edward Fitzgerald, one of the leaders of

the 1798 rebellion, is buried in the vaults.

Whitefriar Street Carmelite Church, Aungier Street.
19thC church standing on the site of a 16thC Carmelite Priory. The remains of Saint Valentine are buried here and there is a 15thC oak statue of the Virgin and Child, thought to be the only surviving Pre-reformation statue of its kind.
Tel: 01 475 8821

Libraries

Central Catholic Library, Merrion Square.
Of religious and general interest, with a large Irish section.
Open Mon–Fri 11.00–19.00, Sat 11.00–17.30.
Tel: 01 676 1264

Central Library, Ilac Centre.
Tel: 01 873 4333.
Enquiries about other Dublin City Public Libraries (lending, reference and special collections).
Tel: 01 661 9000
Web: www.iol.ie/~dubcilib
Email: dubcilib@iol.ie

Chester Beatty Library, Dublin Castle, Dame Street.
Reopened in 2000 in a purpose designed home in the Clock Tower building of Dublin Castle, the library is a treasure of manuscripts, books, prints and textiles collected by American scholar Sir Alfred Chester Beatty. It has some of the rarest original manuscripts still in existence. The collection reflects the art of manuscript production and printing from many parts of the world and from early to modern times with picture scrolls, jade books and woodblock prints from the Far East, around 4,000 Islamic manuscripts, and fine books, bindings and manuscripts from Western Europe. With many Early Christian papyri, the library is a major resource for the study of the Old and New Testaments.
Open Tue–Fri 10.00–17.00, Sat 11.00–17.00, Sun 13.00–17.00. Admission is free.
Tel: 01 407 0750
Web: www.cbl.ie
Email: info@cbl.ie

Genealogical Office, Kildare Street.
Part of the National Library, the genealogical office offers a service to assist in the task of tracing family history, familiarising people with the relevant records and procedures.
Open Mon–Fri 10.00–17.00, Sat 10.00–12.30.
Tel: 01 603 0200

Gilbert Library, Pearse Street.
Books and manuscripts relating to Dublin which were accumulated by 19thC Dublin historian Sir John T Gilbert and now in the care of Dublin Corporation. The collection includes rare early Dublin newspapers, 18thC bindings, Irish Almanacs, manuscripts of the municipal records of the City of Dublin and the records of the Dublin guilds. Closed for refurbishment until 2002.
Tel: 01 661 9000

Goethe Institute Library, Merrion Square.
German cultural information centre and library.
Open Tues & Thurs 10.00–19.00, Wed 14.00–19.00, Fri 10.00–13.00.
Tel: 01 661 1155

Irish Architectural Archive, Merrion Square.
Open Tues–Fri 10.00–13.00 & 14.30–17.00.
Tel: 01 676 3430

Marsh's Library, St Patrick's Close.
Given to the city by Archbishop Narcissus Marsh and opened in 1701, this is Ireland's oldest public library containing many rare books still in their original carved bookcases. The building was designed by Sir William Robinson who was also the architect of the Royal Hospital, Kilmainham. To prevent the theft of rare books readers were locked in wire cages and three of these cages survive.
Open Mon & Wed–Fri 10.00–12.45 & 14.00–17.00, Sat 09.45–12.45.
Tel: 01 454 3511

National Library of Ireland, Kildare Street.
Offers over half a million books, a vast collection of maps, prints and manuscripts and an invaluable collection of Irish newspapers and periodicals. The impressive Victorian building has been home to the Library since 1890, and there is a large domed reading room. Holds temporary exhibitions on Irish writers and books.
Open: Mon–Wed 10.00–21.00, Thurs–Fri 10.00–17.00, Sat 10.00–13.00. Admission is free.
Tel: 01 603 0200
Web: www.hearnet.ie/natlib
Email: info@nli.ie

National Photographic Archive, Meeting House Square.
Only established in 1998, it has over a million photographs recording people, political events, and scenes of Irish cities, towns and countryside. Images from the collection are always on view. There is also a reading room and darkrooms.
Open: Mon–Fri 10.00–17.00. Admission is free. Disabled access/toilet.
Tel: 01 603 037
Web: www.hearnet.ie/natlib/photoarchive
Email: photoarchive@nli.ie

Royal Irish Academy Library, Dawson Street.
One of the largest collections of ancient Irish manuscripts in the country with one usually on display together with a small exhibition. Access may be restricted depending on Royal Academy meetings and large groups need to make a prior arrangement to visit.
Open Mon–Fri 10.30–17.00. Admission is free.
Tel: 01 676 2570

Trinity College Library, College Green.
The oldest and most famous of Dublin's libraries dating from the late 16thC. Entitled to receive a copy of every book published in Ireland, the library also contains an extensive collection of Irish manuscripts including the Book of Kells, a beautifully illuminated copy of the gospels written on vellum in Latin around the year AD800. The Book of Kells is now bound in four volumes and two are always on display in the Treasury, one open at a major ornamental page and the other to show two pages of script. An exhibition explains how the Book of Kells and other manuscripts such as the Book of Durrow (AD675) and Book of Armagh (AD807) were created and illustrates monastic life in the 8thC. The impressive Old Library or Long Room Library is lined with marble busts of scholars and is nearly 64 metres (210ft) long. It rises two storeys with a high barrel vaulted ceiling and contains over 200,000 of the college's books.
Open Mon–Sat 09.30–17.00; Sun 09.30–16.30 (Jun–Sept), Sun 12.00–16.30 (May–Oct). Last admission 30 minutes before closing.
Tel: 01 608 2308
Web:www.tcd.ie

Arts Centres, Galleries, and Concert Halls

Arthouse, Curved Street.
Purpose built multimedia centre for the arts.
Tel: 01 605 6800
Web: www.arthouse.ie
Email: info@arthouse.ie

City Arts Centre, Moss Street.
A multi-purpose arts venue with galleries, exhibition areas and theatre space for local groups and artists.
Tel: 01 677 0643

Designyard, Essex Street East.
A centre exhibiting and selling contemporary furniture, glass, ceramics and jewellery in an 18thC china warehouse.
Tel: 01 677 8482

Douglas Hyde Gallery, Trinity College.
Showing mainly temporary exhibitions of contemporary art.
Tel: 01 608 1116

Gallery of Photography, Meeting House Square.
Exhibitions of contemporary photography. Roof terrace has views over the square.
Tel: 01 671 4654
Email: gallery@irish–photography.com

Hugh Lane Municipal Gallery of Modern Art, Parnell Square North.
19thC and 20thC paintings, mainly Impressionist works, bequeathed by Sir Hugh Lane who was drowned in the Lusitania in 1915, form the nucleus of this collection. The Lane Collection is split with the Tate Gallery in London; each half is alternated between the galleries every 5 years. There is an extensive range of Irish and international paintings, sculpture and stained glass and the acquisition of contemporary work is ongoing. Opening in 2001 is a new exhibition area to include the London studio of Dublin-born artist Francis Bacon, which was carefully dismantled and reconstructed here. Regular 'Sundays at Noon' Concerts are held at the gallery (apart from July and August) with everything from early music to commissioned new works; the music is often arranged to complement one of the temporary exhibitions. The classical building which houses the gallery, Charlemont House, was designed by William Chambers in 1763 for James Caulfield, later 1st Earl Charlemont. It was reconstructed in 1929 to house the Lane Collection and opened in 1933.
Open Tues–Thurs 09.30–18.00, Fri & Sat 09.30–17.00, Sun 11.00–17.00. Admission free except for special exhibitions. Disabled access.
Tel: 01 874 1903
Email: info@hughlane.ie

National Concert Hall, Earlsfort Terrace.
Home of the National Symphony Orchestra of Ireland, but also a venue for international artists and orchestras, jazz, contemporary and traditional Irish music. The classical building was designed for the Great Exhibition of 1865, then became the centrepiece of University College Dublin before opening as Ireland's National Concert Hall in 1981.
Booking office open Mon–Sat 10.00–19.00. Disabled access/toilet.
Tel: 01 475 1572
Web: www.nch.ie (online booking)
Email:info@nch.ie

National Gallery of Ireland, Merrion Square.
Paintings by illustrious 20thC European artists such as Morrisot, Bonnard, Picasso and Monet hang in the National Gallery as well as the work of Old Masters including Titian, Caravaggio,

Rembrandt and Vermeer. There is the National Collection of Irish art, a room dedicated to the work of Jack B Yeats, English paintings, and over 250 sculptures. William Dargan organised the 1853 Dublin Exhibition on this site and used the proceeds to found the collection; his statue stands on the lawn.
Open Mon–Sat 10.00–17.30, Sun 14.00–17.00. Admission free. Disabled access/toilet.
Tel: 01 661 5133
Web: www.nationalgallery.ie
Email: artgall@eircom.net

Royal Dublin Society, Ballsbridge.
Venue for large events including craft and antiques fairs and Ideal Homes exhibitions.
Tel: 01 668 0866

Royal Hibernian Academy Gallagher Gallery, Ely Place.
Showing both traditional and innovative work from both Irish and international artists.
Tel: 01 661 2558

Solomon Gallery, Powerscourt Centre.
One of Ireland's leading contemporary art galleries, situated in an 18thC Georgian townhouse.
Open Mon–Sat 10.00–17.30. Admission free.
Tel: 01 679 4237
Web: www.solomongallery.com

Temple Bar Gallery and Studios, Temple Bar.
A large complex with studios and exhibition spaces.
Tel: 01 671 0073
Email: tbgs@indigo.ie

Temple Bar Music Centre, Curved Street.
Live music venue with recording and rehearsal studios.
Tel: 01 670 9202
Web: www.indigo.ie/~tbmusic
Email: tbmusic@indigo.ie

Taylor Galleries, Kildare Street.
Contemporary art gallery, mainly Irish, with the emphasis on painting and sculpture.
Tel: 01 676 6055

The Ark, Eustace Street.
A cultural centre for children with a child-size theatre.
Tel: 01 670 7788
Web: www.ark.ie
Email: info@ark.ie

Parks and Gardens

Garden of Remembrance, Parnell Square East.
The Garden of Remembrance, opened in 1966, is dedicated to all those who died in the cause of Irish Freedom. There is a sculpture by Oisín Kelly representing the Irish legend, "Children of Lir".
Opens 09.30 May–Sept, 11.00 rest of year. Closes according to daylight hours.
Tel: 01 874 3074 (garden) or 01 647 2498 (head office)

Iveagh Gardens, Clonmel Street.
Designed by Ninian Niven in 1863, this is one of the least known and most tranquil of Dublin's parks. Features include a rustic grotto, cascade, fountains, maze, archery grounds, wilderness and woodlands.
Opens at 08.00 Mon–Sat, 10.00 Sun. Closes according to daylight hours.
Tel: 01 475 7816

Marlay Park, Rathfarnham.
This large park situated at the foot of the Dublin Mountains contains areas of woodland, a large pond, nature trail and model railway.

National Botanic Gardens, Glasnevin.
Established in 1795, these magnificent gardens occupy an area of 20 hectares (49 acres) and contain a fabulous collection of plants, shrubs and trees. Many of the plants come from tropical Africa and South America and are housed in large Victorian glasshouses. Features include a rose garden, rockery and wall plants, herbaceous borders, vegetable garden and arboretum.
Open Summer Mon–Sat 09.00–18.00, Sun 11.00–18.00; Winter Mon–Sat 10.00–16.30, Sun 11.00–16.30. Shorter opening hours for glasshouses. Admission is free. Toilet for people with disabilities, and gardens largely accessible.
Tel: 01 837 4388

Phoenix Park
Phoenix Park, covering over 712 hectares (1,760 acres), is Europe's largest enclosed city park. Its name is thought to derive from the Irish meaning "clear water" and a spring does rise in the park. Enclosed by an 11km (7 mile) long stone wall, the park was laid out in the mid 18thC and was the scene of the Phoenix Park murders in 1882, when the Chief Secretary and the Under-Secretary for Ireland were assassinated. A more recent event was when the Pope celebrated mass in the park in front of 1 million people; a 27 metre (90ft) steel cross marks the spot. The park includes a number of buildings, the most important of which is Áras an Uachtaráin; the Viceroy's Lodge built in 1751 but later becoming the official house of the President of Ireland when Dr Douglas Hyde moved there in 1938. Other important buildings

are the American ambassador's residence and the Ordnance Survey Office. A 60 metre (205 ft) high obelisk, erected in 1817, is a memorial to the Dublin-born Duke of Wellington. The People's Garden by the main entrance on Parkgate Street is laid out with ornamental planting in ribbon borders, much as it would have been in Victorian times. Dublin Zoo is in the south-east corner. The open space covered by playing fields and paths, known as Fifteen Acres but actually covering more than 200, was used in the 18thC as a duelling ground. Phoenix Park is open to the public at all times but the People's Gardens usually close at sunset.

St. Anne's Park, Dollymount.
Once part of the Guinness family estate, the park covers over 110 hectares (270 acres) and is wooded with oak, pine, beech, chestnut and lime. There is a lovely rose garden, opened in 1975.

St. Edna's Park, Grange Road, Rathfarnham.
The park surrounds the Pearse Museum and includes a walled garden, riverside walks and waterfall. Open daily from 10.00, closing time varies according to daylight hours. Limited access for people with disabilities.

St. Stephen's Green
In the heart of the city, St Stephen's Green was originally an open common but was enclosed in 1663. Opened to the general public in 1877, it is laid out as a public park with flowerbeds, an ornamental pond and several sculptures. There is a garden for the visually impaired and there are summer lunchtime concerts.
Open daily 08.00 (Sun & bank Holidays 10.00); closes according to daylight hours.
Tel: 01 475 7816

War Memorial Garden, South Circular Road, Islandbridge.
Dedicated to the memory of the Irish soldiers who died in the First World War, these gardens include a sunken rose garden and herbaceous borders. They were designed by Sir Edward Lutyens. The names of the 49,400 soldiers who died between 1914–1918 are contained in the granite bookrooms in the gardens, access to which is only by arrangement with the management.
Open Mon–Fri 08.00, Sat & Sun 10.00; closes according to daylight hours.
Tel: 01 677 0236 (gardens)
Tel: 01 647 2498 (head office)

Theatres

Abbey Theatre, Lower Abbey Street.
Ireland's National Theatre, founded by Lady Gregory and W B Yeats in 1904. The Abbey quickly became world renowned, staging plays by J M Synge and Sean O'Casey, and played a significant role in the renaissance of Irish culture. It also provoked controversy in Dublin and even riots. The present theatre was built in 1966 to replace the previous building which had been destroyed by fire. The Abbey stages classic Irish plays, while the Peacock theatre downstairs presents new and experimental drama.
Tel: 01 878 7222

Andrews Lane Theatre and Studio, Andrews Lane.
A wide variety of works shown both in the theatre and studio.
Tel: 01 679 5720

Civic Theatre, Tallaght.
New theatre staging everything from drama to variety shows
Tel: 01 462 7477

Crypt, Dublin Castle.
Drama theatre showing Irish plays and international classics.
Tel: 01 671 3387

Focus Theatre, Pembroke Place, Pembroke Street.
Small theatre presenting the classics and new writing.
Tel: 01 676 3071

Gaiety Theatre, South King Street.
Restored Victorian building and Dublin's oldest theatre, founded in 1837. Drama, opera (Opera Ireland have two seasons a year), ballet, musicals, pantomime, comedy.
Tel: 01 677 1717

Gate Theatre, Cavendish Row.
Modern Irish and classical drama, also international plays. Founded in 1928.
Tel: 01 874 4045

Lambert Puppet Theatre, Clifton Lane, Monkstown.
Tel: 01 280 0974

Murphy's Laughter Lounge, Eden Quay, O'Connell Bridge.
Comedy theatre with Irish and international stand-up comedians Thurs–Sun.
Tel: 1800 266 339

Olympia Theatre, Dame Street.
Comedy, drama, pantomime, musicals, concerts.
Tel: 01 677 7744

Peacock Theatre, Lower Abbey Street.
New and experimental work.
Tel: 01 878 7222

Project Arts Centre, 39 East Essex Street.
Moved in 2000 into new custom designed

building with performance and gallery space; generally innovative new work and everything from drama and visual arts to talks and events.
Tel: 01 679 6622
Web: www.project.ie
Email: info@project.ie

Samuel Beckett Theatre, Trinity College.
Trinity College School of Drama theatre with a variety of student productions during term and touring companies at other times. Venue for Festival Fringe events.
Tel: 01 608 2461

Tivoli Theatre, Francis Street.
Modern theatre and rock venue; cabaret and late night gigs.
Tel: 01 454 4472

The Point, North Wall Quay.
Theatre and concert venue including ballet.
Tel: 01 836 3633

Sugar Cube, Lower Leeson Street.
Multimedia theatre with wide range of entertainment; drama, film, cabaret, comedy, music, events.
Tel: 01 478 0012

The Dublin Theatre Festival, held at many venues throughout the city, runs for two weeks every October. **Tel: 01 677 8439**
The Fringe Festival which presents theatre, dance and the visual arts is held for three weeks, commencing around the third week in September. **Tel: 01 872 9433**

Cinemas

Most cinemas offer cheaper seats before 5pm.
Ambassador, Parnell Street,
Tel: 01 872 7000. 1 screen.

Classic Cinema, Harold's Cross Road,
Tel: 01 492 3324. 2 screens.

Irish Film Centre, Eustace Street,
Art house with 2 screens and restaurant converted from old Quaker meeting house. New Irish films and film seasons. The Irish Film Archive, library and special events.
Tel: 01 679 5744.
Web: www.iftn.ie/ifc
Email: ifc@iol.ie

Omniplex, Santry, **Tel: 01 842 8844**. 10 screens.

Ormonde Cinema, Stillorgan,
Tel: 01 278 0000. 7 screens.

Savoy Cinema, O'Connell Street Upper,
Tel: 01 874 6000. 6 screens.

Screen Cinema, D'Oliver Street,
Tel: 01 672 5500. 3 screens.

Sheridan IMAX Cinema, Parnell Street,
Tel: 01 817 4222.

Stella Cinema, Rathmines Road,
Tel: 01 497 1281. 2 screens.

UCI Cinema, Blanchardstown,
Tel: 01 8222 624. 9 screens.

UCI Cinema, Coolock,
Tel: 01 848 5122. 10 screens.

UCI Cinema, Tallaght,
Tel: 01 459 8400. 12 screens.

Virgin Cinemas, Parnell Street,
Tel: 01 872 8444. 9 screens.

Shopping

Opening hours are generally 09.00–18.00 Mon–Sat. Many city centre shops and shopping centres remain open until 20.00 or 21.00 on Thursdays and Fridays and open 12.00–18.00 on Sundays.
The main city centre shopping areas are around Grafton Street and Nassau Street to the south of the Liffey and around Henry Street (off O'Connell Street) to the north of the river. Both Grafton Street and Henry Street are pedestrianised. Many up-market and international designer stores can be found in Grafton Street, while shops around Henry Street are generally less expensive. The Temple Bar area has a number of craft and specialist shops.

Department Stores

Arnotts, Henry Street, **Tel: 01 872 1111.**
Brown Thomas, Grafton Street,
Tel: 01 605 6666.
Clery and Co, O'Connell Street Lower,
Tel: 01 878 6000.
Debenhams, Jervis Centre, **Tel: 01 878 1222**.
Dunnes Stores, Henry Street, **Tel: 01 671 4629**.
Guiney & Co, Talbot Street, **Tel: 01 878 8835**.
Marks & Spencers, Grafton Street,
Tel: 01 679 7855.
Penneys Stores, Mary Street, **Tel: 01 872 7788**.
Roches Stores, Henry Street, **Tel:01 873 0044**.

Shopping Centres

Dún Laoghaire Shopping Centre, Marine Road,
Tel: 01 280 2981.
Ilac Centre, Henry Street, **Tel: 01 704 1460**.
Irish Life Shopping Mall, Abbey Street,
Tel: 01 704 1452.
Jervis Shopping Centre, Jervis Street,
Tel: 01 878 1323.
Powerscourt Centre, South William Street,
Tel: 01 679 4144.
St. Stephen's Green Centre, Tel: 01 478 0888.
There are also shopping centres on the outskirts of Dublin including at Clondalkin

(Liffey Valley), Blanchardstown, and Tallaght.

Markets

Blackrock, Sat 11.00–17.30, Sun & bank holidays 12.00–17.30 (bric-a-brac, china and antiques).

George's Street Market Arcade (second hand clothes, jewellery, records).

Liberty Market (clothes, fabrics, household goods), Meath Street.

Moore Street Market, Mon–Sat (flower, fruit and vegetables), off Henry Street.

Mother Redcaps, Fri–Sun (indoor flea market), Christchurch Back Lane. **Tel: 01 453 8306.**

St. Michan's Street Vegetable Market (fruit, vegetables, fish and flowers).

Temple Bar Square. Food market is open every Saturday from 09.30–18.00 selling organic fruit and vegetables, bread, cheeses, oysters, and smoked fish. Book Market is open on Saturdays in summer from 09.30.

Sport and Leisure

International Sports Venues:

Athletics – Croke Park.
Tel: 01 836 3222

Gaelic Football and Hurling – Croke Park.
Tel 01 836 3222

Rugby and Soccer – Lansdowne Road, Ballsbridge.
Tel: 01 668 4601

Golf (18-hole golf clubs):

Balcarrick Golf Club, Donabate, 16km (10m) north of city centre.
Tel: 01 843 6957

Ballinascorney, 13km (8m) south west of city centre.
Tel: 01 451 6430

Beaverstown Golf Club, Donabate, 16km (10m) north of city centre.
Tel: 01 843 6439

Blanchardstown Golf Centre, Mulhuddart, 13km (8m) north west of city centre.
Tel: 01 821 2054
Web: www.blanchardstowngolf.com
Email: bgc@indigo.ie

Castle Golf Club, Rathfarnham, 6km (4m) south of city centre.
Tel: 01 490 4207

Citywest Golf Resort, Saggart, 16km (10m) south west of city centre.
Tel: 01 401 0500

Corballis Golf Links, Donabate,16km (10m) north of city centre.
Tel: 01 843 6583
Email: corballis@golfdublin.com

Deerpark Hotel and Golf Courses, Howth, 14km (9 m) north east of city centre.
Tel: 01 832 2624
Web: www.deerpark-hotel.ie
Email: sales@deerpark.iol.ie

Druids Glen, Newmountkennedy, 32km (2m) south east of city centre.
Tel: 01 287 3600
Web: www.druidsglen.ie
Email: druids@indigo.ie

Edmondstown, Rathfarnham, 11km (7m) south of city centre.
Tel: 01 493 1082
Email: edmondgc@iol.ie

Elmgreen Golf Centre, Castleknock, 8km (5m) north west of city centre.
Tel: 01 820 0797
Web: www.golfdublin.com
Email: elmgreen@golfdublin.com

Elm Park, Donnybrook, 5km(3m) south of city centre.
Tel: 01 269 3438
Email: golf@elmparkgolfclub.ie

Forrest Little Golf Club, Cloghean, 9km (6m) north of city centre, near to airport.
Tel: 01 840 1183

Grange Castle, Clondalkin, 8km (5m) south west of city centre.
Tel: 01 464 1043

Grange Golf Club, Rathfarnham, 6km (4m) south of city centre.
Tel: 01 493 2889

Hermitage Golf Club, Lucan, 11km (7m) west of city centre.
Tel: 01 626 8491

Howth Golf Club, Sutton, 14km (9m) north east of city centre.
Tel: 01 832 1793

Island, Corballis, Donabate, 14km (9m) north of city centre.
Tel: 01 843 6462
Email: island@iol.ie

Luttrellstown Castle, Castleknock, 10 km (6 m) west of city centre.
Tel: 01 808 9988
Email: golf@luttrellstown.ie

Malahide Golf Club, 13km (8m) north of city centre. **Tel: 01 846 1611**
Email: malgc@clubi.ie

Open Golf Centre, St. Margaret's, Adjacent to Dublin airport.
Tel: 01834 6264

Portmarnock Golf Club, 11km (7m) north east of city centre.
Tel: 01 846 2968
Email: secretary@portmarnockgolfclub.ie

Portmarnock Hotel and Golf Links, 11km (7m) north east of city centre.
Tel: 01 846 1800
Email: reservations@portmarnock.com

Royal Dublin Golf Club, Dollymount, 5km (3m) north east of city centre.
Tel: 01 833 6346
Email: royaldublin@clubi.ie

St. Anne's Golf Club, Dollymount, 5km (3m) north east of city centre.
Tel: 01 833 6471
Email: stannesgc@hotmail.com

St. Margaret's Golf Club, 11m (7m) north of city centre.
Tel: 01 864 0400
Web: www.globalgolf.com
Email: stmarggc@indigo.ie

Swords Open Golf Course, 13m (8m) north of city centre.
Tel: 01 840 9819/890 1030

Greyhound Racing

Greyhound racing is one of Ireland's leading spectator sports. Meetings are held at:

Shelbourne Park Stadium, Ringsend, (Wed, Thurs, Sat at 20.00).
Tel: 01 668 3502

Harold's Cross Stadium, (Mon & Fri at 20.00).
Tel: 01 497 1081

Horse Racing

There are two racecourses on the outskirts of Dublin:

Leopardstown.
10km (6 miles) south of Dublin. National Hunt and Flat racing with 23 meetings including 4 day Christmas National Hunt Festival.
Tel: 01 289 3607
Web: www.leopardstown.com
Email: info@leopardstown.com

Fairyhouse.
19km (12 miles) north west of Dublin. Home of Jameson Irish Grand National.
Tel: 01 825 6167
Web: www.indigo.ie/fairyhse
Email: fairyhse@indigo.ie

Sailing

The Irish Sailing Association, Dún Laoghaire, for information on sailing, windsurfing and powerboating in the Dublin area and elsewhere in Ireland.
Tel: 01 280 0239
Web: www.sailing.ie
Email: isa@iol.ie

Sports Centres

Aughrim Street, Tel: 01 838 8085
Glin Road, Coolock, **Tel: 01 847 8177**

Swimming Pools

Ballyfermot, Blackditch Road, **Tel: 01 626 6504**
Ballymun, Town Centre, **Tel: 01 842 1368**
Coolock, Northside Shopping Centre, **Tel: 01 847 7743**
Crumlin, Windmill Road, **Tel: 01 455 5792**
Finglas, Rathmines Road, **Tel: 01 834 8005**
Markievicz Pool, Townsend Street, **Tel: 01 672 9121**
Rathmines, Lower Rathmines Road, **Tel: 01 496 1275**
Sean, McDermott Street, **Tel: 01 872 0752**

Help and Advice

Embassies

Apostolic Nunciature, Nephin Road. Tel: 01 838 0577
Arab Republic of Egypt, Clyde Road. Tel: 01 660 6566
Argentina, Ailesbury Drive. Tel: 01 269 1546
Australia, Fitzwilton House, Wilton Terrace. Tel: 01 676 1517
Austria, Ailesbury Road. Tel: 01 269 4577
Belgium, Shrewsbury Road. Tel: 01 269 2082
Brazil, Harcourt Street. Tel: 01 475 6000
Britain, Merrion Road. Tel: 01 205 3700
Bulgaria, Burlington Road. Tel: 01 660 3293
Canada, St. Stephen's Green. Tel: 01 478 1988
China, Ailesbury Road. Tel: 01 269 1707
Czech Republic, Northumberland Road. Tel: 01 668 1343
Denmark, St. Stephen's Green. Tel: 01 475 6404
Finland, St. Stephen's Green. Tel: 01478 1344
France, Ailesbury Road. Tel: 01 260 1666
Germany, Trimleston Avenue. Tel: 01269 3011
Greece, Upper Brook Street. Tel: 01 676 7254
Hungary, Fitzwilliam Place. Tel: 661 2902
India, Leeson Park. Tel: 01 497 0843
Iran, Mount Merrion Avenue. Tel: 01 288 0252
Israel, Pembroke Road. Tel: 01 668 0303
Italy, Northumberland Road. Tel: 01 660 1744
Japan, Merrion Centre. Tel: 01 269 4244
Korea, Clyde Road. Tel: 01 660 8800
Mexico, Ailesbury Road. Tel: 01 260 0699
Morocco, Raglan Road. Tel: 01 660 9449
Netherlands, Merrion Road. Tel: 01 269 3444
New Zealand, Leeson Park. Tel: 01 660 4233
Nigeria, Leeson Park. Tel: 01 660 4366
Norway, Molesworth Street. Tel: 01 662 1800
Poland, Ailesbury Road. Tel: 01 283 0855

Russian Federation, Orwell Road.
Tel: 01 492 3525
Slovakia, Clyde Road. Tel: 01 660 0008
South Africa, Earlsfort Terrace.
Tel: 01 661 5553
Spain, Merlyn Park. Tel: 01 269 1640
Sweden, Dawson Street. Tel: 01 671 5822
Switzerland, Ailesbury Road. Tel: 01 269 2515
Turkey, Clyde Road. Tel: 01 668 5240
USA, Elgin Road. Tel: 01 668 8777

Health Centres and Pharmacies

Grafton Street Centre, Open Mon–Fri 09.00–18.00, Sat 10.00–12.00.
Tel: 01 671 2122

Mercer's Medical Centre, Stephen Street Lower, Open: Mon–Thurs 09.00–17.30, Fri 09.00–16.30.
Tel: 01 402 2300

O'Connell's Late Night Pharmacy, O'Connell Street Lower, Open daily 08.00–22.00 (Sun 10.00–22.00).
Tel: 01 873 0427

Hospitals

Beaumont, Beaumont Road. **Tel: 01 837 7755**
Blackrock Clinic (private), Rock Road.
Tel: 01 283 2222
Dental Hospital, Lincoln Place, **Tel: 01 612 7200**
James Connolly Memorial Hospital, Blanchardstown.
Tel: 01 821 3844
Mater Misericordiae, Eccles Street.
Tel: 01 830 1122
Mater Private, Eccles Street. **Tel: 01 838 4444**
National Children's Hospital, Harcourt Street.
Tel: 01 475 2355
Rotunda Hospital, Parnell Square.
Tel: 01 873 0700
St. James's, James's Street, **Tel: 01 453 7941**
St. Michael's, George's Street Lower, Dún Laoghaire. **Tel: 01 280 6901**
St.Vincent's, Elm Park. **Tel: 01 269 4533**

Police (Garda Síochána)

City centre Garda stations:
Pearse Street station, Tel: 01 666 9000
Store Street station, Tel: 01 666 8000
Dublin Metropolitan Area Headquarters, Harcourt Square,
Tel: 01 475 5555
Greater Dublin Area Headquarters, Phoenix Park,
Tel: 01 666 0000
Dún Laoghaire station, Tel: 01 666 5000

Post Offices

General Post Office, O'Connell Street. Open Mon–Sat 08.00–19.00, Sunday 10.30–18.30.
Tel: 01 872 6666
Post offices are usually open Mon–Fri 09.00–17.30 (closed 13.00–14.15) and from 09.00–13.00 on Saturdays.

Welfare Organisations

Citizens Information Centre, 13a O'Connell Street Upper.
Tel: 01 809 0633

Samaritans, 112 Marlborough Street.
Tel: 01 872 7700 or callsave 1850 609 090

Social Welfare Services, Goldsmith House, Pearse Street.
Tel: 01 874 8444

Tourist Victim Support Service, Garda Headquarters, Harcourt Square.
All referrals must go through the Garda.
Open: Mon–Sat 10.00–18.00, Sun 12.00–18.00.
Tel: 01 478 5295
Email: tvss@clubi.ie

INDEX TO PLACE NAMES

INDEX TO STREETS

General Abbreviations

All. Alley
Av. Avenue
Ave. Avenue
Bk. Bank
Bldgs. Buildings
Boul. Boulevard
Br. Bridge
Bri. Bridge
Cem. Cemetery
Ch. Church
Cl. Close
Clo. Close
Coll. College
Cotts. Cottages
Cres. Crescent
Ct. Court
Dr. Drive
E. East
Est. Estate
Ex. Exchange
Ext. Extension
Fld. Field
Flds. Fields
Fm. Farm
Gdn. Garden
Gdns. Gardens
Gra. Grange
Grd. Ground
Grn. Green
Gro. Grove
Ho. House
Hosp. Hospital
Hts. Heights
Junct. Junction
La. Lane
Lo. Lodge
Lwr. Lower
Mans. Mansions
Mkt. Market
Ms. Mews
Mt. Mount
N. North
No. Numbers
Par. Parade
Pas. Passage
Pk. Park
Pl. Place
Prom. Promenade
Rd. Road
Ri. Rise
S. South
Sch. School
Sq. Square
St. Street
Sta. Station
Ter. Terrace
Vill. Villas
Vills. Villa
Vw. View
W. West
Wd. Wood
Wds. Woods
Wk. Walk
Yd. Yard

District Abbreviations

D.L. Dún Laoghaire

Notes

This index contains some street names in standard text which are followed by another street named in italics. In these cases the street in standard text does not actually appear on the map due to insufficient space but can be located close to the street name in italics.

B

E

H

N